GRAND SUMO

GRAND SUMO

THE LIVING SPORT AND TRADITION

by Lora Sharnoff

illustrations by Lynn Matsuoka

New York • WEATHERHILL • *Tokyo*

The photographs are by Baseball Magazine Sha (pp. 9, 123, and 158); Andy Adams (p. 52); Wide World Photo (p. 120, left); *Sankei Sports* (pp. 4, 25, 45, 49, 54, 59, 80, 81, 99, 111, and 142); Clyde Newton (pp. 22, left, 70, top, and 161); Takashi Koguchi (pp. 22, right, and 60); Takashi Nakano (pp. 61 and 156); and Dr. Shimon Otobe (p. 81, right).

First edition, 1989
Revised edition, 1993

Published by Weatherhill, Inc., 420 Madison Avenue, 15th Floor, New York, NY 10017.

Library of Congress Cataloging in Publication Data: Sharnoff, Lora / Grand sumo: the living sport and tradition / by Lora Sharnoff; illustrations by Lynn Matsuoka.—2nd ed. / p. cm. / 1. Sumo. 2. Sumo—History. I. Title. / GV1197.S48 1993 / 796.8'125'09—dc20 / 89–28911 CIP ISBN 0-8348-0283-x

Contents

Preface

"What made you interested in sumo?" I am frequently asked this question, especially by people familiar with my academic background and master's degree in Japanese literature. Since, basically, I have not been a follower of sports, it sometimes seems a bit odd even to me, too, that I have made a name for myself as a writer and commentator on sumo. Yet I often consider it a natural development of my long involvement with Japanese culture.

I originally became interested in Japan at the age of four when I had the chance to see some Japanese art. I was totally entranced, and my dream thereafter was to learn Japanese and visit Japan someday. I read a lot about Japan over the years, but no public secondary schools in Los Angeles taught Japanese at that time.

Finally, in college and graduate school I had the chance to major in Japanese language and culture. Since literature was my field of specialization, I studied Japanese history, religion, and other subjects to better comprehend the social background of the literary works I read. During that time I vaguely heard something about sumo, but remembered it only as a sport performed by enormous men.

As a Fulbright Scholar, I came to Japan to do research at Kyoto University in late 1973. Lacking my own television, I occasionally caught glimpses of sumo at my neighbor's home. At first, almost all the *sumotori* looked alike to me. I could distinguish only Hawaiian-born Takamiyama and Wajima, who had earlier been introduced in an American news magazine as the first grand champion in sumo with a college degree. I still held a prejudice that sumo was primarily a contest of two big bellies pushing against each other.

By chance, on the last day of the tournament held in March 1975, I happened to be visiting my neighbor, whose television was tuned to the sumo broadcast. My eyes were naturally drawn to the screen when the relatively slender Takanohana came into the ring to face the hefty Kitanoumi in a play-off for the tourney championship. It is no exaggeration to say that Takanohana's dramatic victory had a profound influence on my life thereafter.

First, that match made me realize that sumo obviously entails fine techniques, which enable small sumotori to overcome differences in weight against heavier opponents. Particularly since Takanohana was of the second-highest rank in sumo, his defeat of a grand champion could not be dismissed as a mere fluke.

During the next few tournaments, some other small-sized rikishi, such as Asahikuni, Washuyama, and Kitaseumi, also came to the forefront and made sumo all the more interesting to me. I became eager to learn about sumo techniques—about why such lightweight men could emerge victorious against heavyweight opponents.

I also realized that sumo was just about the only Japanese tradition that I had learned absolutely nothing about in graduate school. American scholars of Japan tend to ignore sumo and look down on it as a mere sport. Once I understood that sumo is more than a sport, I decided to fill in this serious gap in my Japanese education.

I started reading almost all the Japanese books and magazines I could find on sumo. After I moved to Tokyo in the autumn of 1975, I began visiting the sumo stadium and the places where the sumotori train. Perhaps being a young, foreign woman gave me an advantage, for some of the sumotori soon remembered my face and began talking to me. One thing led to another, and eventually Corky Alexander, the editor of *The Tokyo Weekender*, heard that I was quite knowledgeable about sumo. He asked me to write a regular column—something that gave me all the more excuse to maintain contacts with the sumo world.

So what is sumo? As an entire way of life in modern Japan, sumo offers a rare glimpse into the topknots, costumes, and life styles of another era. Sumo's valuable tradition is very much alive, a form of entertainment or leisure that has remained popular over many centuries. In this sense, sumo is a remarkable cultural phenomenon. And, yes, it is also a sport—nonviolent and thrilling to watch.

Years ago, despite my involvement with Japanese culture, I could never have imagined that I would end up writing a book about sumo. But I certainly have no doubt or regrets that Takanohana's dramatic victory in March 1975 led me in this direction and opened my eyes to a most fascinating world and a unique sport. I hope this book will help others to appreciate and understand sumo as well.

I am indebted to ex-Ozeki Takanohana (Fujishima Oyakata) and former Yokozuna Kitanoumi (Kitanoumi Oyakata) for first fascinating me with sumo, and am grateful to just about everyone in the sumo world—especially, though, to Naruto Oyakata (former Yokozuna Takanosato) and his wife Noriko, Azumazeki Oyakata (ex-Sekiwake Takamiyama; formerly Jesse Kuhaulua), and Oshima Oyakata (ex-Ozeki Asahikuni) and his wife Yoshiko. In deference to the ways of the sumo world, I will not mention currently active sumotori, but special appreciation also goes to Hanaregoma Oyakata (ex-Ozeki Kaiketsu), Oguruma Oyakata (ex-Ozeki Kotokaze), Oshiogawa Oyakata (ex-Ozeki Daikirin) and his wife Mitsue, Matsugane Oyakata (ex-Ozeki Wakashimazu), Otowayama Oyakata (ex-Komusubi Wakanoumi), and Onoue Oyakata (ex-Maegashira Hidanohana.)

Referees Shikimori Inosuke and Kimura Koichi, who oversee bouts on the *san'yaku* and *juryo* levels, respectively, and match announcers Zenzaburo, Norio, and Yonekichi shared with me much information.

Tsugaruumi, the trainer of apprentice sumotori at Kasugano-Beya, and the sumo hairdressers Tokokatsu (Futagoyama-Beya), Tokotani (Hanaregoma-Beya), and Tokokuni (Kasugano-Beya) as well as managers Inaba (Kokonoe-Beya) and Obayashi (Sadogatake-Beya) were also particularly helpful.

I am especially thankful, for special advice and valuable information about the sumo world, to Sakisaka Matsuhiko, announcer for the Japan Broadcasting Corporation (NHK); Miyazawa Masayuki, former sports reporter for *Nikkan Supotsu*; Kudo Norio, reporter for *Nihon Keizai Shimbun*; Kawahara Takeo, former NHK announcer; Oomi Nobuaki, sports reporter for *Yukan Fuji*; and acupuncturist Ogura Fumimitsu.

Andy Adams of *Sumo World* and Corky Alexander of *The Tokyo Weekender* provided me with the first forums for my sumo articles and greatly encouraged me. Some photographs in this book were kindly lent to me by Ikeda Ikuo, president of the Baseball Magazine Sha, Andy Adams, Clyde Newton, Dr. Shimon Otobe, Takashi Nakano, Jonathan Ellis, Takashi Koguchi of Kobunsha, and Hal Drake of *Stars and Stripes*. Freelance writer Mark Schreiber helped me with the Chinese readings of some names, and the staff of the Sumo Museum was unfailingly patient and helpful. Portions of

Chapters 12 and 14 first appeared in the *Tokyo Journal* (September 1987) and *The Tokyo Weekender* (November 12, 1982), respectively, and were revised and expanded for this book.

Finally, I wish to thank my husband, Tamura Hidetoshi, for his patience when I had to neglect some housework for writing. This book is dedicated to the memory of Jack Stamm and Kintaro the cat, two good friends who passed out of my life in the fall of 1991.

Note on Terminology

The Japanese words for a practitioner of sumo are sumotori (literally, "one who does sumo"), *rikishi* (written with the characters for "strong man"), or *osumo-san* (literally, "honorable practitioner of sumo"). These words can be used interchangeably.

One of these days sumotori may be adopted into the English language, just like geisha and shogun. But regardless of whether it eventually goes into English or not, I prefer to use sumotori and other Japanese terms rather than the common English rendering "sumo wrestler," since sumo is really quite different from wrestling. In fact, it has more in common with judo than with Greco-Roman wrestling.

Most of the sumotori do not understand English, yet they still object to being called "sumo wrestlers." Former Ozeki Takanohana, who was one of the most popular rikishi through the 1970s to early 1980s, once even told me he wished foreigners would give careful thought to whether or not sumo really resembles wrestling before they start calling the sport "sumo wrestling" and its practitioners "sumo wrestlers."

Rikishi is actually the term most preferred by the sumotori themselves. However, since sumotori is probably easier for foreigners unfamiliar with Japanese to remember, it will be the term used most frequently in this book.

All Japanese and Chinese names in this book appear in the traditional Asian order, with the surname preceding the given name. Although one may be used to hearing one of Japan's internationally famous film directors called Akira Kurosawa, instead of Kurosawa Akira in traditional Japanese fashion, it simply sounds funny to this writer to refer to sumotori in anything other than the traditional manner.

Weights and measures are generally given in the metric system, which Japan has adopted from Europe. One kilogram equals 2.2 pounds. One inch can be figured as 2.54 centimeters, so six feet is about 183 centimeters. In mid-1989, the average-sized sumotori in the top division weighed 148 kilograms and was 182 centimeters tall, which made him 326 pounds and just under six feet.

GRAND SUMO

1

Sumotori: Born or Bred

What brings a youth into sumo? The answer to that question is about as varied as the actual number of boys joining Japan's oldest sport every year. Some go into sumo simply because they like it, while others may be intrigued by its possibilities to bring them fame and fortune. Some find the idea of a career in sumo challenging or glamorous; others were originally urged to try it by friends or family members—sometimes to get a sharp taste of discipline—and a few more have even entered the sport by accident.

All professional sumotori are affiliated with a *sumobeya*. Commonly called "sumo stables" in English, the *heya* (*-beya* when used in a compound) are where sumotori train and, unless they are married, also live. As of May 1992, there were forty-four stables, many of which were maintaining a network of scouts, in various parts of Japan with their strongest connections in the head coach's native prefecture.

Scouting and the Right Athletic Background

Sumo scouts tend to be former sumotori from the particular stable, longtime supporters of the heya, and friends or relatives of the coach (*oyakata*). Moreover, the coaches and active sumotori may do some scouting themselves. Sumo scouts keep alert for information about large-sized, athletic, or exceptionally strong

The entrance to the old Tatsunami-Beya.

young men. Particularly in the smaller cities and towns, rumors of an unusually tall, large, or powerful boy soon spread, and the local papers usually give good coverage to the winners of various regional sports events.

Of course, the champions in local sumo competitions are very sought after, but so are those from judo. Several of the techniques in judo have been adapted from sumo, an older sport, and many high-ranking sumotori, including former grand champions Hokutoumi and Onokuni, have backgrounds in judo. On the other hand, although sumo is often referred to as "sumo wrestling" in English, precious few professional rikishi have entered sumo from Greco-Roman wrestling, and none has succeeded in a big way.

In fact, there have been more successful sumotori who have come into sumo from swimming than those from Western-style wrestling. Champion swimmers tend to have strong legs and hips—essential elements in sumo. It may be interesting to note that the most famous rikishi in recent times who were champion swimmers before joining sumo, such as Takanohana and Masuiya-ma II, both former *ozeki*, as well as former Sekiwake Washuyama, have all been on the lightweight side. (Coincidentally, these three all went into sumo on their own accord, in spite of the opposition of relatives who had been or were sumotori at the time.)

Although an amateur scout may make the initial approach, the most effective persuasion usually comes from the head coach or the leading rikishi in the heya. For example, Chiyonofuji decided to go into sumo after Kokonoe Oyakata (former Yokozuna Chiyonoyama) promised to take him back to Tokyo in an airplane—an exciting idea to a youth who had never flown before. Chiyonofuji's Kokonoe-Beya stablemate Hokutoumi, by contrast, never needed convincing, as his ambition from elementary school days had been to become a sumotori.

Onokuni was persuaded by Ozeki Kaiketsu that a living could not be made from judo—words he took to heart since years earlier Kaiketsu himself had switched to sumo for the exact same reason. Former Grand Champion Kitanoumi, who had been approached in his early teens by several sumo scouts, ultimately chose Mihogaseki-Beya because he was impressed by the kindness of the coach's wife, who had presented him with hand-knitted gloves to keep his hands warm during the frigid Hokkaido winters.

Mitoizumi was scouted by Takamiyama (b. Jesse Kuhaulua) while the latter was making a VIP visit to a department store in Mito City, Ibaraki Prefecture, northeast of Tokyo. When the tall youth asked Jesse for his autograph, the Hawaiian-born sumotori looked him over and suggested he give sumo a try. It was undoubtedly difficult for the boy to turn down somebody whom he greatly admired, and Mitoizumi has since been followed into sumo by his younger brother, Umenosato.

Unwitting Entry

Some country boys are lured into sumo unwittingly. For instance, when Futagoyama Oyakata (former Grand Champion Wakanohana I) returned to his native Aomori Prefecture to bring young Shimoyama Katsunori (the future Wakanohana II) back to Tokyo, he heard about another large boy named Takaya Toshihide in a neighboring town. Since he was already in the area, the coach went to see the other boy too. Because Takaya showed no interest at first in becoming a sumotori, Futagoyama Oyakata finally persuaded him to go to Tokyo with him just "to see the sights of the capital and what a sumo-beya is like." That sounded fine to young Takaya, who ended up riding the overnight train to the capital with Shimoyama and the coach.

After about a week in Tokyo, Takaya decided he had seen enough and was just preparing to return to Aomori when he received letters from a teacher and some classmates encouraging him to do his best in sumo. He and Shimoyama were also sent a local newspaper which reported their entry into Futagoyama-

Beya. Takaya thereupon realized to his dismay that if he went home immediately, people would assume he was too weak to endure the rigors of sumo life. Thus, to save face, he stayed with sumo and ultimately went on to become Yokozuna Takanosato, the fifty-ninth grand champion in sumo history. He and Wakanohana II, incidentally, make the only case in which two future grand champions from the same prefecture joined the same stable at the same time.

Undoubtedly the most humorous case of unwitting entry into sumo involves Yoshibayama (b. Ikeda Junnosuke), who had taken a train to Tokyo with the intention of going to school there. By a quirk of fate, a sumotori from Takashima-Beya happened to be on the platform at Tokyo's Ueno Station at that time to meet a sumo aspirant who was supposed to be arriving on the same train. It later transpired that the youth who had been intending to join the stable got cold feet and jumped the train before reaching Tokyo. Young Ikeda, the only conspicuously large youth in sight, was naturally mistaken for him and taken back to Takashima-Beya before he even realized what was happening to him. Ikeda later became Yoshibayama, the forty-third grand champion in sumo history.

Country Boys vs. City Boys

The majority of new sumo recruits, both past and present, come from the countryside—particularly from the cold northern regions such as Hokkaido and Aomori. In these regions farmers and fishermen have difficulty making a decent living throughout the entire year, and during the off-seasons they often venture to Tokyo and other urban areas to seek temporary employment. Since farmers and fishermen in such areas tend to have difficulty supporting a large household, they are usually glad to send sons other than their eldest into sumo. Sumo also happens to be very popular in Aomori, not only as a traditional sport but also as one which, in contrast to baseball, can be practiced indoors during the long winter months.

Between 1926 and November 1988, the nearly sixty-three years of the Showa period (1926–89), 505 men entered the top division of sumo. Forty-five of them, including eight future grand champions, hailed from Hokkaido. The Tohoku region, comprised of six northern prefectures on the main island of Honshu, produced ninety-four: eight grand champions among them.

By contrast, only a small number of high-ranking sumotori

have hailed from temperate Shizuoka Prefecture, located between Tokyo and Nagoya, and Okayama Prefecture in western Honshu. Sumo has by tradition been quite popular on the southernmost main island of Kyushu, however, and the region has continued to produce a number of high-ranking sumotori.

Furthermore, with some notable exceptions such as Yokozuna Tochinishiki (later Kasugano Oyakata and chairman of the professional Sumo Association from 1974 to 1988), a native of Tokyo, city boys are generally viewed as lacking in the patience to put up with the rigors of sumo life in the apprentice stage.

Sumo Families

Recently an increasing number of brothers, sons, or nephews of past or present rikishi have been going into professional sumo. Nevertheless, nepotism can hardly be said to exist in the sport. The sumo world is a meritocracy; promotions are based almost solely on tournament records, and not on family connections. Despite all the publicity given to successful sumo families in the 1980s, more relatives of famous rikishi have actually failed than those who have succeeded over the years. They have absolutely no guarantee of making the grade. A notable case in point was the late Hanakago Oyakata, who trained two grand champions, a champion, and several other high-ranking rikishi; yet his own son was a failure in the sport.

It is safer for a coach who wants to keep his stable in the family to marry his daughter to a reasonably successful sumotori than to count on his own son to take over. Indeed, daughters have traditionally been so prized in the sumo world that *osekihan*, a rice-and-bean dish normally served for felicitous occasions, is customarily cooked whenever a girl is born into a stable. Although the number of marriages arranged between sumotori and coaches' daughters is on the decline, in 1992 eight out of forty-four stables were still under the administration of sons-in-law of previous oyakata. (Hanakago Oyakata himself married his only daughter to Grand Champion Wajima, but that marriage ended in divorce.)

Mihogaseki-Beya is currently the only stable that has been passed down from father to son, both of whom went as far as the second highest rank of *ozeki* under the name Masuiyama. They have indeed been the most successful father-and-son pair in sumo history. Yokozuna Wakanohana I and Ozeki Takanohana, who are twenty-two years apart in age, have been the most successful brothers. As of July 1989, they were still the only fraternal pair ever to have captured a tourney title in the highest division. Yet they, too, had another brother in between them who was a failure at sumo.

In the 1980s, Izutsu-Beya emerged as a class by itself as a successful sumo family. Izutsu Oyakata went as far as *sekiwake*, sumo's third-highest rank, under the name Tsurugamine in the 1950s. His late wife was the granddaughter of the twenty-fifth Grand Champion Nishinoumi II, and Tsurugamine's second and third sons, Sakahoko and Terao, were performing in the top division throughout 1986, 1987, and 1988. Furthermore, in September 1986, the two became the first brothers ever to be awarded tournament prizes together; in March 1989, they simultaneously held the third-highest rank—another first in sumo history. Yet somewhat forgotten in the background of their glory is the sad case of the eldest brother, Tsurunofuji, who was first promoted to a salaried division simultaneously with Sakahoko but plunged greatly in rank due to a series of injuries and illnesses, and ultimately quit sumo altogether in 1990.

In the early 1990s Fujishima-Beya, headed by the former Takanohana, emerged as another exceptional sumo family. In March 1988, the two sons of the stablemaster (and the nephews of Wakanohana I) made their debuts in professional sumo. And in May that year, the elder of the two, Wakahanada, won the tournament in the lowest division.

On the same day the titles in two other nonsalaried divisions were also captured by sons of former sumotori: Oginohana, son of ex-Sekiwake Oginohana (Takasaki Oyakata), and Kotougusa, son of the late Ozeki Kotogahama. An unprecedented event in the history of the sport, this set off a new wave of successful sumo families. By 1991, both Wakahanada and his younger brother, Takahanada, as well as Oginohana and his younger brother, Oginishiki, were all performing in salaried ranks. In January 1992, Takahanada followed in his father's and uncle's footsteps by capturing a tourney championship in the highest division.

Entrance Requirements

Whether a youngster has gotten into sumo on his own accord, at someone else's urging, or by accident, he must meet some stipulations set by the Sumo Association to be formally accepted. These are

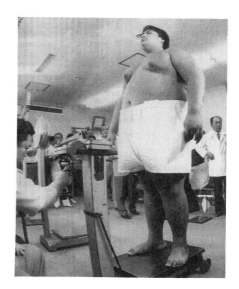

Vincent Divoux of California weighing in at the June 1988 examination for new recruits. He joined Takasago-Beya and was given the ring name Shinnishiki. Divoux is now a rap singer in Los Angeles.

basically to be at least 173 centimeters tall, to weigh a minimum of 75 kilograms, to have completed compulsory education (in Japan, junior high school), and to have the consent of a parent or guardian. Overall physical examinations are also given to check the condition of each recruit's internal organs and blood pressure. Those with problems are usually put on medicine or a health program but are seldom rejected outright.

Before World War II, the entrance requirements were practically nonexistent, allowing boys of almost any size and as young as thirteen to go into sumo, often instead of school. With the establishment of compulsory education in Japan after the war, some thirteen-year-olds even took to commuting to junior high school from their stables. But since it was difficult for such boys to concentrate on both their studies and sumo at the same time, and because their special treatment often proved disruptive to normal life in the heya, the ruling concerning the completion of compulsory education was put into effect in 1972.

Minimum height and weight requirements were also drawn up after the war, and they have been revised a number of times in accordance with the increases in the average size of the Japanese in general. In 1982, minimum height and weight were upgraded from 170 centimeters and 70 kilograms for fifteen-year-olds and 173 centimeters and 75 kilograms for those over eighteen years to the present requirements of 173 centimeters and 75 kilograms for all.

This upgrading has occurred because by the 1980s, 170 centimeters was no longer especially tall for a teen-aged Japanese male.

Those who do not meet the minimum height or weight tend to be rejected outright. Some undersized sumo hopefuls have been known to resort to desperate means to pass the *shindeshi kensa*, the physical examination for new recruits. For instance, some who are on the short side have reportedly pounded their heads repeatedly against a wall or pole to "grow" a centimeter taller by developing a bump. Others who are a bit low on weight have been known to gorge on food and then drink huge bottles of water, all of which is often thrown up right after the examination. Occasionally a youngster who persists after failing the test several times is accepted out of sympathy. On the other hand, Tochitsurugi, a winner of the coveted Technique Prize as well as the Fighting Spirit Prize once each in the 1980s, was allowed to join from the very beginning, though at 168 centimeters he was below the minimum height requirement in 1973. The coaches in charge of the physical faked his papers to give him an extra two centimeters, since Tochitsurugi (then known as Hirano) had been a national high school sumo champion.

In 1990, after a former Nihon University champion named Nagao (later Mainoumi) failed the shindeshi kensa once, the Sumo Association finally created a new ruling to make special exceptions for certain young men who do not meet the height or weight requirement but have a strong background in college or amateur sumo. But in May 1992, the association also established a cut-off age of under 20 for most new recruits and under 25 for those with championships in nationwide amateur or college meets. This ruling took effect in July of that year.

Incidentally, there is somewhat of a jinx against high school sumo champions in professional sumo. Wakashimazu broke it in 1982 by reaching ozeki, the second-highest rank. Nevertheless, most others have not gone far as professional sumotori. For some reason, it appears to be luckier to go into sumo directly out of junior high school, like the majority of rikishi, or else after college.

The Ideal Recruit

Ideally a new recruit should be tall for his age and big-boned— not necessarily fat, but with the capacity to gain weight. Veteran scouts and doctors used to treating sumotori can often tell just by looking at the contours of a youth's chest and stomach area if he can be expected to gain enough weight.

It is preferable for an apprentice to put on weight steadily while learning sumo techniques and movements. Early photographs of some sumotori who later went to the top, such as grand champions Taiho, Wakanohana II, and Onokuni, reveal that they were surprisingly thin at age fifteen or sixteen. The future Wakashimazu was also as skinny as a veritable beanstalk when he finished high school and apparently had reservations about going into professional sumo for this reason. However, Futagoyama Oyakata reassured the youth that he would eventually be able to put on weight after hearing he had no problems with his internal organs. Even though Wakashimazu always remained one of the lighter sumotori, he certainly made a respectable showing as a professional.

As a matter of fact, if a boy is too fat from the beginning, he may not be very athletic and, consequently, have trouble doing the various exercises unique to sumo. Unfortunately, every year some overweight, lazy boys also join under the impression that sumo is going to be a cinch for them. They soon learn otherwise; despite the behemoth proportions sumotori tend to take on later in their careers, boys who are gargantuan from the very outset often do not fare well. Many quit in the first year; others even lose weight in the beginning and then gain it back while also putting on musculature in the sumo way. The bellies of even some of the most rotund high-ranking rikishi tend to be very firm, and hardly the bowls of jelly they may look like. A lot of well-toned muscle exists under all that flesh.

2

Sumo Rankings

The numbers of sumotori are constantly changing; some men leave the sport after each tourney, and other new ones join it. Nevertheless, in recent years the tendency has been for the new recruits to outnumber those who leave sumo annually. Thus, while the average number of sumotori was around 750 in the first half of the 1980s, the figure was generally over eight hundred in 1988 through mid-1992.

The sumotori are divided into a six-division pyramid on the ranking sheets (*banzuke-hyo* or *banzuke*) published thirteen days prior to each tourney. Within the divisions men are further ranked by numbers, with 1 being the top within that group. In general, the rank of a sumotori is only as good as his score in the most recent tourney, which is why most positions within the six divisions are constantly changing. A score with a majority of wins against losses usually means promotion—especially in the lower divisions. A losing record is almost always followed by demotion. (More details about promotions and demotions can be found in Chapter 6.)

Actually, there is something akin to a seventh division called *maezumo*, or "pre-sumo," which is not listed on the ranking sheets. New recruits are tested for their strength and ability in pre-sumo and then ranked accordingly in the *jonokuchi* (introductory) division in the next tourney. But even those who lose all their maezumo bouts will get on the ranking sheets, albeit very near the bottom.

The number of men in jonokuchi is not fixed, varying according to the total number of sumotori. In May 1992, there were 153, with 77 on the east side and 76 on the west.

Jonokuchi is followed by the *jonidan* (second step) division. The number of men here also varies from tourney to tourney. In May 1992, there were 310, divided evenly on the east and west.

In recent years the number of positions in the *sandanme* (third step) division has come to be fixed at 200—100 on the east side and 100 on the west.

The number of positions is also fixed in the *makushita* (literally, "below the curtain") division, where there is a quota of 120 places on the ranking sheets. All the sumotori in the makushita division and below (a total of 783 in May 1992) are considered apprentices and do not receive monthly salaries.

Sekitori

Juryo (also called *jumaime*), the division just above makushita, is where men are first considered to have left the apprentice stage and are treated as full-fledged rikishi. According to one theory, the term juryo derives from the ten (*ju*) *ryo* coins men in this division received as pay in the Edo period (1603–1867). However, since the characters for juryo can also mean "ten each," another theory is that the name stems from the organization of the original twenty juryo—in other words, ten on each side. Later the number of juryo came to be fixed at twenty-six, thirteen on each side; but, claim the proponents of this theory, the old name has stuck.

The sumotori in juryo and the top *makunouchi*, or *makuuchi*, (literally, "inside the curtain") division are called *sekitori*, which means "to have taken a barrier." They receive salaries, have apprentices known as *tsukebito* to wait on and run various errands for them, and are entitled to a number of other privileges as well. During tournaments, for example, they have their hair fixed in the fancier style of topknot fashioned to resemble a ginkgo leaf. They are allowed to wear silk *mawashi* (belts) during tournaments as well as silk kimono when they go out in public. Sekitori are, furthermore, given *akeni* (bamboo trunks) to store their changes of clothing and other accouterments in the dressing room.

Although the juryo are basically entitled to the same privileges as other sekitori, the real glamour and fame tend to come in the top makunouchi division. The quota of positions in this division is "not to exceed forty," but sometimes there are less than this number filled. The men in makunouchi are further divided into rankings, from bottom to top: *maegashira, komusubi*, sekiwake, ozeki, and yokozuna. The number of maegashira usually hovers between twenty-five to twenty-eight but ultimately depends on how many men are ranked at the very top.

The four positions above maegashira (front leaders) are collectively called *san'yaku* (three roles). This term is an anachronism dating back from the times when ozeki was the highest rank in sumo, and yokozuna was just a nickname frequently, but not always, given to especially strong ozeki. There are never less than two komusubi and two sekiwake each, although occasionally three or four men may fill one or both of these slots. These terms can be rendered roughly as "junior champion, second class" and "junior champion"; but as this seems a bit forced, they will be left in romanized Japanese in this book.

Ozeki (great barrier) can be rendered as "champion" in English. The number of ozeki usually ranges from two to five. In May 1992, there were two. Occasionally only one man is deemed qualified to hold the rank, and for a brief time in both 1905 and 1981, there were no ozeki at all.

Yokozuna are also called "grand champions." The name yokozuna is written with the characters *yoko* (sideways) and *tsuna*, the white hawser donned by the grand champion when he performs his special entrance into the ring ceremony. This is the highest a man can go in sumo, and once there he is never demoted. (Retirement is the only option for a yokozuna who is faring badly.) Only one out of perhaps every seven hundred new recruits will ever reach this rank. Ideally, there should be two or three grand champions, but occasionally there is only one or as many as four. During the January 1953 tournament, five men held the yokozuna rank for the only time in history. On the other hand, there were no yokozuna on the ranking sheets after the retirement of Miyaginoyama in 1931 until the promotion of Tamanishiki a year and a half later. A new period of no grand champions on the banzuke-hyo began in July 1992.

Ranking Sheets

All ranks are published thirteen days prior to each tournament on the official banzuke-hyo, although the sheets are sometimes released a bit earlier so as not to conflict with a major national holiday. The layout of the 57 by 44 centimeter ranking sheet is divided into east and west sides, just like the sumotori in tourneys. As the east side is considered more prestigious, the men ranked there most likely did better in the previous tourney than their counterparts on the

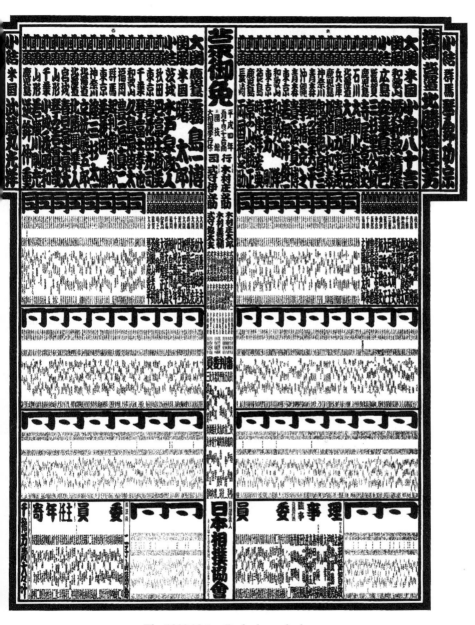

The 1992 Natsu Basho banzuke-hyo.

west. If two men at the same rank had the exact same score in the previous tournament, the one with the better cumulative record for two tourneys or the one who has held the rank longer is most likely to be on the east. The rank, birthplace (or location of the family registry), and name of each man in the makunouchi division appear in that order on the top row. Those on both the east and west sides appear in descending order of rank from right to left.

The only exceptions to this order are the rikishi called *haridashi*, whose names are literally "extended out" of the normal ranking order. This is because while in principle there are supposed to be only two holders of each rank, often in actuality three or four men hold the same rank—especially within the san'yaku. Therefore, the names of the extra men (usually the ones with the lowest scores in the previous tourney or previous two tourneys) are placed outside the normal ranking order, giving the banzuke-hyo the appearance of a patterned shirt with short sleeves.

The lettering for the yokozuna is the thickest. Those for ozeki, sekiwake, and komusubi are still thicker than the characters for the maegashira. The names of the juryo and makushita appear on the next line. The lettering for the juryo is still done in bold ink, though the print is smaller. As the banzuke goes lower in rank, the lettering gets smaller and smaller. By the time it reaches the jonokuchi on the fifth row the characters are so tiny that they can barely be read without a magnifying glass.

Next to the jonokuchi on the bottom row are the names of oyakata belonging to the Sumo Association; they are written in order of rank from right to left. Similar to those of the yokozuna, the name of the top director appears in the thickest and boldest lettering, albeit smaller than that of the actual grand champions. The names of up to the thirteen other executives also stand out. The lettering for the rest of the coaches comes in a smaller size, but hardly as tiny as that of the jonokuchi.

A thin strip of lettering appears from top to bottom in the very middle of the banzuke-hyo. The first line reads *"gomen komuru,"* meaning that all the people listed on the sheet have permission to perform in some capacity in the upcoming tourney. Below that in smaller print are listed the location and dates of the tourney in question. Then appear the names of every *gyoji* (referee) with the lettering getting smaller as it goes down in rank. Below the gyoji are the names of each *shobu shinpan-in*, a coach serving as a judge for tournament matches. There should be no more than twenty of them. At the bottom appear the words Nihon Sumo

Kyokai, the official name of the Japan Sumo Association, and its address.

The oldest extant example of a ranking sheet dates back to 1733 and was issued in Kyoto. The first one for sumo in Edo (present-day Tokyo) was issued in October 1757, and samples can be found for almost all tournaments held thereafter. The banzuke are written in a highly stylized, unique calligraphy known as *sumo-moji* (sumo lettering). The brushwork is done by one of the referees; Kimura Rinnosuke handled the task through most of the 1980s.

Depending on the tourney, the actual number of banzuke-hyo printed varies. The average figure is 420,000 per tournament, and the greatest volume always is released for the one held in January. Sekitori and coaches buy up many banzuke, stamp their names on the right side, and then mail them to patrons and close friends. In January, they tend to be sent especially in substitution for New Year cards, which in Japan serve a function similar to Christmas and Chanukah cards in the West. The remainder of the ranking sheets are sold to the general public at the stadium for fifty yen each.

3

Life as a Sumotori, or the Road to Stardom

Physical examinations for new sumo recruits are given six times a year, just before every tournament. Since the latter part of the 1970s, over a hundred new faces have been coming into sumo each year; the majority of them join just before the spring tournament in March, which is graduation time in Japan.

Once a youth is accepted by the Sumo Association, he is expected to take up residence in one of the sumo-beya. Traditionally, the sumo-beya have been located in the Ryogoku area of Tokyo near the Kokugikan stadium, and even today the greatest number of stables can be found in the vicinity. However, due to the increasing difficulty of obtaining land in the area, several have been constructed in other parts of Tokyo and its suburbs.

Even if a new recruit's home is located in the Tokyo area, he is still required to live in one of the stables at the beginning of his career. A youth who is already living in a stable as the son of the head coach must move from the family's living quarters (usually on the top floor or floors) to a big communal room downstairs for the lowest-ranked rikishi on the day he officially joins the sumo world. Moreover, from the day a coach's son enters professional sumo, he must refrain from calling his parents "father" and "mother." Instead, he will address them as oyakata and *okamisan* (a term used for the coach's wife and also for women shopkeepers), just like the other sumotori in the stable.

Incidentally, all coaches in a stable are called oyakata. The oyakata using the same name as that of the stable is the head coach, or stablemaster. Another way to distinguish the stablemaster from other coaches is by referring to him as *shisho* (master).

Practice

In the sumo world almost everything works or is done according to rank. The new recruit, therefore, must get up earliest in the morning—often before the crack of dawn—to begin training.

The training area, called *keikoba*, may look fairly simple at first glance, as it primarily consists of a rectangular dirt floor with a *dohyo* (ring) 4.55 meters in diameter in the middle, demarcated by rice-straw bales which are 60 percent buried and 40 percent exposed. (Though a few stables have two rings, one is standard.) As the practice area is considered sacred, it invariably has a Shinto altar hanging on one of the walls. Furthermore, the keikoba contains more than meets the eye: strips of dried squid, washed rice, kelp, drops of sake, and various other items associated with long life or good luck are buried in a spot under the dohyo. The ring is remade and refilled with the auspicious items prior to every Tokyo tournament.

Much of the practice consists of bouts similar to those held at regular tournaments—except that they are not preceded by a long series of rituals, and the winner is likely to take on several opponents in succession. Since there are usually more rikishi in the training area than can work out in the ring at one time, many end up standing around watching and waiting for their turn. The coaches generally say that observing others is an important part of the training. Nevertheless, some sumotori prefer doing various basic exercises at the sidelines to watching those in the ring.

Although women visitors are welcome to sit and watch sumo practice from a raised tatami-matted area called *agari-zashiki*, they are not permitted to touch any part of the actual keikoba due to ancient Shinto beliefs about the female body being impure. In any case, few guests ever show up to see practice from the start when it is still dark outside. But as the morning wears on, the agari-zashiki is likely to start filling up with fans and patrons.

Advance permission is usually not needed to view a practice session; even complete strangers to the heya are generally welcome to watch as long as they remain quiet and sit with their legs crossed or kneeling on tatami. However, some stables do not permit visitors other than the press during the tournament seasons; it is also advisable to call in advance when planning to come with a

The two practice rings at Sadogatake-Beya. The overhanging Shinto paper streamers mark the areas as sacred.

An oyakata watches practice from the raised tatami platform above the training area.

Yokozuna Kitanoumi signing his hand-print, shown on the left.

large group. Guests are allowed to take photographs, but generally not with flashes, which can disturb the concentration of the sumotori in the practice ring.

After practice, popular sekitori often start making handprints in black or red ink on thick, square paper boards called *shikishi*, which are later autographed and given to sumo patrons or sold. Visitors desiring an autographed handprint should bring their own shikishi or paper. Those with small children may want to ask one of the sumotori to hold the youngster after practice, following an old Japanese belief that a child who has been held by a rikishi will grow up to be healthy and strong. Most rikishi appear willing to oblige.

Basic Training

Shiko is sumo-style stomping begun in a position with the legs spread far apart. One leg is raised high up and then brought down, while the rikishi exhales. This process is repeated with the other leg. Tyros in professional sumo are recommended to do shiko at least five hundred times a day to strengthen their legs. Asahifuji's father, a former amateur sumo champion in Aomori Prefecture, tried to encourage his son as young boy by giving him ten yen for each

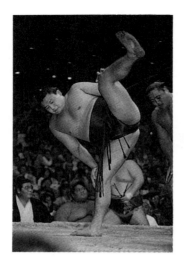

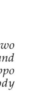

Top, left and right, Takahanada doing two sumo training exercises—shiko stomping and matawari splits. Bottom, hitting the teppo pole with open palms helps improve body strength, timing, and coordination.

shiko he did. The maximum the future ozeki earned in a day as a youngster was apparently ¥3,000.

Matawari are sumo-style splits. While sitting on the ground with the legs spread as wide as possible, the rikishi starts bending the upper half of his body forward to touch the ground. Matawari can be rather painful for all but the very limber; indeed, it has driven many novices, most notably Hawaiian-born Takamiyama, to tears. Anybody who has witnessed sumotori doing such splits is unlikely to dismiss them as mere fat men.

Teppo, a thick wooden pole placed in the ground in a corner of the keikoba, serves as the sumo equivalent of a punching bag. A rikishi slides his feet back and forth, all the while slamming his hands against the teppo pole. This exercise not only strengthens the arms, legs, back, and hands but also improves coordination and timing.

Almost all stables nowadays seem to be equipped with Western athletic equipment, such as barbells and exercise bicycles. Musashigawa-Beya even has a complete weight training room in its basement. Some also encourage their members to jog or take up golf. Yet these are all considered supplementary and are no substitute for the traditional basics.

Every Morning of the Year

As the morning progresses, the training area will continue to fill up with higher-ranked sumotori and perhaps with some coaches as well. The sumotori in the top two divisions are known as sekitori; if the stable has any (not all do), they will generally appear for practice sometime between 8 and 9 A.M. The sekitori wear thick, white cotton-canvas mawashi during practice. The apprentices don black ones for both training and regular tourney matches. During practice both sekitori and tyros have their hair fixed in the same simple *chonmage* (topknot).

The mawashi of veterans in the lower ranks tend to become faded with many washings over the years to a very light grey—sometimes to the point where they are hard to distinguish at a distance from the white ones of the sekitori. But in general even the first-time visitor should be able to tell the sekitori from the others: if not by the mawashi, then by the way apprentices are at the beck and call of the sekitori—wiping dirt out of their hair or off their backs after harsh workouts and otherwise tending to their needs.

The senior rikishi work out among themselves as well as give training to apprentices. The seniors in particular take charge of the juniors on days when no coaches show up. Training is carried out daily all year round; the only vacations are for about five days after each tourney and on January 1.

The most intense practice occurs during the twelve days between the release of the latest ranking sheets and the opening of the tournament. To get a chance to work out with a greater variety of rikishi close to his own rank, a lone sekitori in a heya is likely to go for practice at a bigger, preferably affiliated, stable for at least a week during those twelve days. This is known as *de-geiko* (going out for practice).

Onokuni, for example, used to work out almost every day at the affiliated Futagoyama-Beya until his own Hanaregoma-Beya grew larger by absorbing Hanakago-Beya upon the latter's demise. Asahifuji practiced frequently at Takasago-Beya even after becoming yokozuna. Although Takasago-Beya is not an affiliate of his Oshima-Beya, it was the heya of Asashio, who had been Asahifuji's senior classmate at Kinki University. Some clever sekitori like Chiyonofuji and Hokutoumi did de-geiko, even though their Kokonoe-Beya had other high-ranked men, to gain experience with a wider variety of opponents.

During the twelve days prior to a tournament, several stables

Left, a regular chonmage. Right, a Takasago-Beya stablemate adjusts Mitoizumi's chonmage, which has come undone during practice.

carry out joint practice with their affiliates. This practice is called *rengo-geiko* and usually rotates to a different heya every two days. The Dewanoumi group (consisting of the Dewanoumi, Kasugano, Mihogaseki, Musashigawa, Tamanoi, and Kitanoumi stables) is especially noted for holding joint-training sessions.

The most spectacular joint practice of all takes place once on an unfixed date during the twelve days prior to every Tokyo tournament. The training session is held in view of the Yokozuna Deliberation Council, and the leading sekitori from most stables— even those who are not up for promotion—participate in this practice.

The Finale

Butsukari-geiko (collision practice), another element of basic training, takes place toward the end of the day's workout. This is when an apprentice sumotori charges at the chest of one of the senior rikishi and tries to push him around the ring. A novice may be required to do this repeatedly until he is practically collapsing from exhaustion. Particularly rough treatment of an apprentice during practice is known, somewhat sarcastically, as *kawaigari* (tender loving care). Yet, in a way, such treatment often does

Top, Hokutoumi performing butsukari-geiko at the chest of Chiyonofuji while other rikishi watch and wait for their turns; left, doing deep knee bends under a heavy burden to strengthen the back and legs.

result in a form of care that helps to spur a promising apprentice on. The hazing at a few stables has been known to get out of hand, leading some apprentices to leave the sumo world altogether, but deliberate brutality is rare.

During butsukari the senior rikishi also tosses the novice to the ground a number of times to give him practice in learning how to fall without sustaining injury. Depending on the stable, collision practice may be carried out anywhere from less than ten minutes to nearly a half an hour. It is usually followed by everyone doing leg splits, and then sumo-style stomping several times in unison.

Yokozuna Wakanohana II relaxes in a traditional Japanese bath. His three attendants are reflected in the mirror behind him.

A sumotori performing sonkyo after a day's practice.

Finally, each sumotori squats down in a style known as *sonkyo*: the knees spread open, the back straight, hips lowered, hands on knees, inhaling and exhaling deeply—somewhat reminiscent of a moment of silent prayer. In some stables the performance of sonkyo ends the practice session. In many others this is followed by senior rikishi asking one or more of the novices to recite the sumo code of honor ("I will show respect to my elders; I will take the initiative to perform various chores...."), all the while squatting sonkyo style. A few stables even stage a veritable grand finale with all the sumotori standing up to sing the official Sumo Association song.

Practice sessions generally end between 10:30 and 11:00 A.M., except during tourneys when they are carried out less strenuously and finished much earlier. But the apprentice sumotori is hardly able to relax. After hours of intense training on a dirt floor, the rikishi first enter the bath in order of rank. Apprentices enter the bathing area to serve as attendants to sekitori or the oyakata. In the traditional Japanese bath, the scrubbing and rinsing are performed before actually stepping into the tub. In the sumo world, it is the duty of the attendants to scrub the sekitori. The Japanese think nothing of this practice; however, it apparently was one of the things which upset a Canadian named Kototenzan (John Tenta) during his brief sumo career.

One exception to the rule of entering the bath in order of rank was made briefly for Ozeki Takanohana in 1978. Since he had been

the senior member of Futagoyama-Beya for so long, he was allowed to precede Wakanohana II in the bath until the latter attained his first tourney title as yokozuna.

The sekitori tend to take long baths. In stables with several sekitori, the lower-ranking ones may play catch outside while waiting their turn, go to a nearby coffee shop, or just sit around the agari-zashiki getting their topknots straightened by a sumo hairdresser and chatting.

The First Meal of the Day

After bathing, the sumotori sit down, again in order of rank, in the agari-zashiki or other tatami room nearby to feast at low dining tables which, depending on the stable, are either circular or rectangular. As if the tyros were not hungry enough after being up several hours on an empty stomach (sumo practice can not be done on a full one), next they must stand in the dining area to serve the sekitori. There apparently was often little left for the novices to eat prior to and just after World War II, but that is not much of a problem nowadays. The problem is usually just having to wait until past noon to eat, although that, too, can perhaps serve as motivation to climb to the higher ranks as quickly as possible.

The apprentices who do not appear at the keikoba on a particular day are probably on kitchen duty. Called *chanko-ban*, this involves going out to purchase food supplies for the day as well as fixing the repast. The most famous part of a sumotori's first meal of the day consists of *chanko-nabe*, a sort of stew or chowder, which the rikishi cook themselves by dropping various items chopped up by those on kitchen duty into a big pot (*nabe*) set up before them.

Kitchen chores are generally rotated among all the apprentices, but occasionally a sumotori may grow fonder of cooking than sumo practice. He may even give up training altogether to become the *chanko-cho* (chief chef) of the stable and sometimes is hired privately by the head coach to stay on in that position after quitting sumo. Even though not all rikishi will go as far as chanko-cho, the experience in the kitchen often proves helpful to those who do not make the grade in the sport. Many men who were unsuccessful in sumo find jobs making use of their culinary skills after quitting.

There is considerable misconception, even among ordinary Japanese, about what goes into chanko-nabe. Many imagine that it is just a richer version of *yosenabe*, a potluck sort of stew containing fish, fowl, red meat, and various vegetables. The sumotori do occasionally eat something akin to yosenabe, but generally their stews contain a lot of vegetables and include only one source of protein other than tofu. That is to say, a beef-based stew usually does not contain fish, and vice versa.

In fact, some of the chanko-nabe made in a sumo-beya are no different from ordinary Japanese dishes cooked in a pot such as *shabu-shabu*, and sukiyaki. But when these dishes are consumed in a sumo-beya, they are all called chanko or chanko-nabe. Like most other people, the sumotori would grow tired of eating the same thing every day, so the varieties of chanko are almost endless. (I have eaten chanko-nabe at least one hundred times, yet have seldom been served the same fare twice.) The base in which the dish is cooked also varies from occasion to occasion and from stable to stable. It may consist, for example, of dried fish shavings and soy sauce, miso, or stock made from boiling chicken bones.

In contrast to popular belief, chanko-nabe by itself is not necessarily a high-calorie dish. In fact, when eaten in moderation, those made with fish or chicken in particular can make a nutritious dish for dieters. (A recipe for a chicken chanko is at the end of the chapter.) The difference lies in the amounts consumed of it and with it. Now that Japan has become a wealthy and well-fed nation, its sumotori are also being treated to more side dishes—such as fried

Sumotori on kitchen duty prepare chanko-nabe.

chicken, grilled fish, Chinese dumplings, Western-style salads, omelets, and so on—than their prewar counterparts probably ever dreamed of. All of this is typically accompanied by large bowls of rice and washed down with beer. Hardly a low-calorie meal!

Although the sekitori consume more than the average person, many still do not eat as much as might be imagined from their size. The reasons seem to be that most of them have already reached their working weight and have most of their needs taken care of by apprentices. In contrast, the apprentices not only tend to be hungry from long hours of practicing and running errands for the sekitori on empty stomachs but also usually wish to gain weight. It is generally these younger fellows called *wakaishu* or *wakaimono* who eat legendary, prodigious amounts such as eight giant bowls of rice, 150 pieces of sushi, and twenty-five portions of barbecued beef at one sitting.

The Rest of the Day

After the meal, married sekitori are likely to go home. There are no regulations concerning where married sekitori reside, but

After morning practice, one sumotori visits a neighborhood coffee shop, and Ozeki Takanohana has his back rubbed by an apprentice.

most prefer to live reasonably close to the stable for convenience' sake. Single sekitori may go out for personal business or pleasure or else retreat upstairs to their own private rooms in the stable. In general, only sekitori are allotted their own rooms, although in the more spacious stables senior makushita rikishi might get double rooms to share. Apprentices generally must live in a large communal room.

If an apprentice is not required to run an errand for a coach or a sekitori, the afternoon will be free for him to spend as he pleases. Many of the novices first return to their communal room for a nap. Taking a nap right after the meal helps a sumotori's body store the calories he has just consumed. For this reason, napping is even regarded as an intrinsic part of the training; some rikishi even vie for the longest sleeping record. Several young behemoths snoring away in one room can make quite a sound.

Most young rikishi nowadays possess a number of the gadgets Japan has become famous for; so instead of sleeping in the afternoon, some are likely to watch television or listen to music through head-phones in the communal space. Others might go out to a movie, to a game parlor, or to a coffee shop in the neighborhood.

A fairly simple meal is served in the stable at night. Many go out for dinner if they can. Nowadays both sekitori and apprentices alike, wearing their traditional attire, can often be spotted at movie theaters or dancing at discos.

Rikishi

One unique feature of sumo in contrast with other forms of grappling is the absence of weight classes. While a minimum of 75 kilograms has been set for entry into the sumo world, there are no further weight requirements for promotion to any division. By size alone, it is sometimes difficult to distinguish between the largest new recruits and the smallest sekitori. As of July 1989, the average weight in the top division was 148 kilograms, ranging from Kyokudozan's 100 kilograms (220 pounds) to Konishiki's 241 kilograms (530 pounds). Undoubtedly one of the most exciting aspects of sumo is to see a man face an opponent nearly double his size and then watch the "David" beat the "Goliath." In the mid to late 1980s, for example, Kirishima, who was then about 117 kilograms, had become a major nemesis for Konishiki.

Although the average height of sumotori has hardly changed in recent decades, the average weight has increased rapidly in the 1980s. In 1947, the average height and weight in the top division were 178 centimeters and 115 kilograms; in 1977, they were 182 centimeters and 132 kilograms. Although the average height remained the same between 1977 and 1987, the average weight increased by 14 kilograms. The weights have been increasing in the lower divisions as well. In the 1970s, many of the men in makushita weighed under 100 kilograms; by 1987, very few did. In fact, new recruits weighing over 100 kilograms by the mid-1980s had become the rule rather than the exception.

Even though the average lifespan of former sumotori has been increasing a little in recent years, it is still only in the early sixties— over a decade short of what the ordinary Japanese male can expect to live. Furthermore, sumo doctors fear that, despite the advances of modern medicine, the recent tendency toward increased heaviness in sumotori will lead to health problems in the future.

The Sumo Association maintains its own clinic where all its members can undergo diagnosis as well as treatment for minor problems. Those with serious injuries or problems, such as broken bones, are sent to hospitals for further care. Many stables and individual sumotori also maintain special links with outside acupuncturists, chiropractors, and masseurs, as well as practitioners of modern Western medicine. One Tokyo acupuncturist, for instance, has so many patients in the sumo world that during Tokyo tournaments he receives a special pass to enter the dressing rooms at the stadium, where he treats several rikishi before their bouts.

Finances

The apprentice sumotori do not receive regular salaries—just small stipends from the Sumo Association during tournaments as well as free room and board, clothing, and some spending money from their stable. The amount of that allowance varies widely. All stablemasters receive money from the Sumo Association just for running their heya as well as at least ¥55,000 (in 1989) for each rikishi under their charge. Extra payment is made for each sekitori and, in ascending order, even more for san'yaku (¥100,000 every two months), ozeki (¥200,000), and yokozuna (¥300,000). Other monetary contributions and material gifts come from groups of patrons or supporters known as *koenkai* or *tanimachi*. Koenkai is a normal Japanese term used for various organizations of supporters, including those for politicians. Tanimachi, an expression with the same meaning, is unique to the sumo world. It derives from a doctor living in the Tanimachi district of Osaka in the past who apparently loved sumo so much that he would give medical treatment gratis to any rikishi. Stables with high-ranking or popular rikishi, or those run by a former star, naturally tend to have the greatest number as well as the most generous supporters. Such heya can generally afford to be magnanimous toward their apprentices.

In addition, the sekitori themselves are frequently treated to dinner or a night on the town by their patrons. When they go out with their patrons, they almost invariably receive a gratuity called *goshugi*, which they usually share with or give to their attendants. In addition, sekitori often have one or two apprentices accompany them on such nights out with their supporters, who generally end up giving money to the novices as well. A young sumotori usually welcomes the opportunity not only for the monetary benefits but also for the dinner. The stable's evening meal tends to be a rather paltry affair compared with the chanko brunch.

In this way, some apprentices manage to acquire a lot of their own spending money. One who used to be in a certain heya at the same time as two grand champions and a champion, for instance, apparently saved enough to open his own restaurant in a choice area of Tokyo even though he never reached a salaried rank. Nevertheless, although the treatment of the apprentices has improved considerably in the past two decades, most are not quite as lucky as he was.

The monthly salary of the sekitori in the juryo division in 1992 was ¥645,000, and for maegashira in the top division it was

¥829,000. During the same year komusubi and sekiwake both received ¥1,077,000 a month, while the monthly wages for champions and grand champions were ¥1,497,000 and ¥1,800,000. Grand champions and champions were also allotted ¥200,000 and ¥150,000, respectively, as *basho-teate*—stipends for each tournament they participated in. Sekiwake and komusubi received ¥50,000 as basho-teate.

Prior to each Tokyo tournament, grand champions receive further compensation for the remaking of their yokozuna hawser. They all used to get the same flat rate; however, since 1980, the amount has been based on the actual weight of the cord. In mid-1988, 203 kilogram Onokuni, the heaviest yokozuna on record, was allotted ¥400,000 for his twenty kilogram hawser.

An additional stipend called *mochi-kyukin*, *kyukin*, or *hoshokin* is granted to sekitori for each win and winning tournament they have had since entering sumo. Although the wins are calculated from the lowest division, this stipend is not paid until a rikishi becomes a sekitori. All the more incentive to train hard!

Incidentally, as of July 1989, Grand Champion Chiyonofuji had the highest mochi-kyukin of any active rikishi: ¥3,163,750 per tournament. Ozutsu, a onetime sekiwake and longtime veteran of the top division, had a mochi-kyukin of ¥472,500—more than that of the youngest ozeki at the time, Konishiki.

Mawashi

In addition to all the differences in treatment, there are further distinctions between what wakaishu and sekitori are allowed to wear. All sumotori are supposed to don nothing but mawashi when fighting or in practice. Those with injuries, however, are permitted to be bandaged and may wear tabi.

The mawashi weighs four or five kilograms and is an average of nine meters (ten yards) long and sixty centimeters (two feet) wide. It is folded into six parts and wrapped, depending on the wearer's girth, from four to seven times around the waist, hips, and under the groin. Mawashi are also called *shimekomi*, a term originating from the way they are wrapped.

Sagari, the strings hanging from the front of mawashi, are made of the same cloth as the belt and are stiffened with a glue called *funori*. As the function of the sagari is purely ornamental, the referee simply throws them aside should they come off during the course of a tournament match. Nineteen is the standard number

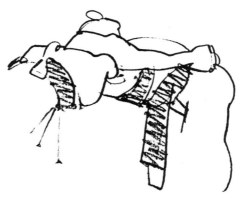

*Practice mawashi sometimes become loose
during rigorous practice and must be retied.*

of strings, but some sumotori have seventeen or twenty-one. Because they are patterned after the sacred ropes hanging in Shinto shrines, their number must always be odd.

Up through the makushita division, sumotori fight in the same heavy black or gray cotton mawashi used for practice in the stables. Sekitori appear in tournaments as well as in public exhibitions in colored belts made of fine silk. According to the rules of the Sumo Association, these mawashi should be either in a shade of purple or dark blue.

Maegashira 14 Tamanoumi (who later went as far as the sekiwake rank and served as Kataonami Oyakata from 1961 until his death in 1987) was the first to break this regulation by wearing a gold mawashi in the Kyushu tournament of 1957. Perhaps because he won it with a perfect score of 15–0, and also because more colorful mawashi look good on television, many sekitori have followed his precedent by wearing belts in colors like gold, green, red, baby blue, and so on. This is one of the few rulebook violations which the Sumo Association overlooks.

The colors are chosen by the sumotori themselves, or perhaps by a patron who has paid to have the belt made at a cost of about ¥300,000. Sometimes a rikishi starts wearing a different colored mawashi to celebrate an elevation in rank, or in hopes of changing his luck after a losing spell. Former Ozeki Wakashimazu switched from his favorite kelly green to light blue after a streak of bad tourneys starting in November 1985, but returned to green after the color change failed to produce any discernible results.

Two views of an oicho-mage, a fancy topknot resembling a ginkgo leaf.

Chonmage

All professional sumotori, except the newest recruits, have their hair fixed in a topknot called chonmage. The hair of new recruits, of course, is still too short for this, so getting it put into a topknot for the first time is a memorable milestone in the career of any sumotori. The topknot is fixed with a fragrant pomade called *bintsuke* by a sumo hairdresser. Just by the lingering smell of the pomade, one can often tell that a sumotori has visited a place even some minutes after he has actually left.

The chonmage worn by the sumotori during practice and their free time are all in the same simple style, but sekitori have their hair arranged in an *oicho* or *oicho-mage*, the fancy topknot resembling a ginkgo leaf, when appearing in the ring at one of the stadiums used for tournaments. A sekitori also has his hair done up in this elaborate topknot for his wedding or promotion party, while his sumotori guests appear in simple topknots.

Other Sumptuary Regulations

Nowadays most sumotori have taken to donning training wear in their private quarters and in the immediate vicinity of the stable. However, they are expected to wear traditional Japanese dress when otherwise appearing in public. In public only the sekitori are permitted to wear silk and carry umbrellas (or have apprentices hold them) in case of rain. Unless they do not mind getting wet,

Training wear after practice is permitted in the stable or nearby neighborhood, but apprentices must don cotton kimono (yukata) when in public.

the apprentices may occasionally duck under the sekitori's umbrella, or find some other form of protection when alone.

Apprentices are required to wear cotton kimono called *yukata* throughout the year. It is only after reaching the makushita division, just below sekitori, that they are even allowed to don *haori* (kimono coats) over their kimono in cold weather. Even the footgear for sekitori and makushita rikishi is better. All the more incentive to reach a select spot. Yet, with so much competition, only about one-tenth of new recruits will ever become sekitori.

Good Luck Chanko
(Serves 4–5)

This recipe, courtesy of former Maegashira Iwatora (Matsuoka Kazutomo) of Kasugano-Beya, was the preferred stew during tournaments. Eating four-legged animals was considered bad luck during a tourney, because their form symbolized the loser in a match—"down on all fours." Fish were not viewed as auspicious either, as they have no hands and feet.

All quantities are estimated, as the sumotori cook by feel rather by precise measurements. Thus, they tend to keep filling the pot with the ingredients they want to eat most.

Ingredients

1 medium chicken
2 medium onions
3 or 4 carrots*
2 or 3 negi onions (substitute large leeks)

1 daikon radish*
1 medium or large potato
10 to 12 shiitake mushrooms (Dried shiitake may be used;
    reconstitute in tepid water and drain.)
1 medium cabbage
1 or 2 cakes *aburage* (deep-fried tofu)
1 cake *koyadofu* (dried tofu) or fresh tofu
½ cup soy sauce
½ cup *mirin* (a sweet sake for seasoning) or ½ cup sake with
    1 tablespoon sugar
½ teaspoon salt
1 or 2 packs *udon* (wheat noodles; substitute egg noodles)

Bone the chicken and cut meat into 1½ - to 2-inch chunks; save the bones for soup stock. Slice negi (or leeks) and all but one of the carrots into bite-sized pieces.

Fill a large stew pot with water and place over medium-low heat. Add the bones with the negi and sliced carrots and simmer, uncovered, about 3 hours to make soup stock.

Slice the daikon and potato and parboil in a separate pot. Reserve. Cut the onion and shiitake into quarters, chop the cabbage into small pieces, and cut the cakes of tofu and remaining carrot into bite-sized chunks. Add all sliced ingredients and soy sauce to the stock pot and simmer until the fresh vegetables are cooked, then add the parboiled vegetables. Season to taste with mirin or its equivalent, and salt. Simmer a few minutes more.

Serve hot. After finishing the chanko, reheat the soup with udon noodles and serve in deep soup bowls.

*Carrot and daikon tops are optional. If used, wash, cut into 1½-inch lengths, parboil and add together with other parboiled vegetables.

4

Sumo in Days Gone By

The sport of sumo has existed in Japan throughout the nation's history. The gods are said to have engaged in it. Emperors and shoguns patronized it; ordinary people have either practiced or enjoyed it.

The Earliest Matches

The earliest written mention of sumo is found in the *Kojiki* (Record of Ancient Matters), a book from 712, which is the oldest extant example of Japanese writing. The *Kojiki* relates a legend about how possession of the Japanese islands was determined by a sumo match. According to the book, about two thousand five hundred years ago, the gods Takemikazuchi and Takeminakata grappled on the shores of Izumo along the Japan Sea coast in what is now Shimane Prefecture, until the latter finally lost. Thus control of the archipelago was ceded to the Japanese people led by Tatemikazuchi, who is said to have established the imperial family from which the present emperor traces his ancestry.

Since the Japanese did not keep any written records until the eighth century, it is impossible to know, aside from legend, exactly when sumo first developed in Japan. However, ancient wall paintings indicate that its origins are very old indeed. In prehistoric times, sumo appears to have been performed mainly as an agricultural ritual to pray for a good harvest.

It is also impossible to determine whether sumo is a completely indigenous sport or whether it was influenced by similar forms of grappling from China, Korea, Mongolia, India, Babylonia, and other parts of Asia and Eurasia. Grappling seems to be a rather basic, instinctive sport played mostly by men. (In regions along the Amazon River women wrestle in a style somewhat similar to sumo.)

Sumo in its early days tended to be violent with no holds barred—often a veritable fight to the finish. The *Nihon Shoki* (Chronicles of Japan), written in 720, records the first bout between lowly mortals as taking place in 23 B.C. Emperor Suinin (r. 29 B.C.–A.D. 70) is said to have made a special request to Nomi no Sukune, a potter from Izumo, to fight Taima no Kehaya, a bully and braggart from what is now Nara Prefecture. The two grappled for quite a while until Sukune finally rendered some devastating kicks to Kehaya's stomach and solar plexis. Kehaya was mortally wounded, and Sukune, the victor, has been immortalized ever since as the "father of sumo."

At the Imperial Court

There are several other legends about sumo matches held in the imperial presence before Japan adopted the Chinese writing system in the seventh century. The first historically authenticated bout took place in 642, when Empress Kogyoku (r. 642–45) assembled her palace guards to perform sumo to entertain envoys from the Paekche court of Korea. Later records mention sumo being performed at the functions of the imperial court, including at coronation ceremonies. The custom of *tenran-zumo* (sumo in the imperial presence) is still carried out at present, albeit in different form.

During the reign of Emperor Shomu (r. 724–49), *sumaibito* (sumotori) were recruited from all over the country to perform in the Imperial Palace garden at a festivity called *sechie* held each year on the seventh day of the seventh lunar month (early August under the contemporary Western calendar). At the same time cultured people would gather as well at the palace to display their skills at writing poetry. With the establishment of *sechie-zumo*, sumo expanded from an agrarian ritual to a large-scale rite to pray for the nationwide peace and prosperity of Japanese society.

In the late eighth century, Emperor Kanmu (r. 781–806) made sechie-zumo an annual event in his court, and the custom continued through the Heian period (794–1185). During the reign of Emperor Saga (r. 809–23) the practice of sumo was encouraged as a martial art; rules were established and techniques refined.

As a Martial Art

After the establishment of the first shogunate in Kamakura from 1185 to 1392, sumo came to be practiced all the more as a martial art by the warrior class. Minamoto no Yoritomo (1148–99), the most famous shogun of the era, was a sumo fan who watched it along with demonstrations of other forms of military training at Tsuruoka Hachimangu shrine (now a popular tourist site in Kamakura).

During this period jujitsu developed out of sumo. Sumo also continued to be performed as a religious rite in agricultural communities, and both country people as well as warriors in times of peace came to enjoy it as a sport.

Sumo experienced a decline in popularity among the ruling class in the early part of the Ashikaga period (1338–1568), as the shoguns of the time preferred Noh and other forms of entertainment. Nevertheless, rural sumo (*kusa-zumo*) was enjoyed by commoners, and several plays with themes related to sumo were staged.

As the power of the Ashikaga shoguns weakened, internecine struggles for supremacy broke out among feudal lords in various parts of the country. During the Period of Warring States, from 1482 to 1558, sumo reemerged as a type of martial training for warriors. As the flames of war flickered out, and Japan moved from the Ashikaga period to the Momoyama period (1568–1603), groups of semiprofessional sumotori emerged. In times of peace they traveled to various provinces to perform—a precursor of the performance tours of the countryside still held regularly today.

Oda Nobunaga (1534–82), a major feudal lord of the late sixteenth century, was particularly fond of sumo. In February 1578, he assembled over one thousand five hundred sumotori from across the country for a tournament held at his castle. Until then there had been no definite boundaries to the arena in which sumo was held; the space was delineated simply by the people standing around in a circle watching the matches or waiting for their own turn to fight. Apparently because many bouts were to be held on the same day at Nobunaga's Azuchi Castle, circular boundaries were drawn on the ground for the first time to speed up the proceedings. These boundaries also had the effect of making sumo safer for its spectators.

The first documented evidence of a ring demarcated by rice straw bales placed on the ground in a circular pattern can be found in the Empo era (1673–81). In the early eighteenth century, the bales came to be half buried in the ground circling the ring, similar to the way they are at present.

From the Period of Warring States through the Edo period (1603–1867), several daimyo began offering their patronage to the strongest sumotori. Those employed by a daimyo not only received a generous stipend but were accorded samurai status as well. They were also presented ceremonial decorative aprons embroidered with the feudal lord's name. Such patronage guaranteed a good living, so many promising rikishi vied with each other in the ring to catch a daimyo's eye. The ranking sheets listed the name of the fief they served rather than their actual places of birth, as is done today in sometimes noting the prefecture of family registry rather than birthplace.

Professional Sumo

The predecessor of modern professional sumo underwent an almost parallel development throughout the Edo period and was called *kanjin-zumo*, implying that it was to be carried out to collect donations toward the construction or repair of shrines, temples, bridges, and other public works. But some of the money, of course, was also used to pay the rikishi, many of whom at that time were ronin—samurai who had lost their masters. In due time the money collected came to be used primarily as wages for the sumotori.

The Edo period inaugurated a long era of domestic peace in which Japan was cut off from the outside world, except for one small trading post on an island in Nagasaki Harbor. Sumo became a popular form of entertainment among the masses who were enjoying peace and prosperity. Kanjin-zumo originally flourished in Osaka and Kyoto, where the first formal organization known as the Sumo Kaisho (Sumo Club) was formed in the Horeki era (1751–64). Soon thereafter a sumo organization was established in Edo (premodern Tokyo), which quickly developed into the true center of the sport in Japan. Yet, despite the popularity of sumo, tourneys were held only around twenty days a year, and sumotori were sportingly referred to as "lucky guys who made a living out of twenty days of work."

During this period a ranking system and ranking sheets were initiated. In 1761, the name of the sumo organization on the ranking sheets was changed from kanjin-zumo to *kanjin-ozumo*, marking the first time the professional version of the sport was called "grand sumo." The idea to have particularly meritorious rikishi became coaches to train further generations of sumotori took hold around this time, and the first sumo-beya were consequently established. Further developments were made in the arrangement of the ring as well. For a while, a square dohyo was even experimented with, only to be abandoned quickly for the traditional circle.

The Golden Age

The first true golden age for sumo came in the late eighteenth century when two very strong and popular grand champions emerged: Tanikaze Kajinosuke and Onogawa Kisaburo. Three grand champions actually precede Tanikaze on the chart for the rank. However, Akashi Shiganosuke, supposedly the first yokozuna in historic order, was promoted posthumously. In fact, his existence may very well be legendary: he is listed as having been 242 centimeters (eight feet) tall, yet there are no records of his wins and losses or of any other vital statistics. Although not that much is known about the second and third grand champions, Ayagawa Goroji and Maruyama Gontazaemon, at least enough evidence indicates that they actually existed.

Tanikaze had the makings of a legend but also was quite real and popular, both in and out of the ring. In a sense, he can be considered the "first true" yokozuna. Tanikaze stood 189 centimeters at a time when the average sumotori was only 168 centimeters.

He captured twenty-one tourney titles, and lost only twice in his four years and eight months as grand champion. Tanikaze was really way ahead in his rivalry with Onogawa, who chalked up only eight tournament titles. At 176 centimeters, Onogawa was much shorter than Tanikaze, but he compensated for his smaller size by perfecting a rather speedy, crowd-pleasing style of sumo. Tanikaze died of influenza at age forty-five in 1795 while still an active yokozuna. He can be counted among the ten best sumotori in history. Onogawa retired in 1798 to become a coach in Osaka sumo.

The golden age lasted even after Tanikaze's demise and Onogawa's retirement largely because of the presence of Raiden Tameimon. Generally regarded as the greatest sumotori ever, Raiden was trained by Tanikaze and made his sumo debut not long after the latter was promoted to grand champion. After winning his first tourney championship in 1793, he went on to capture twenty-six more titles. Raiden was of prodigious size (even in contemporary Japan—let alone his own time): 197 centimeters and

Eighteenth-century woodblock prints showing Yokozuna Tanikaze (left) and Ozeki Raiden.

170 kilograms. He was so strong that he was prohibited from using certain thrusting techniques because of his exceptionally large hands. Despite these interdictions, Raiden lost only ten bouts (against 254 wins and 14 draws) during his twenty-one years in sumo.

Raiden was never promoted to grand champion. Although the rank was not official until 1890, it nevertheless seems strange not to find the name of perhaps the greatest sumotori in history on the list of yokozuna. There are various explanations why Raiden was never designated to the rank. Perhaps the most plausible is that he was overlooked because of the ill feelings existing between his daimyo patrons, the Matsudaira family of Izumo, and the Yoshida family in Kumamoto who had been entrusted with granting yokozuna licenses. Even after Raiden retired from the sumo world in 1811, for some years thereafter he made performance tours of the countryside, where his name could still draw quite a crowd.

A curious custom of not allowing the men in the top division to fight on the last day of a tournament began in April 1791 and was in effect through 1908. Sumo's popularity ebbed and flowed after Raiden's retirement. Around the middle of the nineteenth century, when debate was raging in Japan over whether to open more of its ports to outside contact for the first time in two and a half centuries, the sumo world was undergoing an exciting change of guard from the old to a new generation of fighters. Jinmaku Kyugoro was the last grand champion promoted in the Edo period.

The End of the Feudal Era

The Meiji Restoration, which began in 1868, witnessed the dismantling of the shogunate, with its system of feudal lords, and returned the emperor to a position of authority. A tournament held on the temple grounds of Eko-in in the Ryogoku district of Tokyo demonstrated that sumo still retained its popularity with the people, yet the sumotori themselves suffered economically by losing their daimyo patrons. To make matters worse, the aftermath of the chaos caused by rebellions against the new social order soon hit Tokyo, leaving most people little time to think about entertainments like sumo. Those who could afford to be entertained tended to be more interested in Western things than in sumo.

In 1873, Takasago Uragoro rebelled against the resourceless Sumo Club and demanded, among other things, reforms in its monetary policies. As he was initially expelled from the organization, he assembled a group of reform-minded rikishi and led them to Kansai (the Kyoto-Osaka region). Five years later the reform group reunited with the Sumo Club in Tokyo, and Takasago Uragoro soon emerged as its most powerful figure.

The presence of Emperor Meiji (r. 1868–1912) at a sumo tournament in 1884 greatly helped to revive interest in the sport and bring it out of its slump. Around this time politicians, industrialists, and cultural figures emerged to offer financial backing to sumotori in the stead of the feudal lords. Moreover, an extremely appealing grand champion, Umegatani Totaro I, appeared in 1884. Although Umegatani I held the yokozuna rank for just a year, he suffered a total of only six losses (against 116 wins and 20 draws) during his career in the top division and is still widely viewed as the best sumotori to emerge after Tanikaze and Raiden.

The name of the Tokyo-based Sumo Club was changed to the Tokyo Sumo Association in 1889. In the following year Yokozuna became an official rank on the ranking sheets. Nishinoumi Kajiro I was the first grand champion to be listed as such. Then, just before the turn of the century, further interest was aroused in sumo as a symbol of strength when Japan emerged victorious in the Sino-Japanese War (1894–95).

The First Proper Stadium

A new golden age came around the time of the Russo-Japanese War (1904–05), as a result of the excitement stirred by the powerful

The old Kokugikan in Ryogoku, reconstructed many times, was the mecca for sumo as a national sport.

rivals such as Hitachiyama Taniemon, Ozutsu Man'emon, and Umegatani II—not to forget the popular Ozeki Araiwa. The word *kokugi* was coined to describe sumo as the "national sport," and the idea arose to build a proper stadium for the sport so that tourneys would no longer have to be canceled because of inclement weather. The first Kokugikan (stadium of the national sport) was constructed next to the Eko-in temple in 1909, and several sumo stables were put up in the surrounding Ryogoku area. Umegatani I (Ikazuchi Oyakata) played a significant role in raising the funds to build the stadium. When asked by one potential backer what he had for collateral, the former grand champion apparently showed his muscles—a move which sealed the deal.

With a seating capacity of some fifteen thousand, the first Kokugikan was unquestionably the most splendid sports stadium in Asia at the time. The original building was destroyed by fire in 1917 and reconstructed only to suffer damage again in the Great Kanto Earthquake of 1923. The Kokugikan incurred damage once more during the air raids over Tokyo in March 1945. But, in any case, the presence of a permanent home for sumo added to its prestige, at least for a while.

A number of exciting figures like yokozuna Tachiyama Mineemon, Otori Tanigoro, Nishinoumi II, Onishiki Uichiro, Tochigiyama Moriya, Nishinoumi III, and Tsunenohana Kan'ichi came to the fore from the end of the Meiji period and through the Taisho period (1912–16). Tachiyama, who never had a losing record during his eighteen years in sumo and only lost three times as a grand champion, even created his own sensational era. He won forty-three bouts in a row, lost the forty-fourth, and then went on to win another fifty-six matches. Years later Tachiyama admitted that one loss to Nishinoumi II was a "fixed match" (yaocho). Thus, if it had not been for Tachiyama's willingness to help out his weak fellow yokozuna, he would have set an all-time record of one hundred consecutive wins. As it is, his fifty-six straight wins was the best record in his time, and it currently stands as the fourth best in history.

Around this time, sumo started diversifying in style with the appearance of an increased number of practitioners of a speedy fighting form based on pushing and shoving, rather than the traditional grips on the belt. Tachiyama was famous for his thrusting power, but he was good on the belt as well.

In 1911, the sumo organization in Kyoto was dissolved after it returned from an exhibition appearance at the World's Fair in London. In the same year new reforms, such as the institution of a retirement allowance for former rikishi, were made by the Tokyo Sumo Association at the demand of thirty-three rikishi, who had threatened to go on strike.

Just as Tachiyama's era was winding down, Tochigiyama and Tsunenohana arose to create another golden era in the early 1920s. Tochigiyama gained recognition by stopping Tachiyama's fifty-six bout winning streak in a fight that was definitely not fixed. A mere 172 centimeters and 103 kilograms, Tochigiyama compensated for his lack of bulk through hard training and well-honed pushing and thrusting techniques. Dubbed the "little giant yokozuna," he suffered only eight losses during his seven years at the top.

A recession toward the end of the Taisho period adversely affected attendance at the sumo stadium. In addition, the Sumo Association itself fell into financial troubles after the Great Kanto Earthquake. For a while, about the only thing that aroused special interest in sumo was the presence of Dewagatake, a man of prodigious size by any standards (203 centimeters, 195 kilograms) who rose to the sekiwake rank.

In an attempt to revive interest in sumo, starting in 1925 a cup from the crown prince came to be presented to the winner of the tourney in the highest division. A year later that crown prince became Emperor Hirohito, and the trophy has been known as the Emperor's Cup ever since. Furthermore, in 1926, the Osaka Sumo

Association was amalgamated with the one in Tokyo. In the following year, tourneys in March and October were added to the agenda, making for four a year (the other two were held in January and May), and live radio coverage of sumo tournaments was inaugurated in 1928.

The Great Futabayama

Nevertheless, sumo remained in a slump until the 1930s, when yokozuma giants like Tamanishiki San'emon and Minanogawa Tozo emerged along with the lean and handsome Grand Champion Musashiyama Takeshi. Then, just when the sumo world seemed on its way to better days, a group of upper-ranking sumotori, led by Sekiwake Tenryu, staged a walkout. They assembled in January 1932 at a Tokyo restaurant named Shunjuen and demanded a number of reforms. In the wake of the Shunjuen Incident, the Sumo Association had to postpone the first tourney of the year until February. It ultimately solved the problem of a lack of upper-ranking fighters by promoting several from the lower ranks.

One of those whom fortune smiled upon was Futabayama Sadaji, who soon proved himself more than worthy of the early promotion. He reigned supreme even after 80 percent of those involved in the Shunjuen Incident returned to the fold. At 178 centimeters and 134 kilograms, Futabayama was not especially large, but he trained very hard and perfected his initial charge. He is said to have never made a false start. Futabayama also had a wonderful sense of balance, believed to have been acquired from working on fishing boats as a youngster. Nobody knew until after his retirement that Futabayama was blind in one eye due to an injury suffered during boyhood.

In the mid-1930s, tourneys came to be held only twice a year again for eleven or thirteen days each. In May 1936, Futabayama won his first tournament as a sekiwake with a score of 11–0. He did not lose another match until nearly three years later. During that time he was promoted to sumo's second highest and then to the highest rank.

Such excitement was stirred when Futabayama lost to Akinoumi that the radio announcer even failed to get correct which side he was tripped on. Futabayama's record of sixty-nine consecutive wins remains unbroken still. His twelve tournament titles would translate into over thirty under the present postwar system of six tourneys a year.

The great Yokozuna Futabayama, who retired in 1945, set an unbroken record of sixty-nine consecutive wins.

Practically lost in the excitement created in 1938 by Futabayama's long winning streak was the news that Yokozuna Tamanishiki, at age thirty-four, had died after a delayed appendectomy. Tamanishiki, who captured nine tourney titles, had been the strongest grand champion in the early part of the 1930s, yet he never managed to beat Futabayama after the latter began his winning streak.

Even though tournaments could not always be held regularly during World War II, Futabayama retained his popularity and supremacy during that period. He retired from the ring three months after Japan surrendered to the Allied forces. While an active grand champion, Futabayama had been allowed to open up his own sumo gym, Futabayama Dojo (later Tokitsukaze-Beya)—a move no longer permitted. He served as the head of the Tokitsukaze-Beya and also, beginning in 1957, as chairman of the Sumo Association until his death in 1968.

Other appealing grand champions, such as Haguroyama Masaji and Akinoumi Setsuo, also emerged during the war years. Although Haguroyama trained quite hard and was so strong that he was said to be "made of steel," he always remained in the shadow of Futabayama, who belonged to the same Tatsunami-Beya. Haguroyama held the grand championship for an all-time record of eleven years and eight months. He probably would have created his own era in sumo if it had not been for Futabayama. Akinoumi, on the other hand, while popular with the public, was far from a spectacular yokozuna. He is in fact remembered more as the man who broke Futabayama's sixty-nine bout winning streak than he is as a grand champion.

Kuramae Kokugikan

Although the Kokugikan suffered some damage during the fire bombing of Tokyo in March 1945, it still held up well enough for a seven-day tourney there in June that year. However, after World War II, the Allied forces occupying Japan took over the stadium for their own use. To make matters worse, several of the stables had burned down during the war, and food was scarce in Tokyo in the early postwar years. The sumotori had to make frequent tours to the countryside for their subsistence.

Finally, rather than keep on holding tourneys in places like the Meiji Shrine and uncovered baseball stadiums (where finishing everything on schedule depended greatly on meteorological conditions), the Sumo Association decided to construct another stadium across the Sumida River in the Kuramae district of Tokyo. The Kuramae Kokugikan opened to the public in 1950.

Kurumae Kokugikan, the home of sumo from 1950 to 1984.

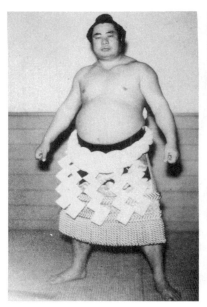

Left to right, Tochinishiki and Wakanohana I,
yokozuna crowd-pleasers of the 1950s.

Postwar Golden Times

In 1953, NHK (Nippon Hoso Kyokai), Japan's national public broadcasting corporation, began live television broadcasts of sumo, which served to arouse all the more interest in the sport. In the same year, the number of tournaments was set at four each year, in January, March, May, and September. The November and July tourneys were added to the schedule in 1957 and 1958, respectively, fixing the number at six a year ever since. Perhaps by coincidence, the 1950s saw the rise of some strong, or at least interesting, grand champions like Maedayama Eigoro, Azumafuji Kin'ichi, Chiyonoyama Masanobu, Kagamisato Kiyoji, Yoshibayama Junnosuke, Tochinishiki Kiyotaka, Wakanohana Kanji I, and Asashio Taro.

The rivalry between Tochinishiki and Wakanohana, both small but very skillful, particularly captured the public's fancy. In March 1960, they became the first pair of yokozuna to go into the last day of a tournament evenly matched with scores of 14–0. Wakanohana won that clash, which significantly influenced Tochinishiki's decision to retire two months later. Wakanohana retired two years after that.

Both Tochinishiki and Wakanohana ended up with ten tourney titles, a record second only to Futabayama at the time. The Tochi-Waka rivalry continued after retirement as well. Tochinishiki inherited Kasugano-Beya from former Yokozuna Tochigiyama (who had legally adopted him as a son) and then produced a yokozuna and an ozeki in the 1960s. Wakanohana branched off from Hanakago-Beya to open his own Futagoyama-Beya, and in the 1970s and 1980s trained two yokozuna and two ozeki. Kasugano (formerly Tochinishiki) became chairman of the Sumo Association in 1974 and passed the position on to Futagoyama (formerly Wakanohana I) in early 1988. (Kasugano and Futagoyama were their names as elders in the Sumo Association; membership requirements are discussed in Chapter 9.) Thus, Futagoyama came to head the Sumo Association, while Kasugano remained as a special advisor to the Sumo Association and the director of the Sumo Museum (located within the grounds of the Kokugikan) until his death in 1990.

Taiho and Kashiwado

The 1960s saw the emergence of another appealing pair of yokozuna rivals: Taiho and Kashiwado were promoted to sumo's highest position simultaneously in 1961. In contrast to Tochinishiki and Wakanohana, who both stood under 180 centimeters, Taiho and Kashiwado were tall at 187 and 188 centimeters respectively. Taiho, a handsome Eurasian born to a Japanese mother and a Russian father, enjoyed a special popularity with women and children. He also conscientiously trained with special diligence and was exceptionally powerful and skillful on the belt. His record of thirty-two tourney championships has yet to be broken.

Kashiwado, by contrast, was injury prone and in the end took only five tourney titles. Sadanoyama, who was promoted to grand champion during this period, actually ended up with one more title than Kashiwado. Yet the era is still named Hakuho after a combination of characters from Kashiwado's and Taiho's names. (*Haku* is another reading of the character *kashi*.) Kashiwado appealed to those who found Taiho simply too strong and pretty, and many saw in him a tragic sense of potential never fully realized.

Taiho and Kashiwado opened their own stables after retirement. In the 1980s they were among the ten members of the board of directors of the Sumo Association. Kashiwado's Kagamiyama-Beya was the first to produce a rikishi in the top division as well as a

A bout about to begin between the great yokozuna rivals of the 1960s, Kashiwado, left, and Taiho.

tournament champion (Tagaryu in 1984). But, as Dewanoumi (formerly Sadanoyama), also on the board of directors, was in better health in his postretirement years, he, and not Taiho or Kashiwado, was chosen to succeed Futagoyama to the chairmanship of the Sumo Association.

In the late 1950s through the 1960s, several reforms were initiated by the Sumo Association under the leadership of Tokitsukaze (formerly Futabayama). These moves included the establishment of fixed monthly salaries for sumotori in the top two divisions, mandatory retirement ages for referees and certain other positions in the Sumo Association, minimum height and weight requirements for new recruits, and a system of six tournaments a year. A Sumo School was established in 1957; all new recruits must study subjects such as sumo history and calligraphy for six months while undergoing basic training. The sumo organization also formally adopted its present name, Nihon Sumo Kyokai (Japan Sumo Association), in that year. Subsequently, revisions were made in the regulations concerning matches so that, since 1965, sumotori from affiliated heya could be pitted against each other in a tournament.

The 1970s

The 1970s began with the simultaneous promotion in January of another pair of yokozuna rivals: Tamanoumi Masahiro and Kitanofuji Katsuaki. Although at 177 centimeters, weighing 130 kilograms at his peak, Tamanoumi was not especially large, he had developed strong legs and hips—not to mention considerable technique—as a practitioner of judo in junior high school. Moreover, early in his career he had trained in the same sumo stable as Taiho. (Later, after following the coach who discovered him into a new independent stable, Tamanoumi repaid his debt to Taiho in true sumo style by beating him in their first official bout in 1965.)

Only three months after capturing his sixth tourney championship in July 1971 with an unblemished 15–0 record, Tamanoumi suffered a fatal heart attack following an appendectomy—the fourth man in history to die while an active grand champion. He was twenty-seven years old and just coming into his prime. As Tamanoumi's winning percentage as yokozuna was .867—second only to Futabayama in this century—many people think he might have become one of the greatest sumotori ever if he had only lived longer.

Kitanofuji has widely been regarded as the first modern-minded yokozuna. Good-looking with an outgoing personality and a fine singing voice, which he was not hesitant about displaying in public, he naturally became rather popular. Yet, instead of taking advantage of the gap left by the death of Tamanoumi, Kitanofuji fell into a slump after the loss of his good friend and rival. He won the last tournament of 1971; the following year he became the first grand champion ever known to sit out a tourney due to insomnia.

In fact, 1972 was the first year since the establishment of the system of six tournaments annually in which each tourney title was captured by a different man. Among them was Hawaiian-born Takamiyama (Jesse Kuhaulua), the first foreigner to win a tournament in the highest division. Another was Wajima Hiroshi, who in 1973 became the first college graduate to reach sumo's highest rank.

Kitanofuji retired in July 1974 with a respectable record of ten tourney championships behind him. Kotozakura, who had been promoted to grand champion in January 1973 at age thirty-three, also called it quits during the same week. After that tournament in July, Kitanoumi Toshimitsu was promoted to sumo's highest rank at age twenty-one years and two months—the youngest yokozuna ever. Although the five-year age gap between Kitanoumi and Wajima was greater than that of previous pairs of yokozuna rivals

An entrance to the ring ceremony by grand champions Tamanoumi, left, and Kitanofuji.

such as Tochinishiki and Wakanohana, Taiho and Kashiwado, and Kitanofuji and Tamanoumi, the two generally dominated the sumo world for the rest of the 1970s.

Not that sumo was lacking for interesting players of lesser rank. In 1975, when Wajima was going through a slump, Takanohana, who had been promoted to ozeki simultaneously with him in 1972, took two tourney championships. After the comparatively lean and handsome Takanohana defeated the hefty Kitanoumi, the ecstatic audience threw what was undoubtedly a record number of seat cushions into the ring. Takanohana's oldest brother, Futagoyama Oyakata (former Grand Champion Wakanohana), was among the representatives of the Sumo Association who presented him with a trophy during the ensuing awards ceremony. The two were the only pair of brothers to win a tournament title in the highest division, and many sumo fans naturally hoped that they would also become the first sibling grand champions.

But Takanohana, who was dubbed the "Prince of Sumo," could not beat Kitanoumi and a recuperated Wajima on a regular basis and thus never became king. Nevertheless, he held the ozeki rank for a still unbroken record of fifty tournaments and was a greater crowd attraction than some grand champions.

Takamiyama also remained popular through the 1970s and the

Yokozuna luminaries of the 1970s, clockwise from the top: Wajima, Wakanohana II, Mienoumi, and Kitanoumi in poses from their entrance to the ring ceremony.

first half of the 1980s. Because of his tremendous girth (205 kilograms at his peak), Takamiyama made a spectacular show in both winning and losing. Although he became a true nemesis for Wajima, Jesse amusingly had trouble with some of the smaller rikishi like Asahikuni and Washuyama.

Not that Takamiyama was the only high-ranking sumotori to have problems with these little dynamos who created a sensation in their own right in the latter half of the 1970s. Asahikuni was nicknamed the "Ph.D. of Sumo" because he seemed to know almost every technique in the book. He had to know them to get ahead, as he was only 174 centimeters tall and suffered from chronic pancreas trouble. He sometimes even commuted to tournaments from the hospital. Washuyama, though approximately the same height as Asahikuni, practiced a different kind of speedy sumo. At his best, Washuyama circled around his opponent so quickly that it almost seemed as if an attack were being made from several corners, which is why he was dubbed the *chibikko gangu* (midget gang).

In the latter part of the 1970s Wakanohana II, who was only a month older than Kitanoumi, was for a while regarded as his natural rival, and sumo enthusiasts were expecting a Kita-Waka Era. However, it was never to be. Wakanohana was plagued by a series of injuries and illnesses—not to mention personal problems, particularly after he had been talked into marrying his coach's elder daughter. He won no tourney titles during his marriage and was often sidelined. (The couple divorced shortly before Wakanohana II retired from the ring in January 1983 at age twenty-eight.)

The 1980s

A rival for Kitanoumi finally emerged at the outset of the 1980s in the person of Chiyonofuji. Comparatively slim and good-looking, Chiyonofuji was initially called the "second Takanohana." The eternal ozeki-prince himself took special interest in Chiyonofuji and gave him helpful advice, such as to give up smoking. Although Takanohana himself could never break away from his nicotine habit for long, Chiyonofuji quit on the spot. The move helped him to put on a little needed weight; the extra poundage, in turn, combined with a careful exercise program, served to cure him of his unfortunate tendency to dislocate his shoulder. Chiyonofuji was promoted to ozeki after the January 1981 tourney—the same one in which Takanohana announced his retirement. By the time Chiyonofuji reached sumo's highest rank six months later, he was no longer being compared with Takanohana.

Kitanoumi for years had declined to take advantage of the privilege of a yokozuna to sit out a tournament without effect to his rank, and he set an all-time record for attendance at the top. But years of wear and tear in the ring caught up with him; he finally withdrew from a tourney for the first time in November 1981 and from several more thereafter. Kitanoumi won only two tournament titles after that first absence, yet that still gave him a total of twenty-four—a postwar record at the time second only to that of Taiho.

Fortunately, during Kitanoumi's long slump, a suitable rival for Chiyonofuji developed in the late-bloomer Takanosato, who was promoted to ozeki in January 1982 and to yokozuna in the following year. Nearly thirty-two when he reached sumo's highest rank, Takanosato became the first yokozuna since Futabayama to win a tourney with a perfect score during his debut in sumo's highest rank. Similar to Futabayama before him, he also carried a secret which he did not disclose until he felt the time was right—he had

Yokozuna Chiyonofuji, "The Wolf," who dominated sumo in the 1980s.

been suffering from diabetes for years and had devised a special diet to keep the debilitating illness under control.

Given Takanosato's age at the time of his promotion, his period as a competitor for Chiyonofuji did not last long. Yet for four straight tournaments from July 1983 to January 1984, the two faced each other evenly scored on the last day—the only time such a thing has happened in the history of sumo. Takanosato won three out of the four crucial bouts, and until his retirement in 1986 he

Yokozuna Takanosato, Chiyonofuji's archrival from 1983 to 1986.

remained Chiyonofuji's number-one nemesis. His book on how to bring diabetes under total control has become a sort of bible for other sumotori suffering from the problem. Within a year after his retirement from the ring, Takanosato had shed over forty-five kilograms (almost one hundred pounds) on a semivegetarian diet and was appearing in natty attire on television as a sumo commentator.

The New Kokugikan

Ever since the original Kokugikan was requisitioned by the Allied forces, many figures in the sumo world cherished a dream of returning to the sport's traditional heartland in Ryogoku. Finally the dream started to take shape as reality when the Sumo Association learned in the early 1980s that the deficit-ridden Japan National Railways (JNR) was trying to improve its fiscal situation by selling off some of its unneeded property, including one choice plot adjacent to Ryogoku Station. Negotiations between the JNR and the Sumo Association proceeded fairly smoothly, and ground was broken on the construction site in April 1983. The new stadium was completed on schedule in November 1984 and opened for tournaments in January 1985.

Four days into the first tournament held in the new Ryogoku Kokugikan, Kitanoumi announced his retirement losing the chance of ever winning a bout in the stadium. Chiyonofuji went on to win the tournament and all subsequent tourneys held in the new stadium for the next two years. Takanosato won several matches in the new Kokugikan but never a tournament title. He retired a year after Kitanoumi. Futahaguro, who had been a runner-up in a few tourneys, was promoted to grand champion in the wake of Takanosato's retirement. Yet Futahaguro failed to win any tournaments; thus, he proved not to be true competitor for Chiyonofuji during his brief reign in sumo's highest rank.

Finally, in May 1987, Ozeki Onokuni defeated Chiyonofuji as well as fourteen other opponents to become the second man to emerge victorious in the new Kokugikan. Hokutoumi, who came in second place in that tournament, was promoted to yokozuna, and Hawaiian-born Konishiki (Salevaa Atisanoe) became the first non-Asian to reach ozeki.

Sumo tournaments returned to Ryogoku when the new Kokugikan opened in January 1985.

Wakahanada practicing with Fujishima-Beya stablemate Takatoriki.

After Hokutoumi won his first tournament championship as yokozuna in September 1987, Onokuni, runner-up in the tourney, was promoted to grand champion. At 201 kilos, he became the heaviest holder of sumo's highest rank. Asahifuji was simultaneously promoted to ozeki.

Despite this wave of promotions, the year 1987 ended tumultuously for the tradition-bound sumo world. On December 27, Futahaguro fled his stable after an argument with his head coach, Tatsunami Oyakata, who three days later told the press that the yokozuna had struck his wife as he was leaving the heya. On the last day of 1987, the Board of Directors of the Sumo Association, without listening directly to Futahaguro's side of the story, voted to accept his "resignation"—an unprecedented event in sumo history. Futahaguro, thus, became the first yokozuna not only to be forced out of the sumo world but also the only to leave without any tournament championships to his credit. Tatsunami Oyakata was punished for his inability to discipline and control his most famous charge with a 30 percent pay cut and probation (to stay away from functions at the Kokugikan) for three months.

In the wake of Futahaguro's ouster, Ozeki Asahifuji brought a

Left to right, Akebono, Kirishima, and Musashimaru entering the ring.

little glory back to the Tatsunami-Isegahama camp of stables by capturing the tourney championship in January 1988—the first one for the group in nearly nineteen years. He became the fourth man after Chiyonofuji, Onokuni, and Hokutoumi to emerge victorious in the Ryogoku Kokugikan. Yet his victory was hardly enough to end Chiyonofuji's dominance of the sumo world in 1988, and he failed in his own drive for promotion to yokozuna that year.

After a poor start in March, with two losses during the first three days, Onokuni went on to win the rest of his matches, including a play-off against Hokutoumi, to emerge as the surprising victor in Osaka. Although Chiyonofuji was sidelined with an injury during that time, he broke Kitanoumi's record of twenty-four tournament titles, which had been the second best (after Taiho's thirty-two) under the system of six tournaments a year. He also went through a fifty-three bout winning streak, thus creating the second best record of consecutive wins during the sixty-three-year Showa period and the fifth best in history. At age thirty-three, Chiyonofuji showed few signs of slowing down; if anything, like fine wine, he seemed to be improving with age as 1988 came to a close.

The opening of the first tournament of 1989 was postponed by one day out of respect to the memory of Emperor Hirohito, who died the day prior to its scheduled start. With Hirohito's death and the ascension to throne of his elder son, Akihito, Japan passed from the Showa to the Heisei period.

Chiyonofuji and Kokonoe-Beya continued to dominate sumo in 1989. Hokutoumi, returning to the ring after being sidelined for three tournaments because of severe injuries to his hips and lower back, captured the first championship of the new period in a play-off with Asahifuji.

In March, despite fine performances during the first eight days by all the yokozuna and ozeki, except Ozeki Asashio, who announced his retirement, Chiyonofuji once again emerged the solid winner. His score was 14-1, and the one loss was a default. He dislocated his shoulder in toppling Onokuni on the fourteenth day and was forced to sit out the last day of the tournament.

Chiyonofuji's continued absence allowed his stablemate Hokutoumi to win in May, once again after a play-off with Asahifuji. But Chiyonofuji came soaring back in July and defeated Hokutoumi in a play-off on the final day—the first time in history that two yokozuna from the same stable had challenged each other in the ring for the tourney title.

Chiyonofuji was victorious again that September. However, in November, the final tournament of the 1980s, Konishiki (Salevaa Atisanoe) became the second foreigner in history to capture a tourney championship. He also ended Chiyonofuji's complete dominance of the title in the Kyushu Basho since 1981.

The first tournament of the 1990s was captured again by Chiyonofuji. Making their makunouchi debuts at that tourney were Dewanoumi-Beya stablemates Ryukozan and Oginohana, the elder son of former Sekiwake Oginohana (Takazaki Oyakata). Both came through with winning records, but Ryukozan collapsed during a practice session and died a few weeks later—the first sekitori to die while still active since Tamanoumi in 1971.

Konishiki's expected race toward yokozuna promotion in 1990 proved unsuccessful. Instead, Asahifuji, who had seemed out of the picture from the latter half of 1989 because of chronic pancreatic trouble, reached the rank after two consecutive tourney championships in May and July.

Moreover, after tying for the title (which was ultimately taken by Hokutoumi in an unusual three-way play-off that also included Konishiki), the handsome and muscular Kirishima was promoted to ozeki just a few weeks short of his thirty-first birthday. The ninety-one tournaments it took him was a new record for slowness to reach that rank.

On the other hand, in May 1990, seventeen-year-old Takahanada, the younger son of popular former Ozeki Takahanada (Fujishima Oyakata), became the youngest member ever of the top division. Takahanada's older brother, Wakahanada, made his debut in makunouchi in September, along with stablemate Takatoriki, former collegiate champion Daishoyama, and Hawaiian-born Akebono (Chadwick Rowan). That tournament turned out to be the first one in history in which all four new maegashira came through with winning records.

Nevertheless, the sumo world continued to be dominated by Kokonoe-Beya in 1990 with Chiyonofuji and Hokutoumi winning two tourney titles each. The one captured by Chiyonofuji in November turned out to be his thirty-first (a record second only to Taiho's thirty-two) as well as his last.

In January 1991, Ozeki Kirishima won his first tournament championship, followed by victories by Hokutoumi and Asahifuji respectively in March and May. Yet while seemingly off to a good enough start, 1991 proved to be perhaps the most chaotic year in sumo history.

The May tournament opened with eighteen-year-old Takahanada's dramatic upset over thirty-five-year-old Chiyonofuji. Takahanada thereby managed to avenge his father, who had quit eleven years earlier after losing consecutively to Chiyo. Two days later, Chiyonofuji announced his retirement—exactly twenty years to the day the great Taiho left the ring for good. At the tourney's end, Takahanada became the youngest recipient of one of the three prizes awarded on the last day.

Onokuni announced his retirement during the Nagoya Basho in July. The tournament itself was captured by an unheralded maegashira, Kotonofuji, with a solid 14–1 record. Hokutoumi and Asahifuji gave lackluster performances and finished with 9–6 and 8–7 respectively—the worst record ever for a tourney with two yokozuna. Musashimaru (Fiamalu Penitani) made his juryo debut in July and became the first foreigner ever to take the tourney title in that division.

Both of the remaining yokozuna, Hokutoumi and Asahifuji, were sidelined during the September tournament, which was captured by Kotonofuji's stablemate, Kotonishiki. It marked the first time in sumo history that not only consecutive titles had been captured by maegashira but by maegashira from the same stable (Sadogatake) as well.

During the autumn tournament, the Sumo Association instituted a few measures to reform behavior in the ring. It promptly began fining members of makunouchi who engage in false starts (*matta*) ¥100,000 and fining juryo ¥50,000. At first, both players were fined; but after protests from the rikishi, only the guilty party came to be punished. The association also decided to formally chastise those whose matches appeared lacking in fighting spirit, and in the worse case not allow such offenders into the ring for three days. (The latter has yet to happen, as of July 1992.)

In the Kyushu Basho in November, Konishiki emerged victorious for the second time in his career. In this way, 1991 became the first year since 1972 in which every single tourney championship went to a different man.

In March 1991, Akebono defeated Konishiki in the first official bout ever between two Americans in makunouchi. However, Konishiki won all their matches in the ensuing year. With Musashimaru (Fiamalu Penitani) in the top division in November 1991, bouts between Americans no longer seemed unusual as the year turned into 1992.

Chaos has continued to reign in the sumo world in 1992, with each of the first four tourneys of the year being captured by different players. Asahifuji announced his retirement in January, the tournament in which nineteen-year-old Takahanada became the the the youngest ever to take the top division title. He was too young, in fact, to be allowed under Japanese law to take part in the traditional victor's toast with liquor.

Konishiki proved victorious again in March but was not promoted to yokozuna. At first, he seemed resigned to the idea that the standards for such promotions had become stricter in the aftermath of the Futahaguro incident of 1987. However, after a member of the Yokozuna Deliberation Council published an article in a monthly saying that foreigners lack the dignity and presence befitting a grand champion, Konishiki allegedly complained to a few reporters that racism is what really prevented him from reaching sumo's highest rank. On the day the ranking sheets for the Natsu Basho were released, Konishiki held a press conference in which he denied making such remarks to the newspapers in question.

Another important press conference was held prior to the opening of the tournament in May. Hokutoumi announced his retirement from active competition. Although he had already been sidelined for the previous four tourneys, his announcement meant the loss of all four yokozuna in just one year.

During the May tournament, Konishiki failed again in his attempt at yokozuna promotion. Meanwhile, another foreign hero emerged in Akebono, who captured the title with 13–2 and was subsequently promoted to ozeki.

The tournament in July 1992 saw no yokozuna on the ranking sheets for the first time in sixty years, and nobody was likely to reach the rank before the end of the year at the earliest. However, the two top ozeki spots in July were occupied by foreigners (Akebono and Konishiki) for the first time in history. Musashimaru had also reached a high rank. Therefore, the eventual promotion of a foreigner to yokozuna seems only a matter of time. Time will only tell, too, which of the young Japanese contenders will eventually help Akebono, Konishiki, or Musashimaru create a new golden age of sumo.

5

Grand Tournaments

Grand tournaments take place just ninety days of the year, yet these are what a sumotori lives for. It is no exaggeration to say that his treatment and very existence in the sumo world depend on their outcome.

Since 1958, fifteen-day grand tournaments have been held regularly six times a year during the odd-numbered months. In January, May, and September, the tourneys are held at the Kokugikan stadium next to Ryogoku Station in Tokyo. In March, the tournament takes place at the Osaka Furitsu Taiikukan (Osaka Prefectural Gymnasium); in July, at the Aichi Kenritsu Taiikukan (Aichi Prefectural Gymnasium) in central Nagoya; and in November, at the Fukuoka Kokusai Sentaa (Fukuoka International Center) in northern Kyushu—the only tournament held outside Honshu. All the tourneys, except the one in Nagoya, begin on the second Sunday of the month and close on the fourth Sunday. The Nagoya tournament opens on the first Sunday, supposedly so that it can end before the worst summer heat sets in and also to give the leading sumotori more time to go on a long tour of northern Japan afterwards.

Sumo tournaments are called *basho*. The January tournament is the Hatsu Basho, literally meaning the first one of the year. The March tourney is officially known as the Haru Basho, meaning spring tournament, although it is also called the Osaka Basho. The tourney held in May is called the Natsu Basho, the summer tournament. Although the appellation may seem more appropriate for the July tournament, one has no choice but to remember it the way the

Sumo Association has named it. The tourney which takes place in July is called the Nagoya Basho. In September comes the Aki Basho (autumn tourney), and in November, the Kyushu Basho. Each of these tourneys is referred to as a *hon basho*, meaning "proper tournament." The hon basho held outside of Tokyo are also known as *chiho basho*, meaning regional tourneys.

The Stadium

The present Kokugikan in Ryogoku, where three of the tournaments are held annually, serves as headquarters of the Sumo Association. The stadium is a 35,342-square-meter building with a seating capacity of 11,098; it stands 39.6 meters at its highest point. It has three floors aboveground and two underground. The stadium was constructed to withstand earthquake tremors up to ten on the Richter scale and is equipped with computerized temperature control, fire prevention equipment, and sensors to detect gas leaks. It also has a 1,250-ton tank designed to store rainwater and divert it to the toilets and air-conditioning system inside. The stadium, furthermore, contains a sumo museum open to the public and reception rooms, which may be rented for various functions. The Ryogoku Kokugikan was built at a total cost of ¥15 billion.

On the second floor the seats are Western-style chairs. However, except for some tables with lounge chairs in the very back, the first floor is given over to traditional Japanese seating arrangements on tatami. Most of this consists of cushioned box seats, known as *masu-zeki* or *sajiki-seki*, generally holding four persons. These seats usually must be purchased through one of the twenty teahouses (*chaya*) lined up along the northern entrance to the stadium. Their cost will come to far more than the price of the ticket, as the teahouse will add charges for food and drink as well as some sumo souvenirs onto the bill. These are all brought to the masu-zeki by a *dekata* (usher) dressed in traditional Japanese workman's clothing. (When sumo is not in season, most of these men work on farms or with construction companies in the Tokyo area.)

The first five rows around the ring are individual seats called *tamari-seki* or *suna-kaburi*. The latter, meaning "sand-covered," comes from the fact that spectators sitting in this area occasionally take in some of the sand kicked up on the dohyo or flying off the body of a falling rikishi. Despite the unglamorous appellation, the suna-kaburi are the most sought-after seats.

The ring, as seen from the four-person box seats, reserved through teahouses near the Kokugikan's northern entrance.

Behind the sumotori awaiting their bouts, the first five rows of suna-kaburi, or "sand-covered," seats closest to the ringside action, are the most desired.

Except for some differences in the number of seats as well as in the arrangements in the last row and second floor, the interior layout of the other stadiums used for sumo generally follows the same pattern.

The seats as well as the tickets are labeled *shomen* (main side), *muko-jomen* (opposite main side), *higashi-gawa* (east side), and *nishi-gawa* (west side). The present labeling in the Kokugikan is actually the opposite of the actual compass points and traces its origins to the tradition of the emperor always sitting facing south. The area in which he sat was designated the main or northern side, and everything to his left was deemed the "east side," and to his right the "west side"—a pattern which can be seen in the old capital of Kyoto. Thus, what is supposed to be west from his perspective is actually east on the compass, and vice versa. In the Kokugikan the emperor's box is actually located on the second floor in the middle of the building's southern side, which in respect to tradition is called the main or northern side.

On the walls above all the seats on the second floor are life-size colored photographs of all tournament winners from the past five and a half years. Written on the frame is the month and year of the tournament, and the rikishi's name and rank, as well as his score. The photographs of the winners of the two most recent tourneys are unveiled in a brief ceremony on the opening day of each Tokyo tournament.

The four aisles leading to the ring are collectively called *hanamichi*, or "flower paths." This appellation stems from a Heian period custom of decorating the aisles in which the rikishi appeared for the special matches in the imperial court with hollyhock and calabash flowers. The hollyhock symbolized the eastern aisle, and the calabash the west. Technically all four aisles leading to the ring are hanamichi, but many people still use the term only in reference to the two used by the rikishi and call the other two tsuro, the ordinary Japanese word for aisle.

The two true hanamichi lead from the ring to dressing rooms (*shitaku-beya*), one each on the east and west sides. The dressing rooms are dominated by two elevated rows of tatami where the sumotori keep their changes of clothing and rest or watch television while waiting their turn to go out. Each sekitori has a painted bamboo trunk, with his name written on the side, to hold personal effects. Some rikishi—particularly the sekitori—use the slightly narrow aisle between the rows to practice certain moves, often on their attendants. In front of the wall at the far end is another elevated tatami-matted area which is reserved for the yokozuna or the

The head of the Sumo Association, flanked by the san'yaku, greeting the audience on the last day.

Center left to right, Chiyonofuji, Asahifuji, and Hokutoumi sit before Chiyonofuji's bamboo trunk in the dressing room.

leading yokozuna, if there are two in the same dressing room. A door on the other side of the room leads to the bathroom.

The Ring

The center of any sumo stadium is the dohyo, demarcated by *tawara*, rice-straw bales filled with earth and small stones and covered with sand. The dohyo in fact gets its name from these cylindrical bales. The character for tawara is also read as *hyo* in some compounds, and one reading for the character for earth is *do*.

The dohyo in the stadium is the same size as those used for practice in the heya. The main difference is that the one in the stadium lies on top of a square mound, between fifty-four to sixty centimeters high, which is similarly delineated by straw bales. Prior to the opening of the new Kokugikan, the mound was always made of Arakida clay from Saitama Prefecture near Tokyo. However, land development in the suburbs of the capital has rendered Arakida clay scarce in its native region, so a similar type of moist and porous clay from Tsukuba in Ibaraki Prefecture is frequently used instead. (Each time a sumo entourage goes on tour, some men are sent in advance to the locality to search for clay of similar quality.)

The ring is made anew by twenty men prior to each tournament. Requiring three days, the work starts with the dismantling of the old ring. Eight four-ton trucks may be required to carry away the old clay if the entire ring is destroyed; but nowadays often only its surface is redone, in which case two trucks will suffice. At the end of the first day's work the inner core of the old ring is covered with new clay, sprinkled with water, and left overnight for the two soils to settle well with each other.

On the following day, the twenty workers (almost invariably *yobidashi*—the men who call sumotori up for their matches) build up an eight-ton mound and pound it down, perhaps with empty beer or soda bottles, without the help of any machinery. They mark a 4.55 meter diameter with nails and rope, dig small trenches around the circle, and fill them with rice-straw bales. By the end of the next day the yobidashi will have placed the sixty-six order-made tawara very firmly into all points of the trenches.

One bale is set two millimeters higher than the others and slightly outside the circle in the middle of each of the cardinal points. This was originally done to drain rainwater from the ring in the days when sumo was held outdoors. These bales later came to be called *toku-dawara*, or beneficial bales, as occasionally a rikishi who would have gone out of the ring, if it were an unbroken circle, lucks out by having his foot land on one of them.

The finishing touch to the new ring comes with painting of the *shikiri-sen*, the starting lines on the east and west sides. These white lines, ninety centimeters long and six centimeters wide, are painted thirty-five centimeters from the very center of the dohyo.

The day after the ring is completed a *tsuriyane*, a suspended roof modeled after the roofs over Shinto shrines, is hung over it. Weighing about six tons, this roof is 9.9 meters wide and 8.8 meters high. In the past it not only had religious significance but also served as protection from meteorological elements.

The roof used to be held up by four wooden pillars; however, for years people complained that these blocked their view of the matches. Thus, in 1952, the roof came to be suspended from the ceiling on steel cables. As each of the pillars had been wrapped in a different colored cloth with symbolic significance, they were replaced with giant tassels (*fusa*) in the same hues and hung from corners of the roof. The tassel lying at the east and shomen (north) corner is green, representing spring and Seiryu—a green dragon god of the east. A red tassel lies at the east and muko-jomen (south) corner, representing summer and Shujaku—a red sparrow tutelary god of the south. At the southwest corner is a white tassel symbolizing autumn and Byakko—a white tiger god of the west. The black tassel at the northwest corner represents winter and Genbu—a snake-encircled turtle god of the north and of water. Smaller tassels in the same colors are also hung in the middle of each side of the roof.

The large tassels weigh eighteen kilograms; they are ten centimeters thick and 2.10 meters wide. Apparently the initial ones dropped to just under two meters over the ring, but that occasionally caused problems when the topknots of rikishi over two meters tall, like Ozeki Ouchiyama and Sekiwake Fudoiwa, accidentally hit them. At present the tassels hang down to a point 2.12 meters above the ring.

Gigantic cushions that are for the judges are placed on each side below the dohyo. Two judges sit on the muko-jomen side; the one below the red tassel also serves as timekeeper. The chief judge sits on the shomen side. On the left and right of the judges on the east and west sides are places for rikishi to sit while waiting for their bouts. In the lower divisions the seats consist of simple straw matting, but large cushions are set up for the last five makushita and all juryo bouts. Each man in makunouchi is entitled to his own

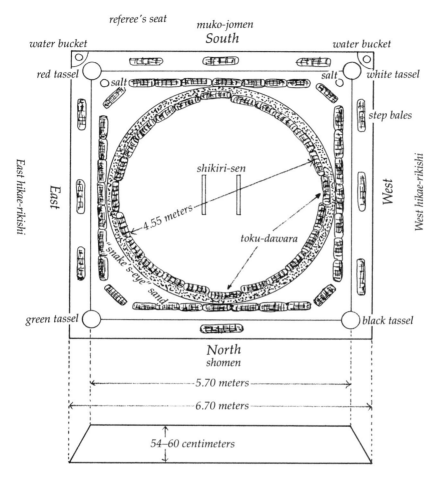

Figure labels:

referee's seat   muko-jomen

South

water bucket   water bucket

red tassel   salt   salt   white tassel

step bales

East hikae-rikishi   East

shikiri-sen

4.55 meters

West   West hikae-rikishi

toku-dawara

"snake's-eye" sand

green tassel   black tassel

North

shomen

5.70 meters

6.70 meters

54–60 centimeters

A scale drawing of a tournament ring.

cushion in a color of his choice. This cushion is laid out by one of the apprentices two matches prior to the sekitori's own bout.

Large baskets filled with salt are set up at the southeast and southwest corners of the ring practically under the red and white tassels. Not long before the sekitori-level bouts begin, buckets of water are also affixed to niches in the same corners of the ring. The salt and water are for purification in the rituals preceding upper-level matches. Occasionally the judges may even indicate to low-ranking makushita rikishi to throw salt.

On the morning before the opening day of a tournament, a ring festival (*dohyo-matsuri*) is held in the Kokugikan and, in somewhat different form, in the stables to bless the ring and pray for no injuries during the ensuing two weeks.

Daily Proceedings

Tournament matches called *torikumi* begin around 9:30 A.M. every day. They steadily work their way up from the lowest to the top division and end with a yokozuna fighting (or an ozeki match if there are no yokozuna present) just before 6:00 P.M. The last bout is known as the *musubi no ichiban* (the match tying everything together).

Except for three brief changings of the judges sitting around the ring, the action is continuous until around 3:00 P.M. when the men in the juryo division perform their entrance into the ring ceremony (*dohyo-iri*). On most days, NHK starts televising the action from around this time. The judges change again after the juryo perform their ceremony. This is followed by the last five matches in the makushita division, which go on while the juryo are undoubtedly changing from their ceremonial aprons into their fighting mawashi (*tori-mawashi*). The bouts move from the makushita division into juryo without any fanfare—except that the names of the judges, who have already been sitting there for five matches, are finally read over a loudspeaker. The juryo bouts proceed without break, except on the first and last days, when the chairman of the Sumo Association, flanked by all the ozeki and yokozuna (or all the san'yaku in tourneys with few yokozuna and ozeki) in their tori-mawashi, appears in the ring between the third and fourth-to-last juryo fights to greet the audience and thank them for their patronage.

Just after the last juryo fight, around 4:00 P.M., four white banners bearing the characters *man'in onrei* (full house, thank you) are electronically lowered from the ceiling on days when the tickets have been sold out. The house may not actually be full, since the decision to display the banners is made according to ticket sales up to about 2:30 to 3:00 P.M.

Promptly after the banners descend (or right after the last juryo bout, if the banners are not lowered), the makunouchi men appear for their own dohyo-iri. They are followed by the yokozuna doing his, or their, special dohyo-iri if there are any grand champions participating in the tourney. After that, one of the two top-ranking referees climbs into the ring to read the next day's matches in the

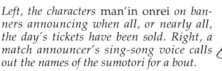

Left, the characters man'in onrei *on banners announcing when all, or nearly all, the day's tickets have been sold. Right, a match announcer's sing-song voice calls out the names of the sumotori for a bout.*

top division. What follows is the first and only real break of the day. For about ten to fifteen minutes the ring area is devoid of all sumotori and judges for the only time until the completion of the tournament day.

Between 4:25 and 4:30 P.M., four sumotori and five judges take seats below the ring, and the initial bout in the makunouchi division begins within four minutes after a yobidashi has summoned the first two rikishi into the ring. There is one more brief changing of the judges halfway into the top division matches around 5:10 P.M., but the bouts and their accompanying routine continue without break. The close of the day is marked by a bow-twirling ceremony.

The bouts are likely to start with mae-zumo during part or all of the first week of a tournament, depending on the number of newcomers. Otherwise, the day begins with jonokuchi. In either case, the stadium will be only sparsely illuminated while the lowest divisions perform, and generally only the most true-blue sumo fans and friends or relatives of these sumotori show up to see them. More lights come on between 1:30 and 2:30 P.M., depending on the season (i.e., earlier in the winter). The ticket price is based on where a person sits; it is the same if one shows up at 9:30 A.M. or 4:00 P.M.

Those who have watched only the sekitori perform might be surprised to see how slender some of the tyros are as well as the lack of ritual preceding their matches. In the lowest divisions the rikishi virtually jump at each other right after climbing into the ring in a style known as *tobitsuki*, or "leaping."

Makushita rikishi get two minutes for warming-up rituals called *shikiri*. In juryo, the time limit is three minutes; in makunouchi, it is four minutes. Rikishi used to be able to spend as much time as they wanted for warming up and psyching each other out—an important part of this ritual—but time limits were instituted in 1928 with the launching of live radio broadcasts of sumo. The initial time limit for makunouchi was ten minutes. This was subsequently lowered a few more times and set at the present four minutes in September 1950.

In all divisions, the winner of a match is the one who manages to get his opponent onto the ground or out of the ring first.

Entrance into the Ring Ceremony

Every day before the juryo and makunouchi bouts, the rikishi in these divisions perform their dohyo-iri, the colorful entrance into the ring ceremony dating back at least to the Genroku era (1688–1704). The juryo, in reverse order of rank, make their way down an aisle and are led by a juryo-level referee onto the ring. The referee enters the ring first. Then each juryo gets in as his name, hometown, and stable are announced. A yobidashi claps small cherrywood boards (ki) together before each name is read.

The first juryo in the ring circles almost back to the spot where he entered it, while the others proceed to take their places. Once the highest-ranking man is in the ring, they all turn inward, clap their hands, raise their right arms, hitch up their aprons slightly, raise both arms, turn outward, and leave the dohyo quickly in the order in which they came in. Then the juryo on the other side mount the ring to perform the same ritual.

The hand clapping is meant as purification. The arms are raised to show that the rikishi is not holding any weapons, and the aprons are hitched to symbolize stomping—a move which supposedly drives demons away.

On the first and all subsequent odd-numbered days of the tournament, those who will be fighting on the east side that day perform the ritual first. On even-numbered days those on the west side go first. These numbers are calculated by the basho's start. Whether a tourney begins on an even- or odd-numbered day of the month, the opening day is always called shonichi (first day), and all subsequent days are numbered in relation to it.

The dohyo-iri ritual for makunouchi follows the same pattern as the one for juryo—except that they are led by a referee for their own division. An ozeki or occasionally a sekiwake is the last to mount the ring, for a yokozuna performs a separate ceremony.

Only for sumo held in the imperial presence is the dohyo-iri

The makunouchi sumotori entering the ring before the matches.

routine changed. When the emperor or crown prince is attending sumo—usually on the middle Sunday of a Tokyo tourney—the makunouchi men, after following the referee into the ring, form rows facing the emperor's box in the very middle of the front row of the second floor on the shomen side. They are not introduced until the last one has taken his place, and they all do the usual stomping and clapping. After the name, birthplace, and stable of the individual rikishi are read, he lowers his head, climbs down from the ring, and files out. This style of dohyo-iri is called *gozen-gakari*.

Once the makunouchi men leave the ring on both normal and imperial presence days, a yobidashi claps his boards again. Then a grand champion appears, wearing his majestic yokozuna hawser. He proceeds down the aisle following a *tate-gyoji* (one of the top two referees) and two attendants, a sword-bearer (*tachi-mochi*) and a dew-sweeper (*tsuyu-harai*)—a role harking back to the days when sumo was performed outdoors.

The two present styles of yokozuna dohyo-iri, *unryu* and *shiranui*, both begin with the grand champion taking a position between his two attendants, who are squatting in two opposite corners of the side of the ring (east or west) that they mounted. While still squatting, the grand champion claps his hands twice to attract the attention of the gods and then extends his arms out horizontally with his palms up. Known as *chiri o kiru* (or *chiri*), this motion stems from an old samurai way of purifying the hands and also demonstrates that the grand champion does not possess any weapon. The yokozuna next stands up and moves to the ring's center facing the shomen, where he swings his arms out and claps again. He then sets his feet wide apart and places his left hand on his rib cage, while extending the right one out horizontally. Reversing the positions of his hands, the yokozuna raises his right leg as high as possible and then stomps hard in shiko style. Next he inches his feet forward, while slowly bringing his torso up.

The divergence in the styles comes with this raising of the torso called *seri-agari*. A practitioner of the more common unryu style keeps his left hand at his chest and spreads the right one slightly out forward, while he moves up. In the shiranui style, a grand champion spreads both hands out.

Once up, the practitioner of either style again stamps hard twice in a symbolic move to drive demons out of the ring. This usually brings cheers and shouts of *Nippon ichi* ("the best man in Japan") from the audience. The grand champion then turns to the side and saunters over to his original position between his two attendants, whereupon he squats down to do the chiri motions

A yokozuna, attended by a sword-bearer and dew-sweeper, during his special entrance to the ring ceremony.

once more. Finally, he gets up and leaves the ring, followed by his attendants and the referee.

Any other grand champions will mount the ring to perform the same ritual. The eastern proper (*higashi sei*) yokozuna appears last on the opening day of the tournament. If there are other grand champions, the eastern proper yokozuna will appear first on the second day, and the western proper yokozuna will be the last to perform. The order is rotated daily.

The yokozuna dohyo-iri was first performed by Tanikaze Kajinosuke and shortly thereafter by his rival Onogawa Kisaburo in the late eighteenth century. Tanikaze's attendant tachi-mochi carried a sword during the ceremony as a sign of the grand champion's samurai status.

The present styles are named after Unryu Hisakichi and Shiranui Koemon, two grand champions of the early nineteenth century. Through the Meiji period actually several individual styles of dohyo-iri were practiced. It is difficult to prove which, if any, of them were actually transmitted by Unryu and Shiranui. However, when Haguroyama, upon promotion to grand champion in 1941, took to doing a dohyo-iri imitating the form of Tachiyama, a yokozuna from 1911 to 1918, it was labeled shiranui. Another style,

*Yokozuna hawsers are tied behind in one of
two styles—unryu, left, or shiranui.*

which had been favored by Nishinoumi II, yokozuna from 1916 to
1918, and some others after him, came to be named unryu. While
there is no Sumo Association regulation forbidding grand champions
from creating a new style of dohyo-iri, tradition appears to have set
in, and only the unryu and shiranui forms have been performed
during the major part of the twentieth century.

The shiranui style is said to be most becoming to a yokozuna
who is unusually large or powerful. Unfortunately, there also
seems to be a jinx against its practitioners, for their careers at the
top do not last long. While Tachiyama and Haguroyama retained
the rank for a fairly long time, their postwar successors to the
shiranui style (Yoshibayama, Tamanoumi, Kotozakura,
Takanosato, Futahaguro, and Asahifuji) have had either short or
checkered careers at the top.

Ideally, the two attendants should be members of the same
stable as the grand champion and be ranked sekiwake or below.
However, since not all heya have enough other men in the top
division (or they have enough but one is an ozeki), often someone
is called in from an affiliate. Occasionally one of the attendants is
not even from an affiliate. He may be serving out of a special
friendship with a grand champion (such as Mutsuarashi attending
Kitanofuji in the 1970s) or because he has trained a lot with a
yokozuna (such as Koboyama with Chiyonofuji in the 1980s).

The man serving as sword-bearer must be higher in rank than
the dew-sweeper. An attendant who does not belong to the
yokozuna's stable will not serve in the dohyo-iri on a day he is

Kotogaume's kesho-mawashi, left, has a design using only English, whereas Akebono's features Japanese characters, a U.S. flag, and Kintaro, a folk hero.

scheduled to face that grand champion or the other attendant in the ring. A substitute is found for such occasions.

Kesho-mawashi

Kesho-mawashi are the ceremonial silk aprons worn by sekitori during the juryo, makunouchi, and yokozuna dohyo-iri. They are embroidered with various designs or calligraphy, and sometimes even inlaid with jewels. Most kesho-mawashi have gold or silver fringe at the hem; only ozeki, yokozuna, and the latter's attendants during his dohyo-iri are permitted to have purple fringe. These aprons typically cost around ¥400,000 to ¥500,000 and sometimes even millions of yen. Although outwardly they resemble decorative aprons, they are really one long piece of cloth—an oversized variation of a woman's obi, the sash worn with a kimono.

For the yokozuna dohyo-iri the grand champion and his two attendants use a set of matching kesho-mawashi. The pieces in the set are generally not of the exact same design, yet each one goes with the others, such as pictures of three different seasonal flowers or guardian gods, or the characters for spirit (*shin*), skill (*gi*), and body (*tai*)—the three essential qualities of a rikishi.

The aprons are usually presented to a sekitori by a group of patrons, and the name of the organization which donated it often appears just above the fringe at the hem. The most popular sekitori have several; some even wear a different one every day.

Rituals

One major distinguishing feature of sumo in comparison with other sports is that each match begins and ends with decorum. Upon climbing into the ring, the two opponents begin shikiri, the ritual warming up, by doing shiko stomps. Next they go to their respective corners at the muko-jomen side of the ring, where they receive *chikara-mizu* (power water) from the victor of the previous match or the one who is to fight next: the *hikae-rikishi*. Since the water is both for good luck and purification, someone who has already lost that day cannot give it to the next man in the ring. Therefore, on one side the winner of the previous bout offers the water, but on the other it is given by the next man up. Even if that man loses his own match eight to ten minutes later, his record for the day was still unsullied at the point he ladled the water.

When two rikishi come down the aisles to replace the two men who have climbed into the ring, ideally the lower-ranking one should take his seat first; occasionally, however, they do not manage

Left, a judge and one of the referees on the south side of the ring. Right, the victor of the preceding match offers a ladle of "power water" to the next competing sumotori.

Two sumotori size up each other in a staring showdown known as niramiai.

to synchronize their timing properly. During all bouts, there are always supposed to be four rikishi, two each on the east and west sides, sitting below the ring. The opponents in the third-to-last match in juryo and makunouchi remain by the dohyo instead of going back to the dressing rooms after fighting. The winner of that match may be required to offer water to the last man to fight if the second-to-last rikishi on his side lost. If, as often happens, both the second-to-last and the third-to-last fighters on the same side have lost, leaving no one qualified to offer chikara-mizu, then an attendant of the final man comes down the aisle in his mawashi to ladle the water.

No matter who gives him the water, the rikishi (in most cases a sekitori) in the ring will use it for rinsing his mouth; then he most likely spits it into *chikara-gami* (power paper). Some rikishi are also known to use pieces of this paper to wipe sweat from their armpits. After purifying their bodies in this way, the two fighters throw some salt for more purification and squat opposite each other in the middle of their edge of the ring. They clap their hands and extend their arms out horizontally with their palms open—the same chiri done during the yokozuna dohyo-iri for purification as well as to prove that no weapons are carried.

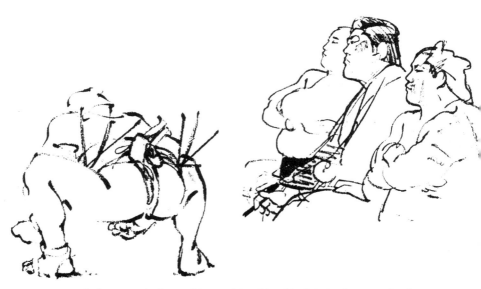

Left, a sumotori crouching and touching his fists to the ground prior to the start of his bout. Right, one of the judges sits between Chiyonofuji, on his left, and Takanosato as they await their bouts.

Next the two get up, take a few steps forward, do some more stamping, and squat behind the starting lines on their sides. The referee will approach them at this point and shout, *"Kamaete"* ("Take your places"). They then lower their fists, crouch down, and stare hard into each other's eyes. This psychological confrontation is called the *niramiai* (mutual staring). Despite their length, these rituals contain a lot of drama; often it is possible to predict the loser of a bout just by watching his facial expressions or eyes or both during this showdown.

The rikishi finally rise again and return to the corner for more salt. Some grab a fistful, while others take just a tiny pinch. The audience often roars when the two opponents have completely contrasting salt-throwing styles or stare long and hard at each other.

The entire ritual may be repeated around five or six times during the allotted four minutes prior to a makunouchi match. The judge sitting under the red tassel will indicate to the referee to tell the men in the ring that their preparation time is up. Before the actual bout begins, the two rikishi will go back to their corners on the muko-jomen side and perhaps accept towels to wipe themselves off. Then they proceed to their positions behind the two

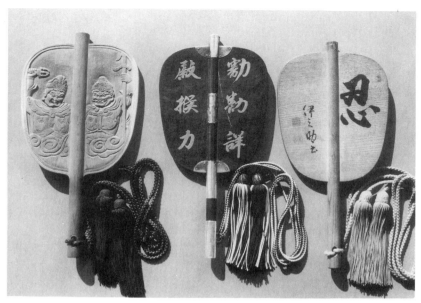

Referee war paddles.

starting lines near the ring's center and crouch down opposite each other. Some squat down far away from the white line, others right in front of it.

The moment the referee holds his *gunbai* (war paddle) flat back against his torso, the two rikishi know it is time to stand up for the initial charge (*tachiai*). The fighters should have both hands on the ground for the tachiai. But steadily this ideal came to be widely ignored, and in the mid-1970s to mid-1980s several high-ranking sekitori would charge without putting even one hand on the ground first. This ultimately prompted the Sumo Association to issue a ruling, in September 1984, that all rikishi must have at least one hand on the ground when beginning the tachiai and that the judges around the ring or the referee could stop the match if it began improperly. Special lectures, with films of greats from the past like Futabayama, were given to the sekitori in preparation for the tournament that month.

The ideal tachiai should be synchronized, so that the two sumotori rise together. Standing up too quickly or in too low a position can be rather disadvantageous. Occasionally two opponents will both feel ready to fight before the time limit (*jikan ippai*) and will rise for the initial charge after indicating their intentions to each other through eye contact. This is not only perfectly acceptable, but is in fact generally regarded as laudable.

Occasionally a false start occurs when one sumotori calls *"matta"* ("wait") if he does not feel ready to join his opponent's initial charge. This act itself is called matta as well. Although technically not sanctioned, for a long time it was allowed to happen more often than not. However, once in the Nagoya Basho of 1976, after Arase and Wakamisugi (later Wakanohana II) had seven matta, the judges became rather angry and called an unprecedented conference to deliberate on its abuse. Moreover, in the fall of 1991, the Sumo Association decided to fine makunouchi rikishi guilty of doing matta ¥100,000, and to fine juryo ¥50,000. Yokozuna, in particular, are expected to set a good example by not initiating matta. The great Futabayama is said never to have done matta, and Taiho and Kitanoumi did it only a few times.

Compared with the time spent on the ritual preliminaries, the actual bout itself is likely to be over very quickly—often in less than a minute, sometimes in a split second. If the mawashi of one of the opponents becomes too loose during the fight, the referee may halt the action briefly to retie or tighten it. This is called a gyoji matta. If a rikishi's belt comes off during his match, he is automatically declared the loser. This has not happened since the 1960s, yet some people still joke about how the television cameras blacked out when Wakachichibu lost his belt.

If the match should reach a long stalemate, with both rikishi locked in a grip for three or four minutes, the judges or the referee may order the fight to be halted temporarily for a breather called *mizu-iri* or *mizu ga hairu*. The referee stops the bout, carefully measures the hold the sumotori were in with his arms, and checks the position of their feet. Once he has the exact positioning in his mind, he lets the two sumotori out of their hold and has them go to their corners for water offered by a hikae-rikishi. About a minute later, the referee carefully locks the two back in their original positions and directs them with his paddle to start again. There are no set time limits for calling a mizu-iri; the matter is left to the discretion of the judges or the referee.

Should the two fighters reach another impasse after the first water break, the bout may be stopped and rescheduled for a little later or after the very last match. Another option is to call a draw (*hikiwake*). Both occurrences are rare. The last case of a rescheduling in the top division occurred in a fight between Kaiketsu and Asashikuni in March 1978, and the last draw was in a bout between Minenoumi and Futagodake in September 1974.

A victorious sumotori, swinging his hand like a sword cutting toward the cardinal points, expresses gratitude to the three gods of creation.

After the referee points to the winner's side with his paddle, the fighters return to their places near the edge of the east and west sides of the ring. The victor's name and the technique he used to win are announced over a loudspeaker; in the top two divisions, the win is also announced on lighted boards just below the second-floor gallery on the east and west sides. Both fighters are expected to act courteously and not display any outward signs of emotion, although nowadays this ideal is not always followed.

Back in their places behind the starting lines, the sumotori must lower their heads to each other before leaving the ring. The loser leaves first. The winner must express thanks to the three gods of creation: Amenominakanushi no kami, Takamimusubi no kami, and Kamimusubi no kami, by swiftly swinging his hand in the four cardinal points while crouching on his heels before the referee's paddle. This is called *tegatana o kiru* (cutting with the hand like a sword), and it must be performed by the winner of each match, whether or not some white envelopes have been presented from the referee's paddle.

Each envelope contains money, and their number depends on how many banners were carried by yobidashi circling the ring at the start of the warm-up rituals. The banners represent companies, groups of patrons, and other sponsors who offered ¥60,000 (in 1992) as special prize money called *kensho-kin* (encouragement money) for the bout. Some companies are mainly interested in the name value of the association with sumo. Others intend to sponsor one of the sekitori. A winner takes all on the paddle, although only ¥30,000 is actually in each envelope. The Sumo Association keeps ¥5,000 as expenses for printing a sponsor's name on the program for the day and announcing it over the loudspeaker. The remaining ¥25,000 is set aside in a fund to help the rikishi pay his taxes at the end of the fiscal year. (This system was instituted apparently because in the past many sekitori tended to spend their money as soon as they got it and would later find themselves unable to pay their taxes.)

The practice of giving kensho-kin to the winner of a match dates back to the Edo period, and was especially popular in Kyoto and Osaka. Later—particularly during World War II—items of food and clothing were even flung to the winners. After the war the kensho prizes were standardized at a specific amount of money.

The amount of kensho-kin a sekitori receives each tourney is viewed as a barometer of his popularity, although, of course, some men win many envelopes that were really meant for their opponents. The most kensho-kin ever placed on a bout was twenty-six for Yokozuna Taiho versus Ozeki Tochinoumi in January 1964.

Mono-ii

If a fight does not seem to have a clear-cut winner, or if the referee appears to have made a mistake in his decision, one or more of the five judges sitting below the ring may call a *mono-ii*, a conference to discuss the matter. The judges climb into the ring to deliberate, perhaps checking for telltale footprints at or over the edge. A rikishi sitting below the ring is also allowed to call a conference, but he cannot join the judges in their deliberations. (It is very rare that a hikae-rikishi initiates a mono-ii.) The referee may join the discussion, but only if expressly invited to.

The judges can make one of three decisions: (1) to call a replay (*torinaoshi*) because the two rikishi went out or fell down simultaneously (*dotai*), (2) to overrule the referee's decision as wrong (*sashichigai*) so the gunbai must be pointed at the other man, or (3) to reaffirm the gyoji's original decision as correct (*gunbai-dori*).

For disputed bouts in the top division, one of the judges will be linked up by earphone to a monitor room where the match is played back in slow motion on videotape. The information obtained from the monitor room will be used for reference in the discussion. This monitoring system was launched in May 1969 after a controversial bout in March between Taiho and Toda (later Haguroiwa), who was judged the victor. The referee had originally declared Taiho the winner, but the judges reversed his decision. Yet photos in the newspaper the next morning showed that Toda's foot had briefly stepped out of the ring first.

Quite a furor erupted in the wake of that misjudgment, as it had put an end to Taiho's forty-five-bout winning streak. (Decisions concerning wins and losses cannot be reversed the next day.) The incident prompted the Sumo Association to start using videotapes, although the gesture was too late to help Taiho, who dropped out of that tourney three days later with bronchitis. Since the video playback system is not turned on for the lower divisions, it does not help those in disputed matches at such levels. Nor is the monitoring system of any use when no one calls a conference for what may look like an extremely close bout or a wrong decision to those in the audience. Nevertheless, it is better than nothing.

Yumitori-shiki

The *yumitori-shiki*, the bow-twirling ceremony following the final bout of each day, dates back at least to the late eighteenth century, when Yokozuna Tanikaze was presented with a bow by the shogun, Tokugawa Ienari, for winning a tournament in Edo Castle. The victorious grand champion responded by twirling it around in all four directions. During the Edo period, the komusubi, seki-wake, and ozeki who won on their final day participating in a tournament were respectively given a fan, a bowstring, and a bow. This custom apparently later developed into the yumitori. At first the ceremony was performed only on the last day of the tourney, but since 1952 it has come to be carried out every tournament day.

Since 1896, the ceremony has been customarily performed by someone ranked in the makushita or a lower division and belonging to the same, or at least an affiliate, heya as one of the yokozuna. Although an extra stipend is given for doing the yumitori-shiki, many rikishi are loath to accept the role since it is widely believed to be a jinx against a successful career in sumo. In January 1991, Tomoefuji, a former performer of the yumitori-shiki, effectively broke this jinx by winning the Fighting Spirit in the top division.

The performer of the ceremony dresses in a decorative apron

The bow-twirling ceremony following the last makunouchi match of the day.

and has his hair done in an elaborate topknot like a sekitori. He must mount the dohyo from the same side as the person who won the final bout. If he accidentally drops the bow during the ceremony, he must pick it up with his feet, for putting a hand on the ground symbolizes a loss.

Organization of the Matches

Generally a rikishi is likely to be pitted against anyone close in rank to himself, except those from his own stable. Only in the case of a tie for the division championship on the last day do opponents from the same stable face each other. As of May 1992, this had happened only twice in the makunouchi division (in 1949 and 1989), though it occurs fairly frequently in the lower divisions.

All bouts for the first and second days are drawn up two days prior to the opening of the tourney by the judges' committee. Thereafter, sekitori-level matches are drawn up on the afternoon before they are to take place. Bouts in the four lowest divisions are often drawn up two or three days in advance, as the men in them fight only seven days per tourney.

Since it is too late to change the arrangements for a bout that has already been announced, a rikishi who suddenly drops out, due to illness or injury, must forfeit to his scheduled opponent. Absences are known as *kyujo*; a win by default is called *fusensho*; and a loss by default is *fusenhai*. When a bout is being forfeited, a yobidashi carries into the ring a white banner with the characters fusensho, which he holds up for the audience to see. The rikishi who wins by default makes the same signs of thanks to the referee's paddle as any other victor. Normally a defaulted match comes in the order in which it was originally scheduled. However, as it is considered inauspicious to end the day with a default, if the rikishi getting the fusensho had originally been scheduled for the final match, he will appear on the dohyo before the second-to-last bout.

On the first day of a basho most of the maegashira face other maegashira ranked at the same or a very close number. The yokozuna almost invariably faces a komusubi or a sekiwake on the opening day.

A komusubi tends to have a rough first week, as he is pitted mostly against the upper-ranked rikishi—especially the yokozuna and ozeki. A komusubi who gets through the first week with a score of 3–5 or better is likely to chalk up a winning record, because in the final seven days he will face mostly maegashira. On the other hand, occasionally a komusubi or sekiwake who has earned a reputation as a "giant killer" for beating most of the upper rankers in the first week will ironically have trouble with maegashira in the next seven days. In any case, komusubi is widely regarded as a difficult position—especially for a person reaching it the first time. Indeed, rare is the man who achieves a winning score during his first attempt at komusubi.

The yokozuna and the ozeki will mostly be matched against komusubi and the upper maegashira during the first week. Each loss is called *kuroboshi* (black star). A win is normally known as *shiroboshi* (white star), but when a maegashira upsets a yokozuna, that is referred to as *kinboshi* (gold star). As long as the victorious maegashira is active in sumo, he will receive a bonus of ¥15,000 (as of 1992) in his tournament stipend for each kinboshi attained in his career. One kinboshi is worth more in a sekitori's calculations for his additional stipend, or *mochi-kyukin*, than an ordinary win or even a winning record. As of July 1992, Akinoshima held the all-time kinboshi record of fourteen.

Kinboshi in sumo slang has also come to mean a beautiful woman—something as desirable as a victory over a grand champion. When a maegashira wins by default against a grand champion, that is treated just as an ordinary (shiroboshi) win. A maegashira victory over an ozeki is informally dubbed *ginboshi* (silver star), but the Sumo Association neither rewards nor keeps special records of them.

Except for the January 1989 tournament, whose opening was postponed by one day out of respect to the memory of the late emperor Hirohito, the middle day (*nakabi*) has always fallen on a Sunday. Most Japanese businesses have that day off, and some potentially exciting matches—such as a yokozuna versus an ozeki, or a yokozuna or ozeki against a lower-ranking nemesis—are put together. Such scheduling is especially common on the middle day of a Tokyo tournament when the emperor or the crown prince has announced his intention to attend.

New recruits who have passed their trials of the first week in mae-zumo will be introduced on this day in a ceremony known as *shusse-hiro*, occurring well before the sekitori-level matches. (If there are many new recruits, the ones with poorer records will be introduced on the two subsequent days.)

During the second week, the yokozuna are mostly pitted against other grand champions and the ozeki, but they may have some bouts with sekiwake and maegashira as well. A low-ranking maegashira who does exceptionally well in the first week is likely to have his strength and skill tested against some of the san'yaku—sometimes including a yokozuna or two—during the final seven days. In the postwar period such testing came to be done partly to prevent a maegashira from winning the tournament without facing any ozeki or yokozuna.

In the lower divisions, high-ranking juryo and others who seem ready for promotion are likely to face low-ranking maegashira during the second week. In the same way, some in the upper part of the makushita division will be pitted against those at the bottom of juryo. For any bouts against a juryo, a makushita man must have his hair arranged in the elaborate topknot donned by sekitori but continues to wear his regular dark cotton mawashi. Similarly, a high-ranking sandanme may have a match or two with makushita opponents, and rikishi in the upper level of jonidan may face some sandanme sumotori.

East and West Bouts

In the past, sumotori ranked on the east did not face others on that side; the same held true for those on the west. However, the present arrangement mainly indicates that the man on the east side probably had the higher score in the previous tourney.

When there is a bout between east and east, or west and west, the man who is higher in rank is allowed to stay on the side in which he is listed on the banzuke. This arrangement is at least in part made so that two men who are going to fight each other in the ring will not have to meet in the dressing room that day. Only the two top grand champions are likely to remain on the same side every day during the tourney.

Through 1964, sumotori did not face any opponents from affiliates of their own stable. This practice was changed so that the Sumo Association could cut down on the number of sekitori by allowing them more possible opponents close in rank to themselves.

The move has also undoubtedly made sumo more exciting since it allows a greater variety of strong opponents to face each other. In January 1965, during the first tournament held under this new system, Tamanoshima (later Yokozuna Tamanoumi) of Kataonami-Beya beat Yokozuna Taiho of the parent Nishonoseki-Beya. This match, which could not have occurred just two months earlier, created considerable excitement. In fact, since 1965 some of the best bouts each tourney, such as Wajima vs. Wakanohana II and Kitanoumi vs. Mienoumi in the latter half of the 1970s, or Chiyonofuji vs. Konishiki and Onokuni vs. Takanosato or Wakashimazu in the 1980s, or Akebono vs. Konishiki in the early 1990s, have taken place between opponents from the same group of stables.

Physical and Mental Preparation

In sumo, like in all other sports, a person's performance may depend a lot on the physical condition he is in. Being injured or coming down with a cold, needless to say, can have ill effects on a man's final record, sometimes even forcing a person to drop out. On the other hand, there have been cases of sumotori managing to do well despite physical pain or a fever; some have even been known to commute to the tournament from a hospital. Undoubtedly the degree to which a sumotori's physical condition affects performance depends a lot on the individual and the nature of the problem.

Former Ozeki Wakashimazu, for instance, quickly recovered from a broken leg in March 1984 and had a winning record in the following tourney. Yet the same problem has led to the ruin of a number of sumo careers, such as that of Maegashira Konuma who, until breaking his leg in May 1976, had been widely regarded as the "second Kitanoumi." Former Ozeki Kotokaze, in contrast, seriously injured his knee twice; the second time caused him to drop into the makushita division, but he later managed to go as far as ozeki.

A sumotori is generally allowed to sit out a tournament if he has a fever or has been injured, but he is expected to fight on even after a death in his family or other disturbance in his life. Some claim that mental condition plays an even bigger role in determining a man's performance. Former Grand Champion Takanosato makes one interesting case in point. While a sekiwake in March 1981, he came down with a high fever during the tournament and was planning to drop out. But, upon hearing that Ozeki Masuiyama II, his opponent scheduled for the fifth day, was announcing his retirement, Takanosato decided that he may as well remain in the tourney one more day to pick up the win by default. He ended up staying in for the duration of the tourney and earning eight consecutive wins as well as a final score of 10–5.

About two years later, Ozeki Takanosato was in fine physical condition during the May tourney and indeed appeared to be a leading contender for the championship. Yet he dropped two surprising losses to lower-ranked opponents to end up in second place, even though he was the only one to beat Hokutenyu, the winner of that tournament. Takanosato ultimately went on to win the next tourney in Nagoya and become grand champion. But a few years after his retirement, he revealed to me that he had been in an argument with the woman he later married the night before the crucial bout in May, and this distraction had led to his upset in the ring.

Takanosato's head coach, Futagoyama Oyakata (formerly Yokozuna Wakanohana I), was dubbed *dohyo no oni* (the demon in the ring) during his heyday for his dauntless fighting spirit. Yet he, too, collapsed in September 1956, when his four-year-old son was scalded to death after a boiling pot of chanko-nabe spilled on him. Wakanohana appeared in the ring wearing Buddhist rosary beads as he chalked up twelve consecutive wins, but he came down with a high fever that forced him to withdraw on the thirteenth day. Wakanohana undoubtedly would have been promoted to yokozuna if he had won that tourney; the tragedy forced him to wait another two tourneys to reach sumo's highest rank. (Ever since that incident, small children have been strictly kept away from the areas in the sumo stables where chanko is prepared.) On the other hand, former Yokozuna Tochinishiki managed to capture the *yusho* (championship) in July 1959, even though has father was fatally hit by a truck on the tourney's fourteenth day. Thirty years later, Chiyonofuji beat stablemate Hokutoumi in a play-off to win the tournament following his youngest daughter's death by sudden infant death syndrome (crib death).

The Last Day

On *senshuraku*, the last day of a tournament, written poetically with the characters for "pleasures of one thousand autumns," the matches begin later, as most of the lower-ranked sumotori have already had their seven bouts by the thirteenth day. The matches also end about thirty minutes earlier to allow time for the awards ceremonies. (The bouts are likely to begin a bit later on the final Friday and Saturday as well.)

If there are any ties for the yusho in juryo and the four lower divisions, play-offs—followed by the awards ceremony—are normally held just before the makunouchi dohyo-iri at around 3:30 P.M. The play-offs in makushita and below often involve two or three sumotori tied at 7–0; sometimes three to seven or eight, or even more, apprentices will be tied at 6–1. If a juryo, tied for the best score in his division, is scheduled to face a low-ranking maegashira on the last day, the play-offs and the awards ceremony will be delayed until after the makunouchi dohyo-iri and that pivotal bout. In 1989, the winner of the championship in juryo received ¥1 million in prize money, and those in the lower divisions were awarded lesser amounts.

After the awards ceremony, the makunouchi matches proceed as normal. However, prior to the last three bouts, the six scheduled fighters perform a ceremony called the *san'yaku soroi-bumi*. First, the three men on the east side climb into the ring. The highest ranking among them (usually the eastern yokozuna) takes a position in center back, the second-ranking man stands in front on the west, and the third man is in front on the east. They clap their hands in unison and do some stomping with one arm out to the side. Their respective positions symbolize ozeki, sekiwake, and komusubi, although in reality they are now most likely to be taken by a yokozuna, ozeki, and sekiwake. After the men on the east side climb down, those on the west go into the ring to perform the same ritual—except their ranking is the highest behind on the east side, the second on the west, and the third alone in front.

The fighters in these last three bouts are most likely sekiwake, ozeki, and yokozuna, although occasionally a komusubi or a maegashira will appear. The winner of the third-to-last match, in addition to his kensho-kin, receives an arrow from the referee. The second-to-last victor gets a bowstring, and the final winner receives a bow.

The final match of the last day is likely to be carried out between the first and second highest-ranking grand champions. If such a pairing is not possible, the bout will probably be between the highest and third-highest yokozuna or the eastern ozeki. The arrangements ultimately depend on the number of san'yaku rikishi and who was absent that particular tournament. But even if the highest-ranking grand champion had a mediocre performance that particular tourney, his bout still must come last. Thus, it can be a bit anticlimactic when the bout determining the yusho comes second or third to last.

The tournament championship goes to the person with the most wins. In the top division this person is most likely to be a yokozuna, ozeki, or sometimes a sekiwake. Occasionally a komusubi or a maegashira captures the tourney title, but there is a jinx against the latter. Sadanoyama was the first to break this jinx by becoming yokozuna in 1965, about four years after he had captured the yusho as maegashira 13. Kaiketsu was promoted to ozeki, for the second time, after a championship as maegashira in 1976. Nevertheless, the jinx can still be said to exist. For example, Tagaryu took the tourney title as maegashira in September 1984 at the last tourney held in the Kuramae Kokugikan. His record thereafter was less than spectacular. In July 1988, he dropped into juryo and promptly won the yusho again; thus, he became the second man after Wakanami (Tamagaki Oyakata) to accomplish the somewhat dubious feat of capturing the title in the second-highest division after doing it once in makunouchi. Only time can tell what will happen to the four maegashira (Kotofuji, Kotonishiki, Takahanada, and Mitoizumi) who captured the yusho between July 1991 and July 1992.

A tourney championship captured with an unblemished record is called *zensho yusho*. If two or more men are tied for the top score, a play-off will take place ten minutes after the last bout and the yumitori-shiki. This is the only occasion when a bout is likely to follow the bow ceremony. The participants in the play-off go through the same rituals as they would for a normal match.

Prior to May 1947, in the case of a tie for the best score, the tourney title would simply go the person higher or highest in rank.

But in November 1945 the fairness of this policy was publicly questioned when Yokozuna Haguroyama, at 10–0, was chosen for the yusho over new Maegashira Chiyonoyama (later a grand champion), who also chalked up ten wins. One of Haguroyama's wins had come through default, whereas all of Chiyonoyama's had been earned in actual fights.

If only two men participate in a play-off, the one who wins takes the tourney title as well. If the play-off involves three men, they draw lots to determine who goes up first and last. The ultimate victor must win two bouts in a row. Thus, it is possible that the winner of the first bout will lose to his second opponent who, in turn, will be defeated by the loser in the initial match. If that rikishi beats the man who originally defeated him, he will take the tourney title. In March 1990, for example, Hokutoumi lost his first play-off bout but ultimately emerged the winner after defeating Konishiki and Kirishima consecutively in the third and fourth rounds.

After the bout is over, the winner goes back to the dressing room to have his topknot straightened, all the while receiving questions from the press. Once his appearance is in order, he comes to the eastern hanamichi. The audience rises for the playing of *Kimigayo*, the de facto national anthem of Japan, and sits down again. Then the victor and key members of the Sumo Association mount the dohyo. First, the chairman of the Sumo Association reads a brief speech lauding the victor's achievements and then presents him with the Emperor's Cup (*Tenno-hai*) and a large banner with names of past winners. The Emperor's Cup is just the start of an almost endless stream of prizes and enormous trophies from various prefectural and foreign governments as well as several organizations, both domestic and foreign. All the trophies are returned to the Sumo Association in a ceremony on the opening day of the following tournament, and the winner later receives smaller replicas of them to keep.

In 1992, the more unusual prizes included a gigantic jar of dried black mushrooms from the Agricultural Union of Oita Prefecture, a year's supply of gasoline from the United Arab Emirates, and an automobile (for winners of Tokyo tourneys)—all accompanied by monetary awards as well. The prize money from the Sumo Association itself in 1992 was ¥5 million.

After twenty to thirty minutes of trophies and victory speeches, *sansho* (literally, "three prizes") are awarded for Technique (*Ginosho*), Fighting Spirit (*Kantosho*), and Outstanding Performance (*Shukunsho*). This award system was established after World War II, and the recipients are required to have chalked up a winning record and must be ranked below ozeki. The criteria for the Technique and Fighting Spirit prizes are probably self-explanatory, but the Shukunsho is supposed to go to the man who beat the most yokozuna, ozeki, or the strong candidates for the yusho.

Sometimes the same man is simultaneously awarded two of these prizes; as of July 1992, only three men had ever been granted all three at the same time. If the winner of the tournament is ranked sekiwake or below, he will quite likely receive the Fighting Spirit Prize and probably the Technique Prize as well. Occasionally two men share one of the prizes. Every so often one of the prizes (most often the Ginosho) is withheld; in 1988 it was withheld for five consecutive tournaments. Although the Ginosho is considered the most prestigious, all three are worth the same: ¥1 million (in 1992).

The audience is considerably thinned out by the time the sansho recipients are awarded their trophies. Many who attended the bouts are probably not even aware that the end of the tournament inside the stadium is really marked with the *teuchi-shiki*, a ceremony involving hand clapping and exchange of sacred Shinto sake around the dohyo to introduce the new recruits once more and wish them good luck in the upcoming tournament, when their names will appear on the ranking sheets for the first time.

The tournament winner from the top division rides atop an open convertible in a triumphant victory parade. He is flanked by another sekitori or two from his stable or an affiliate. The victor and his sekitori attendants normally change into formal *haori-hakama* (kimono coat and skirt-trousers) for the parade. But once Wakanohana I had so little confidence he would win the tournament that he did not even bring such formal wear to the stadium with him. He and Wakachichibu went into the convertible in their mawashi—an incident dubbed ever since as the "naked victory parade."

All stables, except those in mourning, celebrate the end of the tournament that Sunday night with parties called *uchiage-kai*. Needless to say, the party given at the stable of the tourney victor tends to be the most lively. Typically, a gigantic cup of sake and a large sea bream, among other delights, are placed before the seated victor, and the party does not officially get underway until he touches his lips to the liquor. However, in January 1992, Takahanada, being a nineteen-year-old minor, had to make do with a toast of oolong tea. Aside from being rather tasty, sea bream in Japan is regarded as auspicious because of the play on words between its Japanese name, *tai*, and *omedetai*, meaning congratulations.

It is no particular problem for the stable's okamisan to purchase

The "naked victory parade" of Yokozuna Wakanohana I and stablemate Wakachichibu.

this fish, despite its expense, when the victor of the tournament is already certain. But when the outcome is up in the air until past 5:00 P.M. on the last day, all the stables with a contender for the championship must obtain a sea bream before the party guests start arriving. Yet as it would seem rudely sarcastic to serve sea bream to the person who ultimately did not emerge with the championship, this delicacy is likely to end up in the garbage or in a pet's dish.

The next morning a brief holiday begins for all the sumotori, whether they were among those able to savor the cup of victory or those who drowned their sorrows in the liquor that overflowed at the party.

6

Promotions and Demotions

A sumotori's rank generally reflects his record in the most recent tournament. A score with more wins than losses is called *kachikoshi* and in most cases means an elevation in rank, either within the same division or else to a higher one. A losing score is called *makekoshi* and, except in a few rare cases, leads to demotion either within the same division or to a lower one.

The sumotori in the four lower divisions have matches on only seven days of a fifteen-day tournament, so kachikoshi for them means a record of 4–3 or better. In the three lowest divisions (jonokuchi, jonidan, and sandanme) even the minimum winning score of 4–3 can lead to a promotion of several rungs. With a record of 7–0, or sometimes 6–1, a rikishi can usually advance out of any of these divisions in just one tournament. Thus, it is not unusual for a particularly large or a highly skillful sumotori to get to the makushita division in less than a year.

Makushita

Promotions in makushita are on a lesser scale, and it is nowadays impossible to pass through this division in one tournament, even with a score of 7–0. The fastest a sumotori can go through makushita is with two consecutive records of 7–0 or possibly 7–0 followed by 6–1. (Before World War II, when there were fewer tourneys a year, Haguroyama, a future yokozuna, passed through all the lower divisions, including makushita, in one tournament each.)

Makushita is the division where a sumotori must truly start developing the right combination of power and skill. It is not rare for a man who reached the makushita division very quickly to remain there, going up and down within the division, for many years. Many give up sumo here—some of them after ten years. On the other hand, sometimes a rather persevering rikishi will finally advance to juryo after eight or ten years in makushita.

The one exception to the 120-man limit in makushita is made for sumotori who have just finished college. Because such rikishi tend to be older as well as more experienced than other new recruits, they are usually allowed to skip the three lowest divisions and debut at the bottom of makushita. They are called *makushita tsukedashi*, which means that their names will not appear on the ranking sheets until the next tournament. If a new college graduate chalks up a winning record, he will first be ranked somewhere between mid to upper makushita. If he has more losses than wins, his name will initially be listed in the sandanme division.

Such an inauspicious debut, by the way, does not necessarily bode for a disastrous career in professional sumo. While former Yokozuna Wajima and Ozeki Asashio breezed through makushita in two tourneys, other recent san'yaku figures such as Dewanohana and Ryogoku initially appeared on the ranking sheets in sandanme. Nevertheless, some former collegiate sumotori have also given up in this division.

The one rung difference between makushita 1 and juryo 13, the bottom of the next division, is said in sumo society to be virtually tantamount to the difference between hell and heaven. This is because makushita 1 will most likely have to serve as an attendant to a sekitori, while juryo 13 will have tsukebito to take care of his needs—not to mention a salary and other privileges.

The Sumo Association has a regulation that any man ranked between makushita 1 to 15 who scores 7–0 will automatically be promoted to juryo in the next tourney. However, the decisions concerning other promotions can be arbitrary or based on the circumstances of the times.

Juryo

For example, if three positions in juryo are opening due to demotions, retirements, or both, one of them will go to a person who scored 7–0 in one of the top fifteen makushita ranks. Makushita 1 on the east is also likely to get promoted to juryo, if he has chalked up at least four wins. Yet makushita 1 on the west may not be promoted with a mere 4–3 and may see himself overtaken by a makushita 3 who scored 5–2 or a makushita 4 with a 6–1 record. So what happens to the makushita 1 on the west? He will probably be moved over to the east side in the next tourney, which is the equivalent of a promotion by half a rung.

The east side is the more prestigious in sumo. Therefore, if two men of the same rank have chalked up identical winning records in a tourney, and there is only one opening right above them, it will always go to the man on the east.

Makunouchi

The same principles apply to promotions from juryo to makunouchi—except these divisions have fifteen bouts, so a winning score in them means a minimum of eight wins against seven losses. Thus, if juryo 1 on the east side gets at least eight wins, he will very likely be elevated to the top division in the next tournament. Yet the man on the west side may not go up with the exact same score. If there are, for instance, only three openings in the top division, the other two will probably be allotted, for instance, to juryo 2 with a record of 9–6 and juryo 4, who chalked up eleven wins.

When there are quite a few vacancies in the top division, juryo 5 might even be promoted with a mere 9–6, and the western juryo 1 will also go up with eight wins. This happens because promotions between divisions ultimately depend on the number of people falling or retiring from the higher one. In the meritocracy of the sumo world sometimes a bit of luck helps where even the best connections do not work.

New faces in the top division are called *shinnyumaku*. *Shin* means new, *nyu* is to enter, and *maku* comes from makunouchi.

Promotions, of course, also take place within divisions, and a higher percentage of wins naturally results in a greater leap. For example, a man ranked maegashira 10 is likely to climb to maegashira 7 or 8 after the minimum winning record to 8–7, but with a score of 10–5 or better, he might just go right to the top of the maegashira ranks in the next tourney. With a losing score, he could be demoted back to juryo.

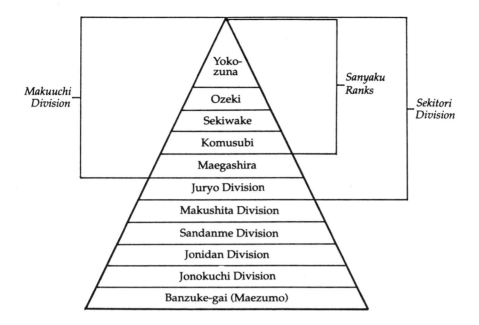

San'yaku

A high-ranking maegashira who chalks up at least eight wins might earn promotion to komusubi if there is an opening. At times when nobody is due to drop to or go up from komusubi, even a maegashira 1 might not move up just because of eight wins. Sometimes, even if there is an opening, a maegashira 3 will probably be favored for it if he has scored 9–6 or better.

Likewise, a minimum winning record does not always guarantee a komusubi an immediate elevation to sekiwake. Such a promotion can be expected only if there is an opening or if the komusubi has scored so well (i.e., 10–5 or better) that the Sumo Association can practically not help deciding to have three sekiwake listed on the ranking sheets. In the mid-1980s, both Kitao (later Futahaguro) and Masurao, for example, were not promoted to sekiwake at first despite records of 8–7 as komusubi.

The situation can be even more frustrating for a sekiwake, because even consecutive winning scores do not necessarily guarantee him promotion to ozeki, which has it own special standards to be explained later in this chapter. Sakahoko, for example, held the sekiwake rank between November 1987 and March 1989 for a record of nine consecutive tournaments without even getting close to ozeki consideration.

On the other hand, once in a blue moon a sekiwake will not get demoted even in the wake of a losing score of 7–8. Tochiakagi, for example, was simply moved in 1979 from the east side in May to the less prestigious west side in July. He lucked out mainly because both komusubi as well as all the maegashira down to rank 7 had losing records that tournament, leaving the Sumo Association hard pressed for men to promote.

A man making his debut as komusubi or sekiwake is referred to as *shinsan'yaku*. Sometimes an upper maegashira is promoted directly to sekiwake, if he has chalked up more than ten wins or if there is no other good candidate to fill the opening. Afterwards, he may plunge back to the maegashira ranks due to a losing record, only to be promoted a few tournaments later to komusubi. But even if his initial appearance in san'yaku comes in the higher of two positions, he is still known as shinsan'yaku.

Absences

Although absences, *kyujo*, are listed as such on the rikishi's record, they are counted as losses when his score is being calculated. An absence does not matter particularly to a grand champion, who is allowed to sit out a tournament without any effect to his rank. However, anyone else who drops out of a tournament before he has achieved at least eight wins (or four in the lower non-sekitori divisions) can expect to be demoted in the next tournament. On a rare occasion somebody drops out with an injury after attaining at least kachikoshi and is even promoted a bit the next tourney.

Others, whose injuries are not too serious, come back after a few days of being sidelined in an effort to stave off a drastic demotion. Such rikishi usually still end up with a losing score, but the one win they may have chalked up after returning to the ring just might make the difference between staying in their present division or dropping to a lower one. In September 1987, Hananoumi accomplished the feat of kachikoshi after dropping out for four days and returning for the last seven. Although it was the first time something of the sort had happened in twenty-two years, the feat was repeated by Takanofuji six months later.

A rikishi who has been injured in the ring during a tournament can apply to be treated under the Public Injury System (*Kosho Seido*). If the four coaches on the committee in charge of such matters accept his application, he will be able to sit out one tournament without effect to his rank. Unless he was one of the rare people to attain kachikoshi prior to the injury, he will be demoted in the ensuing tourney. The system, however, allows him to sit out the tourney in which he was demoted and keep the rank he had for the next tournament. If a sumotori drops out due to injury on the seventh day of the January tournament, for example, he will be demoted in March. But if his case has been accepted under the Public Injury System, he can also sit out the March tourney and remain at the same rank in May.

This system was instituted at the end of 1971 in the wake of massive public sympathy for Ryuko, a popular onetime komusubi who severed his Achilles tendon during the Kyushu Basho. He was thus forced to sit out a number of tourneys, causing him to plunge to the nonsalaried makushita division. The move came too late to help Ryuko; nevertheless, he managed to make a dramatic comeback to komusubi in January 1975—the first time a former san'yaku had managed such a feat after dropping down to makushita. The system is also not entirely helpful to rikishi whose injuries keep them sidelined for several tourneys. Moreover, it does not apply to those injured in practice or while sitting below the ring in a tournament. In September 1989, Fujinoshin had an ankle broken when a rikishi fell on him from the dohyo while he was waiting for his own match. Fujinoshin missed a number of tourneys thereafter and never managed to return to makunouchi.

Ozeki and Yokozuna

New ozeki and yokozuna are called shin-ozeki and shin-yokozuna. Unlike most other sumotori, they are not promoted merely on the basis of one winning score. Promotions to sumo's two highest ranks are first of all based on the candidate's total record in the three most recent tourneys.

While the Sumo Association has not promulgated any absolute cutoff lines for attaining these ranks, it is unlikely that a man could go up to ozeki with a score lower than 30–15 in three tourneys and to yokozuna with less than 36–9. The standard record for ozeki promotion is 32–13 or 33–12, and that for yokozuna promotion is about 38–7. When there is a shortage of ozeki or yokozuna or both, the standards may fall to the minimum records; they tend to be higher when there are three or more holders of the positions.

Ideally the candidate for ozeki should have chalked up at least three consecutive winning records in san'yaku. But occasionally—particularly at times with few ozeki—a man is promoted with one losing record followed by two very good scores, or even with the first of the three kachikoshi earned as an upper maegashira. For example, Kaiketsu had only seven wins as sekiwake in September 1974 but then took the yusho with a 12–3 record as komusubi in November. This was followed by his fine 11–4 record in January 1975. Since Takanohana was the only ozeki at the time, the Sumo Association decided to promote Kaiketsu. In the wake of two consecutive losing records, Kaiketsu was demoted from ozeki in less than a year after attaining the rank.

However, in September 1976, as maegashira 4, Kaiketsu captured the tourney title with an outstanding 14–1, followed by two scores of 11–4 as sekiwake in November 1976 and January 1977. Since, as maegashira 4, he had on the whole faced the same opponents as the men in san'yaku, the Sumo Association decided that he was worthy of promotion once more. Another point in his favor was that his total record in those three tourneys was higher than that of Wakamisugi (later Wakanohana II), who was promoted simultaneously with him.

Capturing the tournament championship as sekiwake often serves as an automatic ticket to ozeki promotion. Chiyonofuji, Kotokaze, Hokutenyu, and Akebono are among recent examples. Yet the promotion of a sekiwake who has won a tournament may be deferred at times when there are already four or five ozeki. For instance, even though Hasegawa captured the yusho as sekiwake in March 1972, the Sumo Association decided to wait and see how he fared in the next tournament, as there were already four ozeki. Hasegawa, unfortunately, managed only eight wins in May and never became ozeki.

Hoshi (later Hokutoumi) was not promoted to ozeki immediately after his first tourney championship, in March 1986, for the same reason. Yet he continued chalking up high marks in the ensuing two tourneys and was promoted to ozeki after the Nagoya Basho in July 1986, at which time Kitao became Yokozuna Futahaguro. Ironically, Hokutoumi's cumulative scores for both ozeki and yokozuna promotion were the same: 36–9.

While winning a tournament title usually increases the chances of ozeki promotion, it is not absolutely necessary. Candidates for yokozuna promotion, on the other hand, are required to have either two consecutive tourney championships or at least "the equivalent" (i.e., runner-up honors) during the same period.

Wakamisugi (Wakanohana II), for example, was promoted after the May 1978 tourney, which he lost in a play-off for the tourney title to Kitanoumi. Wakamisugi had also been the loser in a play-off in March and runner-up in January that year. Although he had no tourney championships during that period, his cumulative score came to 40–5, a total much better than that earned by other candidates who had one or two yusho directly before yokozuna promotion. In fact, Wakamisugi's total ties with those of Yoshibayama and Onokuni for the best cumulative record prior to yokozuna promotion in the postwar period.

Moreover, Wakamisugi had already proven himself to a certain degree by capturing a tourney the previous year. Futahaguro and Terukuni were the only men to reach sumo's highest rank since the end of World War II without any tourney championships to their credit. (Terukuni later attained two, but Futahaguro had none.) Following Futahaguro's abrupt departure from the sumo world at the end of 1987, it is highly unlikely that anyone else will ever earn promotion to yokozuna without some tourney titles on his record.

When someone is up for promotion to grand champion, the Yokozuna Deliberation Council (*Yokozuna Shingi-kai*) is likely to hold a meeting on the day after the close of the tourney to discuss the matter. This committee, composed of up to fifteen prominent men from outside the sumo world (usually including some college professors and executives of the leading Japanese newspaper companies), was established in 1950 to seek public opinion concerning yokozuna promotions. During the first twenty-seven years of the council's existence only ten men were customarily chosen to fill seats in it. In 1988, Futagoyama, after being elected chairman of the Sumo Association, not only broke precedent by appointing an eleventh member but also announced that he would be giving serious consideration to women candidates in the near future.

If the council decides that a candidate for yokozuna is worthy in both his ability and character, it will suggest his promotion to the Sumo Association. Such recommendations are invariably accepted, yet the promotion does not become official until members of the Sumo Association's Committee on Rankings (*Banzuke Hensei-kai*) meet two days later to draw up changes in the rankings. Only the promotions of new juryo, ozeki, and yokozuna are made public immediately; the others are kept secret until the release of the ranking sheets for the next tournament.

An exception is made for a new juryo, because he or his sponsors must order a kesho-mawashi, to be worn during the entrance to the ring ceremony, that can take up to two months to make. New grand champions similarly need time to order the three-piece kesho-mawashi worn by them and their attendants during the yokozuna dohyo-iri.

New ozeki do not especially need to order new aprons, though their patrons usually present some to them in celebration. Promotion to ozeki is treated with special accord primarily because for centuries it was the highest rank in sumo. Until the end of the nineteenth century, yokozuna was just a nickname given to certain ozeki—usually the strongest, but not always even that. Thus, because of its long tradition, ozeki is still treated as a very special rank. Sixty-three men became ozeki between 1926 and 1988, but considering how many men went into sumo during that period, this amounts to only one in over one hundred.

One exception to the principle of the person with the higher score in the previous tournament getting ranked on the east side is made for new yokozuna and ozeki. Usually veteran holders of these ranks are favored for the east side over a newcomer—even a newcomer with a slightly better score in the previous tourney.

Announcement Ceremonies

After the Committee on Rankings votes favorably on a promotion, two coaches are sent as messengers to the new ozeki or yokozuna's stable to relay the tidings. One of the oyakata is always a *riji* (a member of the Sumo Association's board of directors), and the other a shobu shinpan, a judge and member of the Committee on Rankings. Upon arriving at the stable's reception room, they kneel down on the floor, bow, and report the good news to the rikishi, his head coach, and the coach's wife, who bow in return. Right afterwards the newly promoted rikishi "humbly accepts" the glad tidings and promises to do his utmost not to sully the rank. The acceptance speech has pretty much been standardized, but occasionally a rikishi will add an original statement of his own. In January 1982, newly promoted Ozeki Takanosato, who had gotten diabetes under control, promised to be careful about his health. (A year and a half later he was promoted to yokozuna.)

After the acceptance speech, the new appointment is celebrated with a toast of beer. Usually the Association slips its intentions to the mass media in advance of the promotion, so a press conference with the rikishi and his coach invariably follows the toast.

Once that is over, the happy rikishi steps out in front of the stable, where a group of lower-ranked sumotori will then joyfully toss him up in the air—a process called *do-age*. In May 1987, Konishiki was too heavy to be tossed, so he just stood on a metal beer case, while leaning on the shoulders of two lower-ranked sumotori, to give the appearance of it for press pictures.

Tsunauchi-shiki

A new grand champion must have a yokozuna hawser made as well as learn how to do the special dohyo-iri for his rank. Apprentices from his stable and affiliates gather in his heya on the day the promotion is announced to soften hemp cloth, which will later be covered with cotton and twisted into the cord. All the members of the new yokozuna's stable and its affiliates assemble for the *tsunauchi-shiki* (the hawser-making ceremony) the next morning. The rope (*tsuna*) is generally about four meters long and typically weighs around fifteen kilograms, with some variation according to the girth of the grand champion meant to wear it. In November 1987, Hokutoumi had a 13-kilogram hawser, but Onokuni's weighed 20 kilograms.

Usually three strips of cloth are tied to the teppo pole in the practice area. Then they are pulled and twisted by rows of rikishi, dressed in their practice mawashi (sekitori in white and others in black or shades of gray) with felicitous red-and-white bands around their heads and white gloves on their hands in order not to dirty the white hawser. The sumotori shout, "*Hi, fu, mi*" (an old way of saying "One, two, three"), while one of their brethren beats a drum or a metal barrel in time with their movements. This process is repeated several times until the distinct yokozuna hawser takes its shape. Copper wiring is placed inside the hawser to stiffen it.

Once finished, the cord is fitted onto the new yokozuna's torso. If it is too long, pieces will be cut off and given to special guests or patrons. A piece of the hawser is regarded as lucky— especially in ensuring a pregnant woman a safe delivery.

Next the apprentices tie the hawser on the grand champion's back. If it is their first time to do so, more experienced sumotori from another stable—preferably an affiliate—will invariably be on hand to help out. The hawser itself will have one loop in back if the yokozuna intends to do the unryu style of dohyo-iri, or two loops for the more unusual shiranui style.

Once bound into his hawser, the new yokozuna will start practicing the dohyo-iri, usually under the tutelage of a coach, preferably his own or an affiliate stable's coach who used to be a grand champion.

Sumotori at Hanaregoma-Beya braiding Yokozuna Onokuni's hawser and fitting it around his waist. They wear gloves—one seated sumotori has his head wrapped in cloth—to prevent accidentally soiling the sacred white rope.

Onokuni receives a few points on technique from Futagoyama Oyakata (former Yokozuna Wakanohana I) as he practices for his first entrance to the ring ceremony as a yokozuna.

110 PROMOTIONS AND DEMOTIONS

(In July 1986, help from outside the group had to be sought in teaching Futahaguro the dohyo-iri and in making his hawser, as the Tatsunami-Isegahama group of stables had not produced a grand champion in decades and had nobody who was familiar with the procedures.)

Since a new yokozuna obviously does not have his own three-piece kesho-mawashi ready, he must borrow one from a previous grand champion—preferably the man who is teaching him the dohyo-iri. Once the new yokozuna has mastered the steps and movements, he will go through the routine once or twice more flanked by his sword-bearer and dew-sweeper as well as the top referee, all decked out in sumo ceremonial garb.

The entire process from the twisting of the fabric to the final dohyo-iri practice takes about two to three hours. Because the hawser is a symbol of purity, it must stay white; for that reason, a new one is made prior to each Tokyo tourney thereafter for the duration of the yokozuna's career. The tsunauchi procedures continue to be conducted in the same way—except without all the fanfare of the grand champion practicing his dohyo-iri and the media showing up to record it.

Yokozuna Onokuni's dohyo-iri presentation at Meiji Shrine.

The final ceremony for a new yokozuna is when he receives official documents concerning his promotion and makes a ritual dohyo-iri presentation at Meiji Shrine in Tokyo on the first Friday or Saturday after the tourney—that is to say, just one or two days after his hawser was made. Although an ozeki normally does not flank a grand champion during his dohyo-iri, one from the same stable might appear as sword-bearer just for this special ceremony. In 1978, Ozeki Takanohana flanked his Futagoyama-Beya stablemate Wakanohana II during the ceremony at Meiji Shrine, and in 1984 Ozeki Wakashimazu of the same stable was Takanosato's sword-bearer. The proceedings at the shrine are open to the public, and usually quite a crowd shows up.

Demotions

In return for having to wait a number of tournaments for promotion, ozeki and yokozuna, unlike other rikishi, are not automatically demoted after a losing score. An ozeki is demoted only after two consecutive losing records—including losses because of absence, unless the Public Injury System has been applied. No matter how badly an ozeki loses, he will not drop below sekiwake.

In fact, if a freshly demoted ozeki scores 10–5 or better during his first tourney back as sekiwake, he will promptly be repromoted to the ozeki rank. This is not as easy as it may sound, for most fallen ozeki are suffering from ailments or injuries which require more time to heal. As of July 1992, Mienoumi (later a grand champion) was the only man to make a comeback in one tourney (in 1976) since the institution of this regulation.

Yokozuna are never demoted, and they are allowed to sit out tourneys without any effect on their ranking. Yet if a yokozuna continues to do badly for a while, he will undoubtedly come under pressure to retire. Retirement is indeed his only choice.

After dropping out of the March 1953 tournament with a score of 1–5, Chiyonoyama made a special request to the Sumo Association to be demoted from yokozuna and be permitted to begin over from ozeki. Being just 29, which was not old for a yokozuna in those days, he felt he was still young enough to make a new start. But the Sumo Association did not want to create a new precedent by accepting his request. Chiyonoyama ultimately made a respectable comeback in November that year with a score of 11–4, and no yokozuna since him has formally asked to be demoted.

7

The Sumo Calendar

The sumo year is centered on the six fifteen-day tournaments held in January, March, May, July, September, and November. Yet life, of course, goes on in the sumo world between tournaments. Practice is carried out almost daily throughout the year. There are other events and performance tours in the provinces as well. In fact, the upper-ranking sumotori and their attendants spend nearly half of the year on the road.

New Year's time is by tradition the most important holiday in Japan. Most Japanese take five days to a week off. But sumotori, because of the need to train for the first tourney of the year, have only January 1 off. They finally get a belated New Year's holiday for around five days after the Hatsu Basho. In fact, the month following the January tournament tends to be the most relaxed time of the year for sumotori. True, NHK holds a charity sumo show on the first Friday after the tourney, and there may be a couple of topknot-cutting/retirement ceremonies held on Saturday and Sunday. However, there are usually no functions to attend outside Tokyo in January and February. This is probably because in the old days, when sumo tended to be performed outdoors, traditionally not much was scheduled for the coldest months of the year.

A function keeping the sumotori in Tokyo nowadays is the special two-day Ozumo Tournament held annually, since 1977, in mid-February under the sponsorship of Fuji Television, the radio station Bunka Hoso, and a host of other commercial enterprises. One attraction of this tournament is that it offers far more prize money to the sumotori than the regular fifteen-day tourneys, though its results have no bearing on individual rankings. The sumo entourage leaves for Osaka around fifteen to sixteen days prior to the Haru Basho. With rare exceptions, everyone is in Osaka by the time the latest ranking sheets are released on the Monday coming thirteen days before the tournament's start.

After about a week of vacation proceeding the Haru Basho, the sekitori and their attendants begin a tour in which they work their way back to Tokyo along the Pacific coastal area. The spring *jungyo* (exhibition tour) always opens at Ise Shrine in Mie Prefecture and closes in mid to late April with a similar ritual offering at Tokyo's Yasukuni Shrine. The other destinations en route vary from year to year, and the rest of these performances are always for commercial purposes. The only complete deviation in this schedule in recent decades occurred in April 1973, when all the sekitori and some of their attendants made a special friendship tour of China.

Actually some of the sumotori—especially the married sekitori—return home to Tokyo during the week holiday following a *chiho basho* (out-of-Tokyo tournament). In postwar times the sumo world has come to accept the idea of a sekitori wanting to spend more time with his family, as long as it does not affect his normal performance in the ring.

Sumotori have always been expected not to let personal matters interfere with their tournament performance. For instance, they cannot travel far even if there has been a death or birth in their family. Thus, some of them inevitably end up using the break following tourneys to visit a parent's grave or to see the newly born baby for the first time. In 1986, former Grand Champion Kitanoumi faced a real dilemma, albeit between tourneys, when both the coach who had trained him (former Mihogaseki Oyakata) and his own father died within a few hours of each other. As it was physically impossible to attend both the coach's funeral in Tokyo and his father's in Hokkaido, Kitanoumi, in true sumo fashion, chose to go to the former.

Overseas tours are most commonly conducted in June. In the years in which no arrangements have been made to perform abroad, the three weeks to one month following the May tournament can also be relaxed, as jungyo are usually not held in Japan during that time either. The only public appearance a sumotori may be obligated to make, besides in the practice room, during this time might be at someone's *danpatsu-shiki* (topknot-cutting/retirement ceremony).

The sumo entourage heads by Shinkansen bullet train for

Nagoya a few days before the ranking sheets for the July tournament are released. The longest and most important jungyo of the year is launched in northern Japan about a week after the close of the Nagoya Basho. It almost always opens with around five days in Sendai, northern Honshu's most populous city, and at some point during the ensuing month, the sumotori will also perform in Sapporo, the largest city in Hokkaido. The other destinations on this tour differ each year. In some years the entourage will even be divided into two groups following the Sapporo performance; one circles around Hokkaido, and the other tours northern Honshu. They generally return to Tokyo in late August to prepare for the Aki Basho.

Over the first weekend following the September tournament, Television Asahi sponsors a charity sumo program. A danpatsu-shiki or two may also be held that weekend as well. Then a one-day tournament sponsored by Meiji Shrine and its patrons is held on Monday or Tuesday. This tourney used to be carried out within the grounds of the shrine itself, but after being canceled a number of times due to inclement weather, it has come to be held inside the Kokugikan instead. Not sold to the general public, tickets for this event are distributed only to those with connections to Meiji Shrine.

The sekitori and their attendants do not remain in Tokyo long after that event, for they soon must depart on a tour which will lead them through western Honshu and ultimately to Kyushu by late October. Japan's ancient capital of Kyoto is invariably one of the stops en route, but the rest change from year to year. One complete deviation in this schedule took place when a sumo entourage visited Paris in October 1986.

A performance tour of Kyushu follows the Kyushu Basho. The destinations vary each year, and occasionally a stop in Okinawa or Shikoku is included. The entourage always comes back to Tokyo before Christmas (which is not celebrated in the sumo world).

Hanazumo

All public performances of sumo that have no bearing on rankings are called *hanazumo* (literally, "flower sumo"). They include charity tournaments, retirement ceremonies, and exhibition tours. In addition to bouts between sekitori, which are similar (though less spirited) to those in regular tournaments, hanazumo offers a number of unique features such as *shokkiri* (comic sumo), *sumo-jingu* (songs

Takamiyama takes on a trio of youngsters during a sumo exhibition.

about sumo life, touring, and so on), and bouts with groups of children and amateurs (sometimes including American servicemen), as well as demonstrations of the sumo drums, how to fix an oicho topknot, and how the yokozuna cord is bound.

Jungyo

Jungyo not only serve to bring the sumotori closer to the public in areas where tournaments are not held regularly but also provide many chances to scout local youths into the sport. For this reason, the long summer tour of northern Japan is especially important, and many top-ranking rikishi in postwar times have been discovered in this region.

Jungyo, furthermore, offer the sumotori themselves the chance to practice with a wider variety of men than they normally get to work out with in Tokyo. Authorities in the sumo world unanimously say that the efforts of those who practice hard on tour will surely bear fruit in the future. Every year a handful of those who were particularly diligent in their training over the long summer jungyo receive special citations along with a monetary bonus from the Sumo Association.

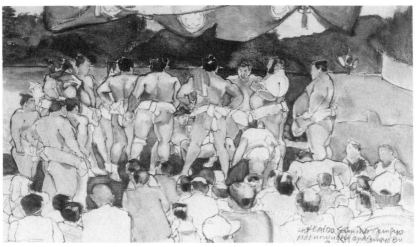

Scenes from sumotori life during jungyo: top left and right, waiting for a train on a hot summer day, and packing up to leave; center, taking an afternoon nap; bottom, sekitori before a joint practice with sumotori from affiliate stables.

The mornings of jungyo are devoted to practice sessions open to public viewing. This is followed by a lunch break in which chanko-nabe and other dishes are served by the wakaishu. Certain regional specialities are also frequently brought in by local patrons and fans. The afternoon session features various hanazumo events such as sumo songs, comic sumo, and bouts with local children; matches between the sekitori in ascending order of rank close the day.

The evenings on the road are free for the sekitori to go out with local supporters or otherwise enjoy as they please, which they indeed do. By contrast, jungyo can be hell for the wakaishu, who not only are kept extra busy running around to buy food in unfamiliar locales but are also involved in packing up and transporting the sekitori luggage.

In the past, jungyo performances were almost always held outdoors, and the rikishi camped during the daytime in colorfully dyed tents set up not far from the ring. For this reason, the entourage was likely to stay in town for a couple of days just in case their scheduled performance had to be postponed because of rain.

But now that many small cities and towns have erected sports stadiums or large gymnasiums, sumo is being held with decreasing frequency outdoors. Without the worry of being rained out, the sumo tour can consequently move on to a different locale almost every day or two, resulting in all the more work for the lower-ranked sumotori. In fact, while the younger sekitori are likely to gain weight on the road, their attendants may even shed a few kilograms during jungyo.

Summer Classes

Not all the sumotori join the jungyo. It would be prohibitively expensive to move some eight hundred behemoths, as well as referees, judges, hairdressers, sumo announcers, and others around Japan. Therefore, only the sekitori (except those who are ill or recuperating from an injury) and about a half of the wakaishu, as well as the necessary number of judges, hairdressers, and others, go on the road. The rest of those in the lower ranks remain in Tokyo and practice with each other in the heya.

Moreover, from late July through part of August, several of the stables are open in the afternoons to groups of children wanting to practice sumo. In this way, some of the wakaishu who do not go on tour spend part of the summer working out with elementary school youngsters, ranging in size from small and scrawny to those who almost look like new recruits—and perhaps they will be some day.

Overseas Tours

Prior to World War II, tours were conducted overseas several times in the colonies of the Japanese empire, such as Korea and parts of China. Since these colonies were then regarded as a part of Japan, such tours were viewed much the same as those to northern Honshu, Hokkaido, and Kyushu. They were different, for that reason, from the overseas jungyo of postwar times.

Yokozuna Hitachiyama was the first sumotori known to have made a public appearance outside of Asia. In 1907, he took three of his Dewanoumi-Beya stablemates on a demonstration tour throughout parts of Europe and the United States. In Washington, D.C., Hitachiyama made a courtesy call at the White House and presented President Theodore Roosevelt with a gold sword. (Some versions of this story also have him giving Roosevelt a gold-studded kesho-mawashi, but this cannot be verified.) The battle-loving president and the muscular grand champion are said to have gotten along famously.

Yet the precedent set by Hitachiyama and his cohorts was not followed through in June 1985, the next time a sumo entourage visited Washington, D.C. A planned courtesy call to the White House was suddenly canceled supposedly because of conflicts in President Reagan's schedule, but the real reason is said to have been because the first lady did not want seminaked behemoths in her garden. Instead, a dohyo-iri was performed by Chiyonofuji, attended by Asashio and Konishiki, in a reception room at the State Department in the presence of Secretary of State George Shultz. (Takanosato, the other grand champion at the time, refused to give a dohyo-iri for anyone other than the president in Washington, though he later performed it on the steps of New York City Hall in the presence of Major Edward Koch.)

The first jungyo outside Asia took place in Hawaii in June 1914; the group was led by grand champions Tachiyama and Otori. In 1916, another group of rikishi, led by retired Yokozuna Umegatani II and Ozeki Nishinoumi, performed in the United States. A tour headed by Tochigiyama and Onishiki Uichiro, both yokozuna, went to both Hawaii and the continental United States in 1921.

The first overseas tour after World War II was to Hawaii, Los

Left, Secretary of State George Shultz flanked by Chiyonofuji, left, and Konishiki during a reception at the U.S. State Department. Right, a poster for the October 1986 exhibition tour to Paris.

Angeles, San Francisco, and Chicago in June 1951. Since Americans tended to be more sensitive about various states of undress in those days, the sumotori were required to wear boxer shorts under their mawashi.

No other performances were given abroad until eleven years later when a sumo entourage visited Hawaii again. Seven more tours were staged in that state between 1964 and 1984.

A friendship tour was made to Khabarovsk and Moscow, where the sumotori performed in the Bolshoi Theater, in July 1965. Yokozuna Taiho, who is half-Russian, apparently tried without success to locate his father during this tour to the Soviet Union. Friendship tours were later conducted to China in 1973, to Mexico in 1981, to the United States in 1985, to France in 1986, to Brazil in 1990, and to the United Kingdom in 1991. A tour to Spain and Germany took place in June 1992, and one is scheduled to Hong Kong in February 1993 and another to California in June.

A distinction is made between tours mainly for commercial purposes and those which come at the invitation of a foreign government, whether at the national or municipal level. The former are jungyo, and the latter *koen*. On the way home to Japan from the Mexico koen in 1981, for example, the sumo entourage stopped in Los Angeles and San Jose, California, for jungyo.

Several koen and jungyo have been canceled for a number of reasons while still in the planning stage. Often the reasons have been financial, but one overseas jungyo schedule that had already been announced to the press was canceled when its promoter was revealed to be under investigation for tax evasion.

When the sumotori travel abroad for performances, they are divided into two groups to ride in different airplanes, just in case a devastating accident were to occur.

8

Sumo Techniques

It is usually fairly easy to distinguish between the winner and loser of a sumo match. The man who is first either to get his opponent out of the ring or force any part of the other's body except the feet down on the ground wins the bout.

Even if just a strand of hair touches the ground first, the man loses. In a famous case in September 1980, the referee declared Ozeki Takanohana the winner over Takamiyama, who appeared to have fallen out of the ring first. However, the judges reversed the decision on the grounds (later verified by photographs) that the tip of Takanohana's topknot had grazed the clay first.

If the two seem to fall or step out simultaneously, one or more rematches may be called until a clear-cut win is established.

Broadly speaking, the methods of winning can be divided into two categories: those which depend on the use of the belt and those which do not. Some writers have even sweepingly defined all the *kimarite* (literally, "winning hands") as "throws"; but certainly tripping or thrusting techniques, or both, do not qualify as "throws." On the other hand, Futagoyama Oyakata (former Yokozuna Wakanohana I), chairman of the Sumo Association since 1988, in his book on the kimarite, divides them into six categories: basic, throws, trips, bending, twisting, and special.

His classifications are probably a bit complicated for novice sumo fans, but everyone should at least remember the two main categories: *yotsu-zumo* and *tsukioshi-zumo*. Yotsu-zumo depends on use of the belt. *Yotsu* means "four" in Japanese, so when sumotori

Ozeki Takanohana loses to Maegashira Takamiyama after the judges, noticing that the ozeki's topknot had touched the ground first, reverse the referee's initial decision.

come to grips, it is literally "coming to fours." Tsukioshi or tsukioshi-zumo is the style of sumo mainly involving pushing and thrusting. Regular practitioners of tsukioshi tend not to be good on the belt and must win quickly before their opponent can get a grip on them.

The Sumo Association officially recognizes seventy ways of winning but has no official classifications for them. For centuries only forty-eight techniques were recognized as kimarite and neatly divided into four categories: throws, trips, bending, and twisting. Therefore, many old-time fans still refer to them as the *shiju-hatte* (literally, "forty-eight hands"). However, since a broader range of techniques was actually in practice, this figure was revised to seventy in 1960. Nevertheless, just over half of the seventy are likely to be seen in a given year nowadays.

The next pages will outline the techniques most likely to be seen in a tournament. I will not attempt to describe them all (though their names will be given), because frankly there are several I have never seen since I started following sumo seriously in 1975.

The Most Frequent Techniques

Yorikiri, in addition to being the most frequently used kimarite, is also one of the easiest to recognize. When the competitors are gripping each other's belts with both hands in yotsu-zumo form, the attacker may press his body against the other's and use his weight and the momentum to drive the other out of the ring.

A related technique, the fifth most frequently used in 1984, is *yoritaoshi*. If the opponent offers too much resistance when driven to the edge of the ring, the attacker may use force to topple him out; the victor lands on top. This is the move Onokuni used to defeat Chiyonofuji on the last day of the November 1988 tournament, putting an end to the latter's fifty-three-bout winning streak.

The process used in *abisetaoshi* is very similar to yoritaoshi, except that the toppling occurs inside the ring. This was declared the kimarite of a famous match between Yokozuna Kitanofuji and Sekiwake (later ozeki) Takanohana in January 1972. Takanohana had applied a frontal leg trip (*sotogake*) to Kitanofuji, who was trying to drive him out of the ring. The two fell together, with light-weight Takanohana underneath. Since Kitanofuji's hand touched ground first, the referee declared Takanohana the winner by sotogake. The judges, however, reversed the decision, declaring that Kitanofuji's hand was *kabaite*—used to break a potentially dangerous fall—for Takanohana and that the yokozuna had won by abisetaoshi. There have been no examples of the permitted use of kabaite since. Abisetaoshi, however, often determines the outcomes of tournament matches.

Oshidashi is another easy-to-recognize kimarite. It literally means "push out," which is precisely what occurs. The pushing is usually done steadily or serially with both hands against the opponent's chest or under his armpits. Occasionally just one hand is used; and even if the other one is on the belt, the technique may still be oshidashi, as long as the main force comes from the pushing.

Oshitaoshi, a fairly common move, is to topple the opponent over the edge of the ring through pushing. In contrast with yoritaoshi and abisetaoshi, only the loser falls.

Tsukidashi is literally to "thrust out." This technique looks looks somewhat like oshidashi—except that left-hand and right-hand thrusts are employed alternately to force the opponent out of the ring.

Tsukitaoshi is variation of tsukidashi in which the attacker thrusts his opponent off his feet inside or outside of the ring.

Tsukiotoshi, the most frequently seen thrusting technique, has

yorikiri

yoritaoshi

abisetaoshi

oshidashi

tsukidashi

tsukitaoshi

tsukiotoshi

hikiotoshi

hatakikomi

traditionally been used as a defensive move when the retreating rikishi suddenly sallies aside and forces his opponent down at a slanting angle. Nowadays some of the shorter sumotori aim for tsukiotoshi from the very beginning. This is the technique Chiyo-nofuji used in beating Hananoumi on the seventh day of the Natsu Basho of 1988, the start of his fifty-three-bout winning streak.

Hikiotoshi can sometimes be difficult to distinguish from tsukiotoshi. Usually, in the course of a tsukioshi bout, the attacker will grab one or both of his opponent's hands to pull him forward and ultimately down to the ground. The attacker may even grip the other's belt while doing this.

Hatakikomi is typically seen in the course of a tsukioshi match when one rikishi suddenly slaps his opponent's shoulder, back, neck, or arm to bring him down to the clay. This technique has come to be used with increasing frequency since the mid-1970s.

Yorikiri generally accounts for 40 percent of the wins in a tournament. In 1984, for instance, it determined 681 makunouchi-level bouts. Its nearest competitors, oshidashi and hatakikomi, were employed 230 and 111 times, respectively, and 31 kimarite were not used by sumotori in the top division at all that year. This information as well as several of the descriptions of kimarite has been translated with permission from Dewanoumi Tomonori and Sakisaka Matsuhiko's *Ozumo o miru tame no hon* (Book for viewing sumo) (Tokyo: Dobun Shoin, 1985).

Common and Uncommon Throws

Uwate-nage, the most common of the real "throws," occurs when a rikishi gets an outside grip on his opponent's belt and throws him down. This has been frequently put into practice by top-ranking rikishi like Chiyonofuji, Onokuni, and Kirishima.

A less common variation is *uwatedashi-nage*. The attacker typically grabs the back of his opponent's belt with his arm above the other's. Then he moves to spread-eagle his opponent's body just before swinging him down.

Sukui-nage is a beltless throw. The attacker generally slips one arm under his opponent's armpit, around to his back, and then tosses him onto the ground in an action similar to scooping, which is what sukui means.

Shitate-nage is similar to uwate-nage except that the attacker gets a grip inside or under his opponent's belt to toss him down.

Shitatedashi-nage is a variation of shitate-nage and uwatedashi-nage. It is used a bit more frequently than the latter.

Kote-nage is another beltless throw. In this case, the attacker locks an arm around the opposite one of his opponent and then swings him down.

Kubi-nage is a throw executed from the opponent's neck or head. This is almost always done defensively by a rikishi who cannot get a grip or has lost it; virtually no one aims for kubi-nage from the very beginning. Tochinishiki (177 cm.) used this move dramatically

uwate-nage

uwatedashi-nage

sukui-nage

shitate-nage

shitatedashi-nage

kote-nage

kubi-nage

kake-nage

in May 1955 to topple new Ozeki Ouchiyama, a gigantic (202 cm.) opponent. (In allusion to the similarity to the way the neck is held during an embrace, kubi-nage is also sumo slang for having sex.)

Kake-nage, a combination arm-leg throw, is seldom used but easy to spot. The attacker locks one arm around the opposite one of his opponent while also wrapping one leg around him. Once the opponent is off balance, the attacker swings him down.

The remaining throws are *tsukami-nage* (lifting throw), *koshi-nage* (hip throw), *harima-nage* (rear-belt throw), *yagura-nage* (pendulum throw), and *nicho-nage* (two-leaf throw). All are rarely seen, although Takatoriki occasionally uses nicho-nage.

Common Techniques

Tsuridashi is employed fairly often and easy to recognize: the attacker simply picks up his opponent, carries him to the edge of the ring, and puts him out on his feet.

Tsuriotoshi is a variation occurring when the attacker is unable to carry his opponent to the ring's edge, so he drops him down inside instead. Occasionally, even when the opponent has landed outside of the ring, the kimarite may be called tsuriotoshi if the move entails dropping him. Despite its resemblance to tsuridashi, tsuriotoshi is used far less often because to bring it off successfully the attacker must be conspicuously stronger than his opponent. Even then, the risk of injuring the other's hips or knees or both is great.

Okuridashi is another easily recognizable kimarite. It is not a move anyone plans as part of his strategy, but is executed quite frequently when a rikishi manages to get behind his opponent and then either drives or pushes him out of the ring from behind. To lose by okuridashi generally makes a man look rather silly.

Okuritaoshi is a variation applied about only one-tenth as often as okuridashi. In this case, the attacker executes a push so hard from behind that his opponent falls down.

Kimedashi is to lock one's arms around the opponent's thrusting or gripping arms and then drive him out in a style similar to yorikiri. This move tends to be favored by exceptionally large or powerful rikishi; recent examples include Takamiyama, Takanosato, Toyonoumi, and Kushimaumi.

Kimetaoshi is a variation in which the opponent is dropped down to the ground.

Katasukashi is when the attacker gets his own arm under that of his opponent to force him down. It is mostly pulled during a tsukioshi exchange and may be difficult to tell from hatakikomi.

Utchari, one of the most spectacular moves in sumo, is carried out as a last resort by a rikishi who has been driven to the edge of the ring. He leans far back, twists his opponent around, and tosses him out of the ring. Due to risk of injuring the hip area, this form of counterattack is no longer used so often these days, when high-ranking opponents are likely to weigh over 150 kilograms.

Makiotoshi is when the attacker grabs his opponent's torso with

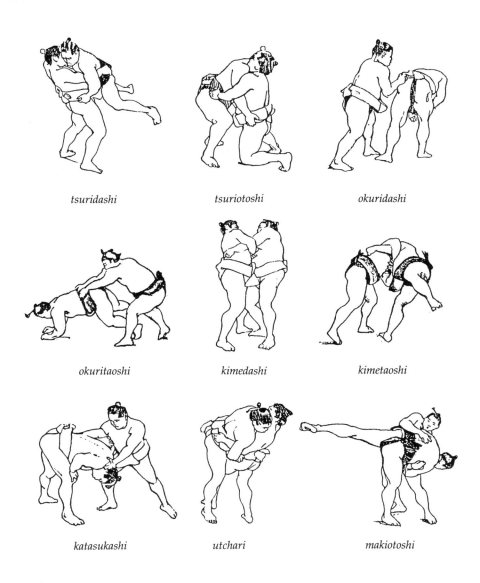

tsuridashi   tsuriotoshi   okuridashi

okuritaoshi   kimedashi   kimetaoshi

katasukashi   utchari   makiotoshi

his own hands and wraps them around his back to twist him down. It is often used in combination with tsukiotoshi, which usually then ends up getting the nod as the kimarite.

Trips

Kekaeshi is usually carried out during a tsukioshi bout, when one rikishi suddenly kicks his opponent's ankle, while simultaneously pulling him forward toward the ground. This trick tends to be favored by the smaller men, such as 174-centimeter Washuyama in the 1970s and 168-centimeter Tochitsurugi in the 1980s.

Ketaguri is a foot-sweep kick also favored by small men. After kicking his opponent's calf in a sweeping motion, the attacker next hits his shoulder or pulls his arm to floor him. This was another move favored by Washuyama and Tochitsurugi as well as 173-centimeter Wakajishi, and more recently Mainoumi.

Uchigake is to bring the opponent toward oneself from a gripping position, while tripping him from the back of his leg. This move is fairly easy to recognize, though its use has decreased markedly since the 1980s. Earlier it had been favored by a number of ozeki such as Kotogahama, Asahikuni, and Kaiketsu, as well as Masuiyama I and II (father and son).

Sotogake is a variation with the trip executed at the front of the opponent's leg. This technique, too, is not seen so often nowadays, although two yokozuna of the late 1970s and early 1980s, Wakanohana II and Mienoumi, excelled at it. Chiyonofuji lost by sotogake twice during the first tournament of 1989. The first of those losses came exactly fifty years and one day after the great Futabayama's sixty-nine-bout winning streak was broken by Akinoumi's sotogake. Tochinishiki also used it in March 1953 to determine a bout with Wakanohana I—a fight so long and intense that the former's chonmage came unraveled.

Kirikaeshi is a backward knee trip executed in the course of yotsu-zumo. The attacker gets the underside of his knee on his competitor's kneecap while holding onto his belt to twist him to the ground.

Kawazugake is a technique used to counter tsuridashi, tsuriotoshi, or sotogake. To defend himself, a rikishi will wrap one of his legs around the back of his opponent's. Simultaneously, he also puts the arm on the same side of his body around his opponent's neck, forcing both of them to fall over backwards; and the counterattacker lands on top, of course. This technique gets its name from Kawazu Saburo, a warrior who was challenged to a sumo match by a champion named Matano Goro in 1176. Though he had just won twenty-one consecutive bouts with other men, Matano promptly lost to Kawazu. Refusing to accept defeat, Matano suddenly lifted Kawazu high off the ground, only to be tripped in the style named after Kawazu ever since. Kirikaeshi was not treated as distinct from kawazugake until 1960, when the number of kimarite was increased to seventy. Nevertheless, in recent times kirikaeshi is seen more often than its parent kawazugake.

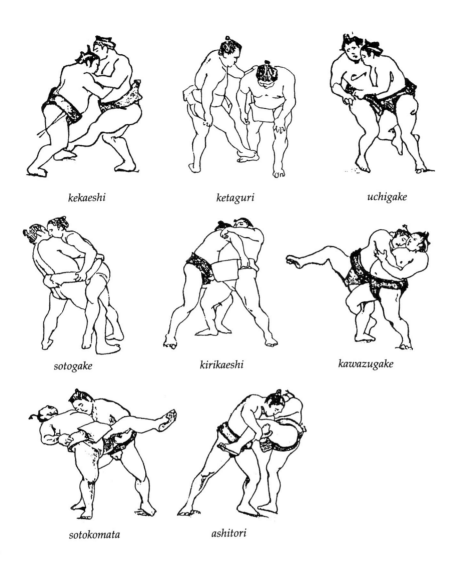

kekaeshi

ketaguri

uchigake

sotogake

kirikaeshi

kawazugake

sotokomata

ashitori

Watashikomi occurs when one rikishi grabs the back of his opponent's calf and pulls it forward, while pushing against his body and ultimately thrusting him out with his other hand. It is usually executed as a defense.

Komatasukui (thigh-scooping) involves executing a *dashinage* (a pulling, arc throw) from the left, then grabbing the opponent's right leg from the knee or above. The attacker tries to keep his balance while toppling the other over. Dewanohana was one of the few recent practitioners of this move.

Sotokomata is a variation also starting from dashinage, but with the attacker wrapping his arm under his opponent's thigh instead of gripping it from above.

Another similar technique is *ashitori*. From the very start of a fight or during an exchange of slapping and thrusting, the attacker will quickly aim to get his hands under his rival's leg, which he then lifts up to break his balance and floor him.

The remaining leg-grabbing and tripping techniques are *susoharai* (literally, "hem sweeping"), *susotori* (hem taking), *omata* (thigh grabbing), *chongake* (heel-shaving trip), *tsumatori* (toe pulling), *nimaikeri* (twofold kick), and *mitokorozeme* (threefold attack). They are unlikely to be seen more than once a year at best, and perhaps not even for over ten years. Some of sumo's trips and throws were adopted by judo, a sport which developed out of sumo. Therefore, sumotori with a background in judo are the most likely to use them.

Twists

Shitatehineri is when the attacker gets a grip inside or under his opponent's belt to twist him down. Some sumotori, like Chiyono-fuji, often apply this move with uwate-nage, which usually gets officially recognized as the winning move.

Uwatehineri is a similar twisting move, except that it is executed with an outside belt hold. Only rikishi with very powerful grips tend to have success with it.

Kainahineri is usually executed in a tsukioshi match when one rikishi grabs onto his opponent's arm and uses both hands to twist him down.

The remaining twists are rarely seen. *Kubihineri* is when one sumotori wraps his own arm around his opponent's neck, then grabs the other's arm with his other hand to twist him down. *Suneburi* is when the attacker puts his own head against his rival's chest, grabs his hand or his elbow, and twists his head down. *Gasshohineri* is when one rikishi holds his opponent's neck between his own hands and twists him down. *Gassho* means "hands clasped in prayer." In September 1987, this move was seen for the first time in twenty-two years in a regular tournament: Kotofuji against Nankairyu in a juryo bout.

Tottari is a sort of arm twist pulled in the course of a tsukioshi

shitatehineri

uwatehineri

kainahineri

kubihineri

suneburi

gasshohineri

tottari

sakatottari

match, when one rikishi gets a two-handed grip on his rival's hand and then twists him down to the ground.

Sakatottari is performed to counter tottari by freeing the hand that has been taken, while twisting the attacker down. Tochiakagi used this move more frequently than anyone else in the late 1970s and early 1980s. Its use declined for a while, but Takatoriki and Mainoumi have been bringing it back.

Seldom Seen Techniques

Hikkake is employed in a tsukioshi bout when one rikishi grabs his opponent's arm from the inside with one of his own hands. He simultaneously grips his opponent's hand from the outside to pull him down on the clay or to twist him outside the ring. This move may or may not be seen in the course of a year.

Amiuchi (literally, "net casting") is to grab the opponent's arms with both hands, spread-eagle his body, and pull him down. This technique acquired the name amiuchi because its form resembles that of a fisherman tossing his net into the sea. It is rarely used nowadays, but once after Chiyonofuji pulled it off spectacularly in 1987, he wittily reminded members of the press gathered around him that he is a fisherman's son.

Uchimuso is executed from a position in which the attacker's arm is over his opponent's. The attacker brushes the area behind his rival's left knee and twists him down toward the left. Since the retirement of Ozeki Asahikuni in 1979, the use of this technique has declined considerably.

Sotomuso is a similar move, rarely seen at present, executed by brushing against the front or side of the right kneecap.

Sabaori (literally, "mackerel folding") starts when one rikishi pulls on his opponent's belt from the outside while they are both at grips. The attacker then leans over on the other with all his weight to bring him to the ground in a bent-knee position. Generally, the largest rikishi have the best luck with this rare move. However, one of its most recent uses was by lightweight Kirishima in September 1987. In May 1986, heavyweight Konishiki seriously injured his knee when forced to the ground in this form by tall Ozeki Kitao, who later became Yokozuna Futahaguro.

Ipponzeoi is a spectacular move in which one rikishi grabs his opponent's arms and then bends a bit to pull him over his own back. It was executed at the sekitori level in tournaments only twice between 1975 and 1988.

Yobimodoshi is a move in which the attacker draws his competitor over to himself and then uses that momentum to thrust the man down. Although Yokozuna Wakanohana I virtually made an art out of yobimodoshi, this technique is seldom seen nowadays.

The remaining kimarite are *waridashi, tasukisori, sototasukisori, kakesori, shumokusori,* and *isori. Sori* means to bend or arch backwards. The sori techniques are rarely used at present.

hikkake   amiuchi   uchimuso

sotomuso   sabaori

Techniques in a Bout

There are also a number of techniques used in the course of a match—often to help win it—but which are not regarded as kimarite themselves. Some of the most popular ones are as listed below.

Inasu or *inashi* is when one rikishi steps aside to parry an opponent who is making a strong charge at him. This tends to throw the opponent off balance, creating a good opportunity to get a strong grip on him or topple him. (In sumo slang inasu also means "to give the runaround.")

Maemitsu (*o toru*) is to grab at the entire front of the opponent's belt. This not only is effective as an offense but can also prove helpful in countering a tsukioshi attack.

Morozashi is when one rikishi slips his arms under his opponent's armpits and his own hands down to get a good grip on the other's belt. Former Sekiwake Tsurugamine (Izutsu Oyakata) and more recently his middle son, Sakahoko, have been regarded as masters of this technique.

Nodowazeme is to push and thrust at the opponent's throat. Several rikishi use it from time to time, but the last men to have been considered true specialists at it were Takamiyama and former Yokozuna Kotozakura. Grabbing at the opponent's throat, however, is forbidden.

Tsuppari is a series of slaps, such as thrusting very high or fast, that are often effective in throwing the opponent off balance just before pulling the winning move.

During practice at the sumo stables, there are no demonstrations of these techniques along the lines of "This is uwatenage; that is yori-taoshi," and so on. Apprentices simply go into the ring and start fighting the best they can. They are expected to learn something about the most common techniques by observing their seniors. But they are supposed to acquire them through actual experience in the ring—what is referred to in the sumo world as "remembering with the body," or in the West as "practice makes perfect." Of course, during practice they may also get advice from their coaches and seniors, such as "Lower your hips," "Get a grip inside the mawashi," "Don't use hataki from that position," and so on.

Nowadays many sumotori also study sumo from video tapes. Typically they tape either their opponents' matches to study the way persons they will face in the ring fight or their own bouts to see where they themselves went wrong or right.

Ways of Losing

In addition to the seventy kimarite, there are four ways a sumotori can be declared the winner without displaying any skill himself—in other words, because of a mistake on his opponent's part.

One is *fusensho*, a default because of the opponent's sudden absence. When a rikishi withdraws from a tourney or retires altogether, the opponent he has already been scheduled to meet gets a fusensho. Sometimes in the lower divisions a sumotori will pick up a default because his opponent did not reach the stadium on time. This especially tends to happen in the out-of-Tokyo tourneys where many of the temporary lodgings for the sumotori are located far out in the suburbs. During the Nagoya Basho of 1987, one jonokuchi rikishi, for example, had a twenty-one-bout losing streak broken only because his opponent showed up too late. (The loss for the opponent is *fusenhai*.)

Hansoku is a violation of the rules. Sumotori are supposed to fight with open hands. Slapping is permitted, but not boxing-style punching. Moreover, rikishi are forbidden to touch their competitor's hair and eyes. Sometimes the forbidden spots are accidentally touched momentarily during the course of a spirited bout, and if the move does not appear deliberate, the authorities may overlook it. However, while in the juryo division in 1980, Itai once pulled the topknots of his opponents on two consecutive days. The judges granted him the benefit of the doubt the first time, but on the second day the match was halted and Hokutenyu declared the winner due to Itai's hansoku. Moreover, perhaps because more is expected of an ozeki, Daikirin lost a match in the early 1970s when he, for the first time ever, touched an opponent's chonmage during a match.

Undoubtedly the strangest hansoku of all was committed in the late 1960s by Maegashira Asaarashi who, during the warm-up, picked up a piece of garbage lying in the ring and walked out of the boundaries to throw it away. He should have signaled one of the yobidashi to remove it, because once in the ring, a rikishi is considered the loser when he goes out first—no matter what the reason.

Isamiashi (literally, "overly mighty feet") is when the seeming winner of a match in the midst of all his fervor inadvertently steps out first. This most often occurs when a rikishi is attempting to carry his opponent out by tsuridashi, but forgets or fails to drop him first.

Koshikudake (literally "broken-down hips") occurs when a rikishi inadvertently loses his balance and falls down on his buttocks. Thus, his opponent, who did nothing or next to nothing to cause the slip, will be declared the winner by koshikudake. Isamiashi and koshikudake are called *kimarite dewa nai kimarite* (kimarite which are not kimarite).

Sumo Words in Japanese

Some of the names of sumo techniques and ways of losing have made their way into ordinary Japanese usage. Utchari is used figuratively to mean "turn the tables on" or "to betray." Katasukashi means "to dodge," and isamiashi is "to step out of bounds." These terms are particularly used in reference to events in the political world; however, by just about any standards, sumo is a far more gentlemanly game than politics in Japan.

9

Life after Sumo

No matter how much glory a rikishi experiences in his sumo career, the time inevitably comes for him to retire. There is no mandatory retirement age for a sekitori; the decision is his, though there may be a bit of nudging from his coach or family. However, the head coach is allowed to fill out the papers for rikishi to resign—a move instituted in the 1970s as a means to get rid of hopeless cases hanging on well into their thirties and other, perhaps younger, men who somehow prove to be burdens on the stable's communal life. The only time a coach has ever used this option against a sekitori was when Tatsunami Oyakata submitted Yokozuna Futahaguro's "resignation" in 1987.

In the past, when only one or two tournaments were held a year, a sumotori's career often lasted well past age forty—sometimes, in fact, for a lifetime. But since the institution of six fifteen-day tournaments a year in 1958, the wear and tear on a rikishi's body have increased considerably, and there is little time to recover from whatever injuries he may incur. Therefore, the typical retirement age has dropped to around thirty-two or thirty-three in the past three decades. Nevertheless, some recent sekitori such as Aobajo and Takamiyama continued fighting until their late thirties. Aobajo retired at age thirty-eight, and Takamiyama one month short of his fortieth birthday. And in January 1988, Oshio finally announced his retirement at age forty after falling into the nonsalaried makushita division. (His former Tokitsukaze-Beya stablemate, Makimoto, after dropping from the sekitori ranks, fought in makushita until age forty-one in 1983.)

Most sekitori decide to retire when their only other choice is demotion to a lower division or rank. Yokozuna, on the other hand, are never demoted, so they tend to retire when they realize, or are forced to realize, that they can no longer earn the marks expected of them. Sometimes, even when a yokozuna's record has not been so bad, losing to a relative newcomer may shock him into a perhaps premature retirement. Sadanoyama, for example, had won the previous two tourneys but suddenly retired in March 1968 after losing to Maegashira Takamiyama and Komusubi Kirinji (later Ozeki Daikirin) on consecutive days. The great Taiho, despite a respectable showing of 12–3 in the March tourney, announced his retirement in May 1971 because he had lost to twenty-year-old Komusubi Takanohana for the second time in a short period of time.

Becoming an Elder

A distinction is made in the terminology to describe those who leave the sumo world altogether (*haigyo* or "quitting") and those who remain after retirement (*intai*) from the ring. In the latter case, the retiring rikishi stays on as an oyakata. Relinquishing an oyakata position is also called haigyo.

The qualifications to become an oyakata or a *toshiyori* (elder of the Sumo Association) are fairly simple on the surface: to have either served one full tournament in the top division or else twenty consecutive tourneys and a total of twenty-five in juryo. Yet, in reality, becoming an elder is not easy.

A rikishi who wants to remain in the Association must purchase *toshiyori-kabu*, stock bearing a time-honored elder's name. Yet by tradition there are only 105 "name stocks," so if none is available at the time a rikishi is retiring, he may end up with no choice but to leave sumo altogether. For this reason, many sekitori make arrangements to purchase stock while they are still active in the ring as an investment for their future.

Arrangements for the stock must be made with its most recent holder or his heirs. One problem is that fewer stocks are readily available now that the average life span of the oyakata is on the increase. The coaches have a mandatory retirement age of sixty-five. Up through the 1970s few of them lived long enough to reach it, but by the 1980s many did.

The decreasing number of available stock has, in turn, caused its price to soar. Although the Sumo Association may have some say in judging who is qualified to assume an elder's position, it has set no limits on the stock's selling price. Therefore, the stock tends ultimately to go to the highest bidder.

The details of such transactions are generally kept hushed; however, it is rumored that the stocks sold in 1986 and 1987 went for well over ¥100 million each. Because not all sekitori have such an amount saved, this is where it comes in handy to have generous patrons, or else to be related to the previous holder of the stock. Marrying a coach's daughter is the most common means to achieve the latter; but a few sumotori have been adopted by an oyakata's widow, and the current Mihogaseki Oyakata (ex-Ozeki Masuiyama II) is the real son of the previous Mihogaseki (Ozeki Masuiyama I).

Retirement Pay

Naturally the sumotori get some benefits in return for the money they paid for stock. First is retirement pay. In 1987, a yokozuna's retirement pay was calculated at ¥8 million for the first tournament participated in at sumo's highest rank, and ¥4 million for each successive basho after that. An ozeki's retirement stipend was figured at ¥6.5 million for his first tourney at that rank, and ¥300,000 for each one thereafter. Sekiwake and komusubi were alloted ¥5.5 million for the first basho in san'yaku, and ¥200,000 for each one after that. Maegashira were entitled to ¥5 million for their first tournament in the top division and ¥150,000 for each one thereafter. The figures for retiring juryo were an initial ¥350,000 and then ¥10,000. Even sekitori leaving the sumo world altogether are entitled to severance pay, yet it hardly compares with that of a person remaining as a coach.

Yokozuna and ozeki, furthermore, receive upon retirement a stipend called *yorokin* for "meritorious service." This amount varies quite a bit, but is worth tens of million of yen and is decided according to factors such as past performance and level of popularity. (For example, former Ozeki Takanohana, who was tremendously popular and also served in the rank for a long time, was awarded the same amount of yorokin in 1981 as Mienoumi, a rather "short-lived" yokozuna.) Former yokozuna and ozeki also do not start out at the lowest rank of oyakata, meaning that they begin as coaches with a better salary than other new retirees.

If a yokozuna has not purchased stock by the time of his

retirement, he can still remain in the Sumo Association for up to five years under the name he used as a grand champion. However, if he does not manage to find suitable stock within that period, he will ultimately be obligated to resign from the Sumo Association. As of May 1992, this had yet to happen.

In recognition of their great achievements, Taiho in 1971 and Kitanoumi in 1985 were permitted to retain their yokozuna names for life or until retirement at age sixty-five—whichever comes first. They are known as *ichidai-toshiyori* (one-generation elder), meaning their names cannot be handed down to anyone else and will pass away with them. In 1989 Chiyonofuji was offered an ichidai-toshiyori but rejected it because he preferred to assume a time-honored name upon retirement.

Sometimes a sekitori ranked below yokozuna who retires without stock of his own will borrow that already purchased by a compatriot still active in the ring. This gives him a sort of reprieve to try to get hold of his own stock until the good Samaritan is ready to retire. Nevertheless, if the borrower does not obtain it by the time his helper retires from the ring, he will either have to leave the sumo world or else arrange to borrow from yet another person. Between May 1983 and September 1988 former Komusubi Wakajishi, for instance, was lent six different toshiyori names while in search of one for himself.

Retirement Ceremony

If a sekitori is planning to stay in the sumo world, he will most likely have a hair-cutting ceremony—danpatsu-shiki—or *intai-zumo* (retirement ceremony) in the Kokugikan after one of the Tokyo tournaments. This usually takes place within four to six months after he has announced his retirement. Following a career steeped in ritual pageantry, the danpatsu-shiki is the last ceremony a man participates in as a sumotori. Whether he was a yokozuna or a lowly maegashira, he is the star of that day.

The retirement ceremony opens with the usual features of hanazumo, such as a comic shokkiri act, singing, and demonstrations of some sort. If the retiring rikishi was a yokozuna, he will appear in his last entrance to the ring ceremony, perhaps flanked by two active grand champions in their white hawsers. The retirement ceremony of a yokozuna is the only occasion when other grand champions can serve as attendants during a dohyo-iri.

*The hair-cutting cere-
monies of Komusubi
Ryuko, left, and Yoko-
zuna Kitanoumi.*

142 LIFE AFTER SUMO

The highlight of the ceremony comes when the retiring sekitori, garbed in a haori-hakama, is seated on a chair in the middle of the dohyo. A referee stands nearby and hands scissors over to a couple of hundred male supporters, celebrities, and friends of the rikishi, who take tiny snips around his topknot, as an announcer dramatically reads the saga of his life. Many brawny and seemingly fearless sumotori have been known to break down in tears during these proceedings, which can take over an hour.

Finally, the sekitori's head coach makes the final cut quickly with a fancy pair of scissors. The former rikishi has only a moment to regain his composure before lowering his newly cropped head to bow to the audience in all four directions of the stadium. At this point the rikishi officially assumes the toshiyori name he has been using for the past four to six months. Most former sekitori preserve their topknots for memories in glass boxes, but a few, like Aobajo, have been known to throw them away. And almost all sumotori comment, after the danpatsu-shiki, how light their heads feel once their topknots are gone.

Although having a danpatsu-shiki on the dohyo may seem like another old tradition of the sumo world, its history actually dates back only to 1937, when former Sekiwake Shinkai had his topknot cut in the ring at Yasukuni Shrine in Tokyo. Yokozuna Maedayama was the first to have a danpatsu-shiki in the Kuramae Kokugikan.

Qualification for Danpatsu-shiki

The requisite for a danpatsu-shiki in the Kokugikan is to have been a sekitori for at least thirty tourneys, and ironically not all men who are qualified to become oyakata meet this. In May 1987, former Komusubi Oyutaka, who had spent only twenty-six basho as a sekitori, got around this stipulation by holding a joint danpatsu-shiki in the stadium with Tokitsukaze stablemate Amanoyama, who qualified in terms of longevity though he never went beyond the rank of maegashira.

Sekitori in such predicaments who do not have a qualified stablemate retiring at the same time are likely to rent a banquet room in the Kokugikan's basement or in a restaurant for the hair-cutting ceremony, as also do some sumotori leaving the sumo world altogether. Since such ceremonies are not being held on a sacred dohyo, even the women guests may join in taking a snip. Most sumotori who leave without ever reaching a sekitori rank have their hair cut in a simple ceremony at their heya.

Wakaimono-gashira and Sewanin

The Sumo Association offers a small number of other jobs aside from oyakata positions to those retiring from the dohyo. On its payroll are eight *wakaimono-gashira* and eight *sewanin* (caretakers) each. Wakaimono-gashira (also called *kashira*), meaning the "head of the wakaishu or wakaimono," has the job of looking after and keeping records of those in his stable and often those in its affiliates as well. A kashira also takes care of various odd jobs and clerical duties around the heya, assists in the making of a yokozuna cord at his or an affiliate stable, and gives a hand in carrying the trophies should a rikishi in his stable or an affiliate win a tournament.

The sewanin are caretakers expressly charged with transporting and taking care of equipment belonging to the Sumo Association, so they tend to be especially busy when the entourage is on the road for jungyo. During tournaments, sewanin may take tickets at the gate to the stadium, just like some lower-ranked oyakata. They are also assigned various random chores and duties, which are hardly distinct from those of the wakaimono-gashira.

In the late 1970s, there was talk in the Sumo Association of phasing these two positions out. However, a wave of new hirings took place between 1986 and 1988, as some of the old-time wakai-mono-gashira and sewanin approached the mandatory retirement age, which was then sixty-three.

The distinctions in the qualifications for the two have become blurred as well. Technically, both the wakaimono-gashira and the sewanin should be former rikishi who went no further, at best, than makushita or juryo. From the Edo period through the Meiji period, wakaimono-gashira were viewed as having the more prestigious of the two positions, and some were even eventually elevated to oyakata status. Thereafter, the level of prestige seems to have fluctuated between the two.

In 1987, for instance, former Maegashira Shishiho and Takarakuni were hired respectively as kashira and sewanin. Not only had Takarakuni gone higher in the maegashira ranks than Shishiho but also, until recently, it would have been unthinkable for someone who had been in the top division to take either of these jobs in the first place. The changes in policy may be an indication that the Sumo Association has become aware of the necessity to keep on men to handle various odd jobs as well as to help the increasing number of sekitori who are unable to obtain oyakata stock.

Aside from these positions within the Sumo Association, some individual stables hire former sumotori as managers. This tendency has grown especially strong in the 1980s and 1990s among newly established heya whose only oyakata is the stablemaster and, of course, who lack wakaimono-gashira or sewanin too. The stable managers technically do not belong to the Sumo Association, so the details of their duties and salaries are strictly between the oyakata who hire them and themselves.

Other Choices

Given the vast numbers of youths who quit sumo every year, it is impossible to keep track of what has happened to them all. Many simply go home to the farm or take over the family business. Many others, with their experience in the chanko kitchen, open or find work in restaurants. Some go back to school and later take jobs commensurate with their education. Several, including a number of former sekitori, have become pro wrestlers, and quite a few have gone into show business. One former sumotori has become a teacher of the samisen, and another is a potter.

Some former sumotori have also gone into politics. As of the end of 1988, at least four ex-rikishi were serving on city councils in various parts of Japan. One famous former sekiwake quit his oyakata position after joining the Jehovah's Witnesses, a religious organization which frowns on fighting. In 1992, he was reported to be running a dry-cleaning shop in a suburb of Tokyo and using his spare time to spread the faith.

10

Sumo Nomenclature

Sumotori have names unlike those of other professional athletes in Japan. They sound more like those used by Kabuki and Noh actors, except that instead of stage names, sumotori take a *shikona* (ring name).

Shikona can conjure up images of real or imaginary locations; some sound fierce, poetic, while others are not much different from ordinary Japanese names. The most popular suffix by far in a ring name is *yama* (mountain), which may seem only natural since sumotori tend to be veritable mountains of men.

Prefixes and Suffixes

Other common suffixes include *ryu* (dragon), *sakura/zakura* (cherry blossoms), *kuni* (country), *shima* (island), *sato* (village), *kawa/gawa* (river), *shio* (tide), and *umi* (sea or lake, depending on the character). Popular prefixes are *waka* (youth/young), *kita/hoku* (north), *o/dai/tai* (large), *tama* (jewel), *asa* (morning), and *taka* (high or noble, depending on the character). Some terms, like *fuji* (Mount Fuji), *nami* (waves), *nishiki* (brocade), *hana* (flower), and *misugi* (three cypresses), are used as either prefixes or suffixes. (It is possible that any of the prefixes could be used as suffixes, or vice versa, in the future.)

Most shikona are composed of two elements, such as Asashio, "morning tide,"and Misugisato, "three cypress village." Further keeping in mind that *no* is generally used in Japanese grammar as a noun modifier, it should be easy to figure out that Hananoumi means "lake of flowers" and Takanonami, "waves of nobility."

The earliest extant record of shikona dates back to the mid-sixteenth century, at which time those based on meteorological forces, such as Ikazuchi (thunder), Inazuma (lightning), and Oarashi (big storm), were in vogue. Though no longer the rage, so to speak, ring names referring to stormy weather still existed in the 1980s. But an equally long tradition of adopting shikona based on the rikishi's birthplace is still practiced rather widely.

Mountains

In recent times former Sekiwake Kurohimeyama and Washuyama, for example, took their ring names directly from mountains in their respective native prefectures of Niigata and Okayama. The moniker Kurohimeyama was borrowed intact; however, in Washuyama's case, the mountain is actually named Washuzan. *Zan* is another reading for the mountain character, but it is not used often in ring names because it is pronounced the same as a different character meaning defeat and, therefore, is considered unlucky. At the peak of his career, Washuyama's fame overshadowed Washuzan's, so that the mountain was frequently called by his name.

Regional Names

Sumotori nowadays do not adopt names intact from mountains in their home prefectures as often as they did in the past, and the formerly common practice of naming based on local rivers appears close to extinction. Nevertheless, several recent ring names, like Kirishima, Toryu, Enazakura, Tagaryu, and Mitoizumi, still come directly from the regions in which their holders were born. For instance, while "misty island," the literal meaning of Kirishima, seems appropriately romantic for such a handsome rikishi, it is really the name of a national park near his home in Kagoshima Prefecture. Similarly, although Toryu, written with the characters for "fighting dragon," sounds suitable for a professional grappler, it is actually taken from a river in his native Hyogo Prefecture.

Enazakura means "the cherry blossoms of Ena," a region in Gifu Prefecture. Taga is an area of Tagaryu's native Ibaraki Prefecture, which made him "the dragon of Taga." Mitoizumi is also a native of Ibaraki Prefecture, from the city of Mito to be precise. *Izumi* (fountain) was actually taken from part of his surname, Koizumi. Umenosato, the name of Mitoizumi's younger brother in a lower division, means "village of plum blossoms."

Many other shikona refer to a rikishi's birthplace in ways recognizable to most Japanese as well as foreigners well versed in Japanese history or geography. For example, the first two syllables of Sasshunada refer to an old name for his native Kagoshima Prefecture (with *nada* meaning "open sea"). The shimazu in the shikona of former Ozeki Wakashimazu is the name of the warlord family that ruled the Kagoshima region.

Samoan-born Nankairyu, literally "South Seas dragon," likewise had a name which conjures up images of his birthplace. Similarly, almost all holders to date of ring names suffixed with kita or hoku have hailed from Hokkaido. This roster has included in recent years rikishi such as Kitakachidoki, Hokutenyu, Kitanoumi, and Hokutoumi. *Kachidoki* literally means "battle cry," while *tenyu* can be translated as "heavenly aid." Hokutenyu was the first in sumo to use those two syllables, which can now be found in other combinations in sumo's lower ranks.

Likewise, Kitanoumi popularized the rare umi reading for the lake character, which is normally read as *mizuumi*. Kitanoumi really did grow up near a northern lake; but the umi suffix in Hananoumi's name did not refer to any actual body of water, and the umi character in Mainoumi, Toyonoumi, and former yokozuna Mienoumi and Hokutoumi means ocean or sea.

Size

References to size play a large role in sumo nomenclature, as can be seen in the prevalence of names suffixed with yama, or prefixed with o, dai, or tai. Many sumotori use a shikona put together simply by attaching "yama" or "o" to their own surname until they reach one of the top two divisions. Ryogoku, for example, was known as Kobayashiyama until he was promoted to makunouchi. His head coach, Dewanoumi Oyakata, a former grand champion, was given the shikona Sadanoyama, based on his surname Sasada. The Sada prefix has since been used by Sadanoumi and others of Dewanoumi-Beya.

The prefix meaning large can be found among the earliest known shikona; however, it became particularly popular after the advent of Yokozuna Taiho (big phoenix). Onokuni (big country),

Daitetsu (large and piercing), Owakamatsu (large, young pine), and Daizen (great goodness) were among the sekitori using this prefix in recent years. However, the *o* in Ozutsu and the *dai* in Daijuyama are different characters (the former of which also translates as large, while the latter means fat).

Undoubtedly some may wonder why Onishiki (active in the 1970s through the mid-1980s), who was about 100 kilograms lighter than Konishiki (small brocade), got the character for large instead of vice versa. This is because Onishiki was the name of a former grand champion from his Dewanoumi-Beya, whereas Konishiki's shikona comes from that of a former yokozuna from his Takasago-Beya.

Certain names, or characters taken from them, are in this way passed down to promising, young sumotori in the same stable. Even though designating Konishiki small may seem a bit humorous, his coach was obviously a better judge of potential than Onishiki's. (Onishiki was komusubi for just one tournament.)

Time-honored Names

Futahaguro's moniker was formed from a combination of the names of two great former grand champions from his Tatsunami-Beya: Futabayama and Haguroyama. Some even say that the psychological burden of inheriting such names is perhaps one of the reasons Futahaguro was unable to capture a tourney championship during his brief reign in sumo's highest rank.

By contrast, Chiyonofuji did not appear the least bit fazed by having a name adapted from those of two previous yokozuna from Kokonoe-Beya: Chiyonoyama and Kitanofuji. Indeed, he captured more tournament titles than his two predecessors combined. *Chiyo* literally means "a thousand years"—a poetic way in Japanese of saying an eternity. His name made him "eternal Fuji."

Stable Associations

While several members of Kokonoe-Beya, such as Takanofuji and Tomoefuji, use Fuji in their ring names, no heya has an exclusive monopoly on Japan's most famous mountain. Asahifuji (Fuji of the rising sun), for instance, hailed from Oshima-Beya. Several other rikishi in his stable also bear names with Asahi, which comes from Asahikuni, the name used by their coach during his ozeki days.

Some other stables also have preferred prefixes for their members, which have been taken from the shikona of the head coach or a leading rikishi. For example, although Kokonoe-Beya does not have exclusive rights to Fuji, it virtually appears to have them for Chiyo. Similarly, many rikishi in Kasugano-Beya carry the prefix Tochi from their stablemaster, former Yokozuna Tochinishiki, who had earlier inherited it from ex-Yokozuna Tochigiyama. Tochigiyama was born in Tochigi Prefecture, but Tochinishiki was a native of Tokyo. In this way, the prefix's associations have ceased to be geographical and have become associated instead with Kasugano-Beya. (Incidentally, the waka in Tochinowaka's and Wakanoyama's shikona does not mean youth, but refers to their native Wakayama Prefecture.)

In Dewanoumi-Beya, many rikishi have names prefixed with either Dewa or Sada. In Kataonami-Beya, the most common prefix is Tama, taken from Tamanofuji and three men named Tamanoumi before him. In Takadagawa-Beya, Mae (forward) comes from Maenoyama; in Azumazeki-Beya, Takami (high view) is from Takamiyama; in Isegahama-Beya, Kiyo (clean, pure) comes from Kiyokuni; in Wakamatsu-Beya, Fusa (tassel) is from Fusanishiki; and in Tatsunami-Beya, Tatsu (standing) derives from the stable's name. Before Hanakago-Beya was forced to close down, it gave shikona prefixed with Hana to several of its rikishi, including Hananoumi and Hananokuni, who were later transferred to Hanaregoma-Beya.

Four heya make sure that all their rikishi are easily identifiable by giving them names with the same prefix. Sadogatake-Beya uses the Koto (Japanese zither) prefix from the former shikona of the head coach, former Yokozuna Kotozakura, and the late Komusubi Kotonishiki before him. The former Ozeki Kotokaze, who broke off from Sadogatake-Beya to establish his own Oguruma-Beya, gives all his rikishi names with *kaze* (wind). In Ajigawa-Beya, Mutsu, an old name for Aomori Prefecture, is taken from Aomori-born former Sekiwake Mutsuarashi and given to all members of that stable even if they hail from elsewhere. In Michinoku-Beya, Hoshi (star) comes from ex-Hoshikabuto. Particularly memorable examples are Hoshitango and Hoshiandesu, the ring names of two Argentinian sumotori. The second halves of these shikona refer to the de facto national dance of Argentina and the famous South American mountain range.

This increasing tendency among heya to give their members such signature shikona may very well become the new wave in sumo nomenclature. In any case, fads seem to come and go in ring names, such as the recent popularity of brocade and sea instead of river, but the mountains always remain.

Names and Luck

As the difference between one win or loss sometimes makes all the difference in a man's treatment in the sumo world, rikishi tend to be very concerned about the whims of fate and are known to change their ring names after a spell of bad luck. Sometimes they do not change the entire name but just part of it. During his record ten years as an ozeki, Takanohana, for example, changed the character *no* in his ring name a number of times but never the whole shikona.

Although sumotori are strongly encouraged to adopt proper shikona upon reaching the sekitori stage, not all do. Sometimes a man does not want to give up his real name. Others may attain considerable fame before a suitable ring name can be found; then it seems too late to change, as in the cases of former Sekiwake Hasegawa and Kurama. Wajima has been the only man allowed to go as far as grand champion under his own surname—perhaps because, written with the characters for "island of rings," it has a poetic ring in Japanese.

Futahaguro was permitted to perform as ozeki under his family name, Kitao. However, when he was being considered for yokozuna, Kasugano Oyakata, then the chairman of the Sumo Association, said he would not be promoted under the name Kitao even if he chalked up sixteen (out of a possible fifteen) wins during the crucial tournament. The name Futahaguro was adopted the week of the promotion.

Itai, on the other hand, was honored with his coach's old shikona, Kotetsuyama, upon reaching the top division. Yet during his first two tries in makunouchi as Kotetsuyama, he ended up dropping out with injuries before chalking up even one win. After switching back to his own surname, he finally managed to produce a winning score in his third try in the top division and has been faring respectably ever since. Given the circumstances, the Sumo Association stopped pressuring Itai to change his name.

Another recent rikishi who was also not pressured to drop his real name was Hachiya. This unusual surname is written with the characters for "bee's arrow"—a perfect appellation for a small-sized sumotori who had to move like a butterfly and sting like a bee. With such a real name, who would need a shikona?

Generally, sumotori are allowed to keep their given name as the second part of their ring name, such as Takahanada Koji (Hanada Koji), Akinoshima Katsumi (Yamanaka Katsumi), and Mainoumi Shuhei (Nagao Shuhei). Foreign rikishi like Salevaa Atisanoe adopt entirely Japanese names (Konishiki Yasokichi) for professional sumo. Moreover, some Japanese rikishi are bequeathed the shikona of a previous sumotori in its entirety; others may be advised by a fortuneteller that a different character combination will bring them more luck in the ring.

Nicknames

Aside from their shikona, many sumotori have nicknames which interestingly almost all come from animals or cartoon characters. Chiyonofuji, for instance, has long been called "Wolf" because of his sharp, often gleaming, eyes. Onokuni was known as "Panda," undoubtedly because of his large frame and gentle countenance. Hokutenyu was referred to as "Polar Bear," due to his fair skin and broad shoulders. Lean and swarthy former Ozeki Wakashimazu was called the "Black Panther" in his prime. And Tochinishiki was dubbed "Mamushi" (viper) because his sumo style was to grab onto an opponent and not let go.

Former Yokozuna Takanosato, Wakashimazu's one-time stablemate at Futagoyama-Beya, was called "Popeye" because of his broad, muscular shoulders and uncanny strength. Two other recent members of Futagoyama-Beya also bear the nicknames of Japanese cartoon characters. Takamisugi is widely known as Doraemon, the plump cat-robot protagonist of an extremely popular series which has also been translated into a number of European languages. Former Sekiwake Daijuyama, because of a facial resemblance, is called Moomin, a cartoon character resembling a cuddly hippo. Though slightly different from a cartoon character, Wakajishi, a former Futagoyama-Beya komusubi, who had only tiny slits for eyes, was called "Itchan," a diminutive for Zatoichi, the blind swordsman hero of a popular movie series.

Addressing a Sumotori

All sekitori should be addressed with "zeki" attached to their ring names. They can also be addressed simply as sekitori—except for ozeki and yokozuna, who should be called by their titles. Sumotori in the lower divisions normally are addressed with "san," just like other Japanese. If you are not sure of the rank of a particular sumotori, he will certainly not take offense at being called sekitori. It is always better to err on the side of politeness when dealing with the sumo world.

11

Foreign Sumotori

As of the Natsu Basho of May 1992, there were thirty-seven non-Japanese men active as sumotori: specifically, twelve Americans, six Mongolians, six Brazilians, four Taiwanese, four Chinese, two Argentines, two Koreans, and one Sri Lankan. Ozeki Konishiki, the first foreigner to reach sumo's second-highest rank, stood at their pinnacle. And Akebono's promotion to ozeki after that tournament meant that in July 1992, the two highest ranks in sumo would be held by foreigners for the first time ever.

Along with their increasing numbers and diverse nationalities, the foreigners in Japan's national sport have come to receive more attention from the media in recent times. However, the presence of foreigners in sumo is hardly a recent phenomenon, for there have actually been ninety-six men with foreign birthplaces during the past fifty-eight years. A foreign-born man first appeared on the official ranking sheets in January 1934. His name was Shoji Hiraga—a Japanese-American from Los Angeles. He was a member of Kasugano-Beya for about three years; his highest rank was jonidan 23.

All the other foreigners who went into sumo prior to World War II were also Japanese-Americans. Actually there were several Koreans as well, but they were not listed as "foreign," since Korea was annexed by Japan from 1910 to 1945.

Toyonishiki (Harley Ozaki)

The most successful of the prewar foreigners was Harley Ozaki of Colorado. A member of Dewanoumi-Beya, he was the fifth

Japanese-American in sumo and the first to achieve sekitori status. Ozaki apparently did not know a thing about sumo when he was led to the stable by a relative during a visit to Japan. In fact, his ignorance of the sport was such that the whitish appearance of the sand-covered ring made him at first think it was made of concrete. He stood 188 centimeters—a height which would make him taller than even the average sekitori of the 1980s. Ozaki, who adopted the ring name of Toyonishiki, never had a losing record during his eight-year career, and scored 6–4 in the top division as maegashira 20 in May 1944, his last tourney before being drafted into the Japanese army.

Ozaki had really wanted to return to fight for the United States when the war broke out, but he could not get passage back. Since he was stranded in Japan, he ultimately changed his citizenship to Japanese at the urging of the sumo authorities. Toyonishiki survived the war and could have gone back into sumo, but quit the sport since not much of a living could be made from it at the time, and he thought he could do better as an interpreter. (He also recovered his American citizenship after the war.) In 1992, seventy-one-year-old Toyonishiki was running a Japanese-style inn in Tokyo with his wife.

Korean Sumotori

The only other foreign-born man to join sumo prior to the war and become a sekitori was Rikidozan—except that, as a Korean, he is not listed among the aforementioned ninety-six. Moreover, even though Rikidozan went as far as sekiwake, and once faced Yokozuna Haguroyama in a play-off for a tourney championship (won by the latter), his greatest fame actually came as a pro wrestler—a precedent he set for several other ex-sumotori. In 1963, he was stabbed by a gangster in a Tokyo nightclub. The wound was shallow, but Rikidozan would recklessly stuff tissue paper into it and sneak out of the hospital for meals. Peritonitis soon set in, and he died at age thirty-nine.

After the war Koreans in Japan lost their Japanese citizenship unless they specifically applied to obtain it again. The new citizenship laws were strictly patrilineal, so that the offspring of Japanese fathers were automatically entitled to be Japanese, but not the children born to a foreign father and a Japanese mother. For this reason, another one-time sekiwake, Kaneshiro, was technically Korean for being born to a Korean father and a Japanese mother. Yet he is also

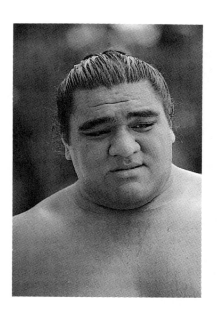

Musashimaru, the fourth rikishi from Hawaii to reach san'yaku.

not included among the foreign sumotori, because he chose to list his actual birthplace, Miyazaki Prefecture in southern Japan, on the ranking sheets.

At the peak of his career, Kaneshiro inherited the ring name of former Ozeki Tochihikari, who also hailed from Kasugano-Beya and Miyazaki Prefecture. However, after slipping considerably in rank, he was no longer considered worthy of being called Tochihikari and reverted back to his own surname.

Kaneshiro was trying to change his citizenship just when he had a series of bad scores in juryo. Although Japan's nationality laws were revised in 1983 to grant citizenship to children of all Japanese, they did not apply retroactively to most offspring born to Japanese mothers and foreign fathers before the changes. He was unable to purchase toshiyori stock in time, as the only one available when he needed it was taken by a higher bidder (Ozeki Wakashimazu). Therefore, Kaneshiro left the sumo world altogether rather than face demotion to makushita.

To date there have been over twenty Koreans in sumo, as well as rumors that several others have hidden their Korean or half-Korean background. In the postwar period only six rikishi have been officially listed as being from South Korea, and none has managed to go further than the makushita division.

Takamiyama (Jesse James Walani Kuhaulua)

A Japanese-Brazilian and a Taiwanese were among the first foreigners to join professional sumo after the war, but they did not go far. In March 1964, Takamiyama (Jesse James Walani Kuhaulua) became the first non-Asian to achieve fame and fortune in sumo.

A native of the Hawaiian island of Maui, Jesse had originally taken up sumo in high school to strengthen his legs, which had been broken by a truck when he was seven, for football. After graduation, he continued with sumo practice while undergoing six months of basic training with the National Guard and then working for a month and a half at a local pineapple cannery. But fate had it that the late Takasago Oyakata (former Yokozuna Maedayama) would spot Jesse during an exhibition tour of Hawaii in February 1964, and encourage him to come to Japan. The Hawaiian youth spoke no Japanese at the time and was so shy that he donned boxer shorts under his mawashi; yet his family had been hard pressed for money since the death of his father, and the idea of seeing Japan intrigued him. Jesse obtained the governor's release from the National Guard, and arrived later that month in Tokyo, where he promptly saw snow for the first time in his life. Since the sumo dormitories were not very well heated back then, the first Japanese word he spoke was *samui* (cold).

Jesse made his debut in maezumo in March 1964, at which time he stood 189 centimeters and weighed 115 kilograms. Though just more than half of what he was to weigh later in his career and not particularly large by today's standards, he was enormous at the time. In May, he captured the yusho in the lowest jonokuchi division at 6–1, and followed it with 7–0 in jonidan in July. At first he performed as "Jesse," but his ring name was soon changed to Takamiyama Daigoro, a time-honored shikona in Takasago-Beya.

The rigors of sumo practice, communal dormitory life, and learning the Japanese language sometimes got to Jesse. He occasionally considered quitting, but his coach had his passport locked away. However, undoubtedly the biggest deterrent was the Vietnam War. Jesse was aware that he was likely to be drafted if he returned to Hawaii; and he had already heard of some of his classmates being killed in the war. Even at its worst, sumo seemed preferable to Vietnam, so Jesse stayed with it.

In March 1967, Takamiyama was promoted to juryo—the first non-Asian sekitori. In January 1968, he reached the top makunouchi

Takamiyama receiving the Emperor's Cup after winning the 1972 Nagoya Basho.

division, where as maegashira 9, he scored 9–6, and was awarded the first of the five Fighting Spirit prizes he was to win in his career. In March, he faltered a bit as maegashira 4, yet, nonetheless, managed to beat Yokozuna Sadanoyama, who retired two days later (some say partly out of the shock of losing to a foreigner). That win marked the first of Takamiyama's many upsets over yokozuna.

Takamiyama remained in the makunouchi division for seventeen years. In November 1969, he became the first non-Asian promoted to komusubi. In the Nagoya Basho of 1972, Jesse achieved the greatest glory of all when he became the first foreigner to capture a tourney championship in the top division. He took advantage of the absence of Yokozuna Kitanofuji and the poor condition of the ozeki to earn thirteen wins (against two losses) and the Emperor's Cup. The congratulatory telegram from President Nixon read by U.S. Ambassador Ingersoll marked the only time English has been officially spoken in the sumo ring. Jesse was also awarded the first of six Outstanding Performance prizes in his career.

Takamiyama was finally promoted to sekiwake in September 1972. Though he failed at 5–10 in his first try, he later held that rank seven times more. In February 1974, he wed Watanabe Kazue. Although they were initially introduced in an *omiai* (a meeting arranged with marriage in mind), Jesse says it was "love at first sight" on his part. Their first child, a boy named Yumitaro, was born that summer; and they later had a daughter, Rie.

When Jesse remained in san'yaku for five tourneys from November 1975 through July 1976, there was speculation about his becoming ozeki. But he was ultimately unable to win consecutively in double figures and hardly perfected his technique beyond tsukioshi and kimedashi. Moreover, his legs were never really strong and were also too long for sumo. Nevertheless, Takamiyama set all-time records for the most bouts in makunouchi (1,398), most consecutive basho in makunouchi (97), and most kinboshi (12), as well as the most kinboshi from one yokozuna (7 from Wajima).

Jesse's popularity was also of champion class. His humorous appearances on commercials and other television spots made him a millionaire as well as recognizable even to Japanese not interested in sumo. His presence served greatly to humanize the previously stern and unsmiling public face of sumo.

In 1976, the Sumo Association announced a new ruling that only sumotori with Japanese citizenship would be allowed to purchase the toshiyori stock necessary to remain in the sumo world as an elder. The Association never offered an official explanation for the move; however, one of the leading coaches commented that it was necessary to prevent sumo from becoming dominated by strong foreigners, as had happened in another traditional Japanese sport, judo. Nevertheless, some of the same coaches responsible for this ruling have not hesitated to accept powerful foreigners, along with all the publicity surrounding their presence, into their heya.

Despite an outcry initially from the public that special exceptions should be made for Takamiyama and Kaneshiro in view of their many accomplishments, the Sumo Association stood by the decision. Jesse agonized for a couple of years over the matter. While he did not want to renounce his U.S. citizenship, as required by Japanese law, he also had qualms about giving up the job he knew best. He ultimately applied for Japanese citizenship, which was granted in June 1980, and adopted a new Japanese name, Watanabe Daigoro, based on his wife's maiden name and part of his sumo name.

Takamiyama retired from the ring on the last day of the Natsu Basho in 1984—only one month short of his goal to fight until age forty. He had seriously injured his elbow, ironically in a match which he won in Kyushu the previous November. The first doctor who diagnosed him did not recognize the extent of the injury, so Jesse did not think of applying for permission to sit out a tourney without effect to his rank under the Public Injury System until it was too late. Lacking the time to recover fully, he was forced to drop out of a couple of tournaments and also fell in rank. Finally he chose retirement over the possibility of demotion to an unsalaried division.

Takamiyama's topknot was cut off on February 3, 1985, in a traditional ceremony attended by a full house at the newly opened Kokugikan in Ryogoku. At that time, he officially became Azumazeki Oyakata. In April 1986, he opened his own Azumazeki-Beya, first with just Japanese rikishi. He later added a total of eight foreigners, although there were never more than five at any one time. Among them, Taylor Wiley (Takamikuni) in March 1988 became the first foreigner to capture the yusho in the makushita division; and English-born Nathan Strange (Hidenokuni) was the first rikishi from Europe. However, they quit sumo in 1989 and 1990 respectively.

More importantly, Akebono (Chadwick Rowan) became the stable's first sekitori in March 1990, and he captured the tourney title in the top division in May 1992—almost twenty years after Takamiyama. Other foreigners in Azumazeki-Beya as of July 1992 were John Feleunga (Takamio) and Troy Talaimatai (Ozora) in makushita, and Percy Kitapa (Wakataisei) in jonidan, all from Hawaii.

Chinese Sumotori

The next sekitori recognized as foreign after Takamiyama was Kiyonohana, born as Zhang Li-hua to Chinese parents in Osaka. By the time he was promoted to juryo in Nagoya in 1974, Japan had restored diplomatic relations with China, so his birthplace came to be listed as Fujian Province on the ranking sheets. Kiyonohana fought in juryo for thirteen tourneys and quit sumo in 1978.

As of July 1992, a total of twenty-one men of Taiwanese or Chinese origins had entered professional sumo over the years. Taiwan-born Tochinohana (Liu Chao-huei) of Kasugano-Beya was originally encouraged to go into sumo by his father, a businessman who had become a fan of the sport during his many visits to Japan. Liu spent most of 1986 and 1987 in juryo, but quit sumo in May 1988—the same tournament in which his fellow countrymen Maitaikyo and Tominohana made their professional debuts. Three other Taiwanese entered sumo between November 1988 and January 1989.

Koo Chun Bong, who fought under the shikona Seiko, was discovered in his grandfather's Chinese restaurant in Tokyo in 1987 by Isegahama Oyakata. Being from Hong Kong, Koo was the first rikishi with a British passport. He quit sumo in 1988.

Konishiki (Salevaa Atisanoe)

Twenty-one other young men from Hawaii as well as six from the United States mainland joined sumo in the wake of Jesse Takamiyama's success. Konishiki (Salevaa Atisanoe) became the first of them to enjoy success, but what a success he has been! Atisanoe, nicknamed Sale (pronounced like "Sally"), was born in Hawaii of Samoan parentage. He stood near the top of his class at the University High School in Honolulu when discovered by Takamiyama. Jesse himself has stated he is not sure how he managed to convince the youth to give up ambitions to go to college and become a lawyer. However, it was probably not easy for Sale to turn down a local hero. In addition, although Atisanoe's father had regular employment with the U.S. Navy, it was undoubtedly not easy to feed a "big" (in more than one sense of the word) Samoan family with several children.

In view of his promise, Atisanoe was immediately given the

Akebono being congratulated by U.S. Ambassador Michael Armacost on his first yusho.

name of a former grand champion from Takasago-Beya, Konishiki Yasokichi, as he made his debut in maezumo in the Nagoya Basho of 1982. In September and November, he took the championships in the jonokuchi and jonidan divisions with perfect scores of 7–0. A year after his name first appeared on the official ranking sheets, Konishiki was promoted to juryo. The only men who had passed through the four unsalaried divisions any faster since the establishment of six tourneys a year were Asahifuji and Itai, who both had plenty of amateur sumo experience.

Konishiki was promoted to the top division in July 1984—only two years after coming into sumo and just one tournament after Takamiyama retired from the ring. In September, he stunned the sumo world and the Japanese public by beating the two yokozuna participating in the tourney (Chiyonofuji and Takanosato) as well as Ozeki Wakashimazu to remain in the yusho race until the very last day. The championship ultimately went to another maegashira, Tagaryu, at 13–2. But, with a record of 12–3, Konishiki was awarded two of the coveted sansho prizes, one of which was shared with Tagaryu.

For the ensuing two years, every time Konishiki seemed on the brink of ozeki promotion, he got injured. The strangest accident occurred just before the Aki Basho of September 1985, when a

Konishiki raising his arms in celebration after promotion to ozeki. In the foreground are Nanyozakura, left, and Nankairyu.

bathing stool collapsed under his gargantuan girth, causing him to break his coccyx and miss all of the tourney.

The May 1986 tournament started off well enough with Konishiki and Onokuni being chosen to meet Prince Charles and Diana, Princess of Wales, during their visit to the Kokugikan. However, on the middle day, Sale badly sprained his leg in a rematch with Ozeki Kitao (Futahaguro). Controversy arose because many people thought Konishiki had clearly won the initial bout and should not have been ordered by the judges to do the match over in the first place.

Konishiki missed the remainder of that basho and all of Nagoya as well. Though a bitter ordeal, he later said the experience made him develop patience.

Konishiki began his comeback in September, and the rest is sumo history. In May 1987, he scored 12–3 to become the first "truly foreign" ozeki. (Maenoyama, an ozeki from 1970 to 1972, for example, never kept his Korean origins secret. But he has not been considered as one of the "foreign" sumotori, because he was born in Osaka and became a naturalized Japanese citizen.)

At the gala party held in September 1987 at a Tokyo hotel to celebrate his promotion, Kasugano Oyakata (former Yokozuna Tochinishiki), the chairman of the Sumo Association at the time, commented that he expected to be attending an even greater soiree in the near future—in other words, the one celebrating Konishiki's promotion to yokozuna.

Although Konishiki did not manage to become yokozuna during the former Tochinishiki's lifetime, he did attain his first yusho in November 1989—just a few months before the great man died. Thus, Konishiki became the second foreigner after Takamiyama to capture the Emperor's Cup, and like Jesse before him, he cried tears of joy, mixed, in Sale's own words, with feelings of "anger" at himself "for coming close yet not managing a yusho earlier." Perhaps symbolic of the changes in relations between the United States and Japan in the seventeen-plus years since Takamiyama's victory, the congratulatory message from President Bush was read by an American diplomat in Japanese, not English. President Bush's subsequent two messages upon Sale's victories in November 1991 and March 1992 were also read in the ring in Japanese.

In February 1992, Konishiki married Sumika Shioda, a former fashion model from Sapporo, in a gala ceremony attended by 1,200 people, including prominent Japanese politicians and show business celebrities. A few months later he applied for Japanese citizenship, indicating his determination to remain in the sumo world after his retirement from the ring.

Around the same time, Sale was also in the news for his alleged statement to a Japanese newspaper that racism is what had kept him from being promoted to yokozuna in the wake of attaining two titles in the previous three tourneys. His supposed charge may have been made in response to questions about an article written by a member of the Yokozuna Deliberation Council for a local magazine saying, "We don't need a foreign yokozuna." When Sale was requoted in the *New York Times*, the issue became an international media event. Sale ultimately held a press conference at which he tearfully denied ever making such a statement.

Being hounded by the press, combined with a lack of practice, seemed to take its toll on Konishiki. In the Natsu Basho of 1992, he turned in a mediocre 9–6 score which completely ruined any possibility of yokozuna promotion in the near future and put him back at peg one—all questions of racism aside.

Akebono (Chadwick George Haheo Rowan)

Just as Konishiki was failing in his fourth attempt at yokozuna, another foreigner emerged to win the tourney championship along with subsequent promotion to ozeki: Akebono (Chadwick George Haheo Rowan).

Nicknamed Chad, Rowan was born near Honolulu in May 1969 to a Hawaiian-Cuban mother and a father of Irish, Chinese, Portuguese, and Hawaiian descent who worked as a taxi driver. Standing over 200 centimeters tall by high school graduation, Chad won a basketball scholarship to a local college. He was planning to study hotel management, but he quit in less than a year in the wake of a quarrel with his basketball coach.

Chad had long been interested in sumo from watching broadcasts of the tournaments in Japan on television. A family acquaintance introduced him to Azumazeki Oyakata, but the former Takamiyama at first thought Chad was too tall for sumo and showed more interest in his 188-centimeter younger brother George. The future Akebono made quite an effort to convince the stablemaster that he was willing to train hard and endure the rigors of sumo life. He also secretly figured that even if he did not make the grade in the sport, he could still benefit from the experience of living in Japan. As he explained it, "I thought I'd probably at least learn enough of the language and culture in two or three years to get a job as an interpreter for all those Japanese who are dropping lots of money in Hawaii nowadays."

As George was still in high school, Azumazeki Oyakata was finally persuaded to take Chad first. The future Akebono made his official debut in March 1988, along with the Hanada brothers and over one hundred other youths. George, incidentally, did join Azumazeki-Beya a year and a half later, only to quit within about four months.

Chad was first given the shikona Daikai (great sea), which was quickly changed to Akebono, meaning "dawn." However, the character was deliberately miswritten with one dot missing on the left. Using the sort of play on words the Japanese tend to love, Azumazeki Oyakata explained that Chad's shikona would receive final dot (*ten o toru*) once he captured the heavenly realm (*ten o toru*)—in other words, a sufficiently high rank in sumo.

Even though Akebono had no yusho in the lower divisions to his credit, he reached the juryo division by March 1990. He breezed through juryo in three tournaments, to move into the makunouchi division in September 1990. Chad was even nominated for the Kantosho then on the stipulation that he win on the final day, which he unfortunately failed to do. However, in the following basho he was awarded the prize.

Early into 1991, Akebono's father, a diabetic, underwent surgery to amputate a leg infected with gangrene. Since this operation meant that his father could no longer drive a taxi, Chad at age twenty-one became the main support of his family in Hawaii.

Akebono went as far as sekiwake without any losing scores on his record. Thus, he set an all-time record of seventeen consecutive kachikoshi tournaments starting from the jonokuchi division, rewriting the previous record of sixteen held by former Ozeki Takanohana. Chad's record is superior also because Takanohana's winning streak ended in juryo.

Akebono finally took in his first makekoshi in May 1991, but with a still impressive 7–8 record. As komusubi in September, he chalked up 7–8 once again. Everything has been uphill since then.

In January 1992, Komusubi Akebono vied for the yusho with Takahanada, another member of the "class" of March 1988. Takahanada ultimately won at 14–1, while Chad was awarded his third Shukunsho and second Kantosho for his outstanding 13–2 record.

Somewhat out of practice after a trip home to Hawaii in February, Akebono could manage only eight wins in March, but that was still good enough to keep his sekiwake rank. Then in May, Chad took a fairly early lead in the tournament, which he never relinquished. His only close competition was Wakahanada, who was awarded the Ginosho.

Akebono captured the tourney championship at 13–2 and received his fourth Shukunsho. In contrast to the U.S. ambassador twenty years before him, Ambassador Michael Armacost read the president's message of congratulations in Japanese. Even more important, the Sumo Association announced that it would consider Chad for ozeki promotion after the tourney.

Three days later, Chad received the news from messengers from the association that his promotion had been approved unanimously. At the press conference held afterwards, he proudly held up a placard with a new version of his name: the dot had finally been added to Akebono. With no yokozuna in July 1992, Akebono held the highest rank on the banzuke.

Musashimaru (Fiamalu Penitani)

Three other foreigners entered sumo in September 1989, along with Chad's younger brother George. Of the four, only Mushashimaru and Ozora, who played on rival high school football teams in Hawaii, remained by 1992.

The future Musashimaru was born as Fiamalu Penitani, the fourth son of a Tongan-German father and a Samoan-Portuguese mother in the eastern part of Samoa in May 1971. The entire family, which later came to include five boys and three girls, moved to Hawaii when Fiamalu was ten years old. His current home is not far from Konishiki's in Honolulu. In high school in Hawaii, Fia (his Samoan nickname; in his stable he is called Maru) took up football and Greco-Roman wrestling. Although he was not particularly fond of schoolwork, his athletic abilities earned him the offer of a football scholarship to Pasadena City College in southern California. The future Musashimaru was hoping that would eventually lead to a career in professional football.

However, his wrestling coach had connections with former Yokozuna Mienoumi and his Musashigawa-Beya and encouraged the youth to give sumo a try. Since Fiamalu had no previous sumo training and Musashigawa Oyakata himself was a bit wary about accepting another foreigner after a bad experience with Musashinobo (William Molina) in 1988, it was decided that the youth would enter the stable for a few months over the summer on an experimental basis. In other words, if he liked sumo, he could formally join later; and if he did not, he could return home without prejudice.

Though the going was rough at first, Fia soon became aware, in his own words, that "nothing in life is easy if you want to be good at it." Meanwhile, Musashigawa Oyakata realized that his charge had great potential and perseverance. The youth was given the shikona Musashimaru, with the Musashi part coming from the heya's name and Maru representing the Japanese pronunciation of the second half of Fiamalu as well as being a name attached to ships. Musashimaru launched his sumo career by capturing the yusho in the jonokuchi division in November 1989—the tourney in which Sale received his first Emperor's Cup.

Fia took the championship in the sandanme division in 1990. He marked his debut in juryo in July 1991 by capturing the yusho in that division—the first foreigner ever to do so. He came close to winning the juryo yusho again in September and graduated from the division in just two tournaments.

Musashimaru made a promising debut in makunouchi in November by receiving his first Kantosho in what turned out to be the second tournament captured by Konishiki. In this way, Fiamalu progressed all the way from makushita to makunouchi in 1991 without any losing records.

He has continued to win in 1992 as well. In January 1992, Musashimaru was ranked high enough to face both Konishiki and Akebono. Although Fia lost those two matches, he came through with a winning record. In May 1992, he chalked up kachikoshi in the difficult komusubi division. Because Musashimaru's body is well-proportioned for sumo with a low center of gravity, sumo commentators generally agree that his future prospects are very bright indeed.

Nankairyu and Polynesian Sumotori

Around a year after Konishiki became juryo, two young men from Western Samoa joined Takasago-Beya. They had been carefully selected from the many youths in the South Pacific island-nation who responded to a television recruitment campaign begun by a Japanese businessman. The older of the two, Kiriful Saba made his juryo debut under the name Nankairyu in May 1987. In November that year he entered the top division—the third non-Asian to do so. Although it took him more time than Konishiki to reach juryo, he progressed through that division to makunouchi one tourney faster. In contrast to Takamiyama and Konishiki, Nankairyu, at 188 centimeters and 143 kilograms, was not significantly larger than most of his Japanese competition. He compensated for his lack of a size advantage with daunting fighting spirit and diligent training.

Nankairyu unfortunately had a drinking problem, which became the subject of considerable adverse publicity after he injured a hotel clerk while inebriated in July 1987. A linguistic gap created further problems between Nankairyu and local reporters, as he did not learn Japanese well, and was not fluent in English either. He ultimately quit sumo in the autumn of 1988, after a heated argument with his head coach, Takasago Oyakata (former Yokozuna Asashio). The stablemaster died about a month later.

Nanyozakura (Fofoga Faaleva), the younger of the two Samoans, was by contrast rather docile and well-mannered. After fighting the makushita division in July 1987, he went to visit his ailing mother in the South Pacific later that summer, never to return to Japan.

For a while in the mid-1970s, there were six Tongans in Asahiyama-Beya. But when they sided with the late oyakata's widow in her dispute with his successor and refused to live in the new heya, they were dismissed from the Sumo Association. One of them, Fukunoshima, had actually been in the hospital with an injury at the time the succession dispute flared up and was never asked for his opinion before being summarily dismissed along with the other Tongans. Although he protested that he was willing to go along with the new coach, the Sumo Association would not let him back in. Fukunoshima ended up as a pro wrestler named Prince Tonga. Apparently one of the other Tongans became a palace guard for the king of the island-nation, and another later returned to Japan for university study.

Caucasians in Sumo

The furthest a Caucasian had gone in sumo up through the 1980s was makushita 9, a rank achieved by black-haired Hakuzan (Pasquale Bosche) a Brazilian of Italian descent. He was diligent about practice; and being a baker's son, he was used to getting up early in the morning. However, he was terribly injury-prone and quit sumo in 1986.

Perhaps the best-known Caucasian was Kototenzan (John Tenta). The first Canadian in sumo, Tenta remained for only four tournaments, yet he did not lose one bout during that time. Ultimately, he could not adjust to the lack of privacy in the sumo living quarters, and was also anxious to have a secure and stable salary as soon as possible. Having been a champion Greco-Roman wrestler in high school and college, Tenta joined the pro wrestling circuit shortly after quitting sumo in 1986.

The other especially well-known Caucasian was Hidenokuni (Nathan Strange) of England, who was in Azumazeki-Beya for about six months until January 1990. Even though Nathan's sumo career was quite short, his presence was highly publicized because he was the first person from Europe in sumo.

The Caucasians in sumo in 1992 were Hoshitango (Marcello Salomon Imach), a former swimming instructor from Argentina; Hoshiandesu (Jose Antonio Flores), another native of Buenos Aires; and Sunahama (William Tyler Hopkins) of Hawaii. Hoshitango, the first Jew in professional sumo, joined Michinoku-Beya in 1987; and Hoshiandesu signed up with the same stable in 1988. Hoshiandesu and Hoshitango both achieved winning scores at the respective ranks of makushita 7 and 8 in May 1992, which brought them close to a sekitori position.

Other Asians

In September 1988, three young men from the Philippines, the first sumotori ever from that country, joined Kataonami-Beya. It seems that a television documentary about sumo had inspired a good number of young Filipinos to write to the local office of the Japan Society to ask how to join the sport. Kataonami Oyakata flew to Manila expressly to interview and select the three he felt had the greatest potential, only to have them run out on him by the end of the year.

Six youths from Mongolia with experience in a Mongolian sport similar to sumo joined Oshima-Beya in March 1992. At the same time, a Sri Lankan, who had originally studied karate in Japan, entered Kasugano-Beya, only to leave some two months later.

Other New Foreigners

In July 1988, Konishiki brought to Japan a distant relative from Los Angeles, Vincent Divoux, who took the shikona Shinnishiki (new brocade). The same tournament also saw the debut of sumo's first

Black (actually half-Black and half-Japanese), Henry Armstrong Miller. He was given the name Sentoryu (fighting dragon), which is also a play of words on his hometown of Saint Louis in Missouri. In the following tourney, Sentoryu beat Shinnishiki in a play-off for the championship in the lowest jonokuchi division.

Shinnishiki returned to Los Angeles to become a rap musician in 1990, but Sentoryu was still active in sumo in May 1992. In addition to William Hopkins, Eric Cosier Gaspar (Koryu) and Kaleo Kekauoha (Nampu) of Hawaii entered Takasago-Beya in September 1990. Brothers George and Glen Kalima, also of Hawaii, joined Magaki-Beya in November 1990 and March 1991 respectively, and in May 1992 were fighting under the shikona of Yamato and Onami.

Five Brazilians of Japanese descent entered Tamanoi-Beya between September 1991 and May 1992. The most famous of them was Luis Ikemori, who two years earlier had become the first foreigner to win the *gakusei* (collegiate) yokozuna title.

The Outlook

When Konishiki nearly captured the yusho in 1984, there was a xenophobic response, with talk of limiting the foreign "meat bombs" and "black ships" (a reference to Commodore Matthew Perry's ships, which shocked Japan into opening up to the outside world in the mid-nineteenth century). Yet, to this date, no limits have been put on the number of foreigners in sumo, unlike in Japanese baseball, which allows only two non-Japanese per team. And even the restriction against foreigners becoming coaches has not deterred many non-Japanese youths from entering sumo.

In the spring of 1992, Dewanoumi Oyakata, the new director of the Sumo Association, announced that foreign recruits would be required to study the Japanese language and some culture for three to six months before being allowed to make their professional debut. Then, at a professional luncheon held at the Foreign Correspondents Club in Tokyo on May 28, Dewanoumi intimated that the association was considering limiting the number of foreigners per heya and in sumo as a whole. He did not mention a precise number, but perhaps because the general reaction from the public and even from the Yokozuna Deliberation Council to this idea has not been positive, no further pronouncements have been made on this issue as this book goes to press.

12

Sumo and Women

A close look at the audience depicted in ukiyo-e prints of sumo matches should reveal no female faces. With the major exception of royalty like Empress Kogyoku, women have been allowed to attend sumo only in this century.

Traditionally, sumo was performed in rings outdoors. Women were not allowed to enter the surrounding grounds set aside for the audience, although undoubtedly in many small villages no barriers existed to prevent them from watching informal amateur matches in the fields.

Sumo indeed appears to have been viewed by some women in the countryside. There is even one old tale about a young village girl who gets an unbreakable hold on a sumotori who had tried to pinch her on his way to a competition in the old capital of Kyoto. In one version of the story, the man, after losing confidence in his strength, relearns the art of sumo from the seemingly delicate yet strong young lady before he dared to face the most powerful rikishi from all over Japan.

While women were barred from seeing professional bouts in the cities, groups of female sumotori began performing in the red-light districts in the late seventeenth century. This style of sumo proved so popular that it grew into a form of entertainment for the general public in the eighteenth century. Nevertheless, the early women's version of the sport apparently stayed close to its red-light origins, and the players assumed suggestive ring names such as Chichigahari (swollen breasts), Tamanokoshi (palanquin of balls), and Kaisato (clam village). Women also performed in matches with blind men, but such exhibitions were often prohibited as "harmful to public morals."

Women's Sumo in the Countryside

Banished from the cities during the nineteenth century, the female version is still performed today in parts of Kyushu. The act appears to have been cleaned up a bit in comparison with what went on during the days of the shogun. Today women sumotori wear mawashi with halter tops and adopt ring names just like male professionals. In fact, they sometimes even borrow the names of great rikishi, past and present, like Wakanohana, Taiho, and Chiyonofuji, but no longer make up vulgar parodies of well-known shikona. Moreover, while several regular sumo techniques have developed around getting a hold on the opponent's mawashi, women's sumo, unfortunately, has not gone further by adding techniques based on grabbing the rival's halter top.

Female Audiences

Sumo first became open to female spectators with the construction of the Ryogoku Kokugikan in 1909. Nevertheless, women were forbidden to sit in the first five rows around the ring until after World War II. Moreover, while many women may have followed sumo on the radio and in the sports pages of the newspapers, "proper" young and not-so-young ladies were not to be seen in the Kokugikan in prewar times.

The women in the prewar audience at the Kokugikan were limited primarily to shopkeepers in the Ryogoku area, geisha, and others in the service and entertainment world called *mizu-shobai* (water trade). The cramped four-person boxes in the stadium, which were later to become the objects of complaints by many foreign fans as well as some of the larger sized, postwar Japanese, were actually deliberately designed that way, according to one former sumotori. He says they were really for the many patrons accompanied by geisha, since the narrow seating virtually assured such dandies about town the chance to bump hands and knees with the geisha by their side.

To Abstain or Not to Abstain

Nowadays, seeing the way hoards of women of various ages hang around the aisles of the Kokugikan and in the sumo-beya, it may be hard to imagine that until fairly recently most Japanese women stayed away. However, just because women were generally kept out of the audience does not mean that sumotori were expected to stay away from the fair sex and lead an ascetic life. To the contrary, an active sex life is encouraged—in fact, even expected.

Of course, the same may be true of most male athletic societies, yet abstention is usually encouraged at least when in serious training or just before an important game. By contrast, abstention of any kind is hardly regarded as a merit in the sumo world. Heavy drinking is not frowned upon—especially if followed by hard practice the next morning to sweat the liquor out through the pores—and sleeping with women is practically considered part of the training.

Former Grand Champion Wakanohana I (Futagoyama Oyakata) has been quoted as saying that having a woman makes for good hip exercise. Haguroyama, a yokozuna from 1941 to 1953, is supposed to have had a woman every night during tourneys because it helped him sleep more soundly. Rikidozan, the sekiwake who went on to great fame as a pro wrestler, often claimed that he got a bloody nose unless he had a woman every night.

On the other hand, Futabayama, who became known as "the god of sumo" for his perfect tachiai and highly disciplined training methods, is said to have refrained from carousing during tournaments in a manner worthy of a saint. Yet once a tourney was over, the great yokozuna apparently always treated himself and his attendants to a night of full service at a geisha house. Even now upper-ranking sumotori are known to offer an apprentice enough money to go to a massage parlor if he wins a crucial bout; but treating a full group of tsukebito to a whole night of sensual pleasures, regardless of tournament scores, is unheard of. Such generosity is perhaps another reason that Futabayama became regarded as a "god" in the sport.

In Futabayama's times the sumotori stayed away from the sort of women who would not venture into the Kokugikan. There was an iron rule for centuries against touching ordinary women. The practice partners for "nighttime sumo" were generally either geisha or prostitutes. Sumotori still play games with geisha today. But, with fewer geisha in postwar Japan, bar hostesses have emerged, along with massage parlor girls, as the predominant female contact for unmarried sumotori.

While many rikishi may simply look blubbery and unappealing to the Western eye, they are generally attractive to Japanese women—especially those in the water trade. Aside from being unusual or a curiosity, rikishi are taller and stronger than the average Japanese male and consequently appear more virile. Of course, some of them happen to be more muscular than fat and are very good looking, even by Western standards.

In addition, a topknot seems to work like a magic charm in attracting Japanese women. Many of the male patrons who put money into the stables take sumotori out at night as bait to draw women to their tables.

Homosexuality in sumo is surprisingly rare by Western standards for a society where so many men live and train together in close quarters. Occasionally a youth with homosexual inclinations does find his way into sumo. However, the pressure to assume a macho appearance is so great in the sumo world that such a young man is likely to be bullied out unless he keeps his sexual inclinations secret until reaching a privileged sekitori rank. (An ozeki of the 1980s, for example, was widely rumored in the sumo world to be bisexual.)

Marriage Partners

Many marriages in Japan today still originate by a meeting arranged by a go-between of two eligible singles, who usually are shown each other's photos and personal histories in advance. While some rikishi do have such traditional omiai, the "arranged marriages" in the sumo world are most likely to be between the coach's daughter and a sumotori, who have undoubtedly known each other for years and hardly require each other's personal histories and photos. Several of these matches have been made purely for political convenience, but at least in a few cases, genuine affection or at least friendship had already developed over the years between the young couple.

Traditionally, sumotori have married the daughters of coaches or people closely connected with the sport (including patrons), women within the water trade (the daughters of innkeepers or restaurant owners), or maybe an especially endearing geisha.

One big merit to marrying the coach's daughter, aside from obviously being the easiest way to inherit a stable, is that a woman brought up in sumo society will already be familiar with its mores as well as used to accomodating many people. The latter point also applies to the daughters of innkeepers and restaurant owners.

Sumotori nowadays are less inclined than their predecessors to marry, or stay married to, a coach's daughter. Nevertheless, as of July 1992, at least seven stables were being run by men married to the daughters of former coaches, whereas only Mihogaseki-Beya was managed by the ex-sumotori son of the previous Mihogaseki Oyakata. Furthermore, Ozeki Asahifuji in the fall of 1988 married a niece of the former Kasugayama Oykata, who does not have any children of his own. The move should allow Asahifuji to rebuild the currently defunct Kasugayama-Beya, an affiliate of his Oshima-Beya. (Oshima Oyakata, in 1988, was still too young to think of choosing a successor; besides, he only has sons.)

Akinoumi, a yokozuna from 1942 to 1946, perhaps set a precedent for divorcing the daughter of a head coach. Although Akinoumi's wife, the daughter of Dewanoumi Oyakata (former Yokozuna Tsunenohana), in true sumo style, accepted his geisha-mistress giving birth the same day she did, she was ultimately abandoned by him. Akinoumi gave up the geisha as well and eventually married an entirely different woman after leaving the sumo world altogether. More recent cases of divorce have resulted in merely forcing sumotori to forfeit their heir-apparent rights to the stable and establish an independent one, such as Wakanohana II, who opened Magaki-Beya after divorcing the daughter of Futagoyama Oyakata (Wakanohana I).

Futabayama was the first major rikishi to break away from the tradition of marrying the coach's daughter or a woman from the water trade. He could have married the coach's daughter, to be sure, but he rejected the offer in order to wed a "proper young lady" of his own choosing. The coach's daughter instead married Haguroyama. (Their daughter, in turn, is married to the present Tatsunami Oyakata, thus keeping the stable in the family for three generations.)

Futabayama's wife was a young heiress living with her grandmother when she first fell in love with him, and can perhaps be called the original sumo "groupie." Although she would not even enter the stadium, she apparently trailed the handsome grand champion with presents for years. They finally became intimate after she visited him while he was hospitalized with an injury. Afterwards, Futabayama took responsibility for touching an "ordinary woman" (one not connected with either the sport or the water trade) by marrying her. His action, along with the full opening up of the stadium to female spectators after the war, established a precedent for women of virtually any social status to marry into sumo society.

Although coaches' daughters and women connected to the sport or the water trade still account for the greatest percentage of sumo wives, an ever-increasing number is comprised of "ordinary women," including stewardesses met on flights, young women from childhood neighborhoods, members of the same religious organization, and even some former groupies.

Some former actresses, singers, and models have also become sumo wives. The initial marriages between two yokozuna (Asashio and Tochinoumi) and women from show business ended in failure—in fact, Asashio's first wife committed suicide. However, since then show-business/sumo marriages have met with success, as long as the wife has been willing to give up her career. Examples include Wakashimazu's marriage to a former pop singer (Takada Mizue), Takanohana's to a one-time starlet, and Chiyonofuji's and Konishiki's to former models. Even Tochinoumi chose for his second wife a one-time member of the Takarazuka Revue Troupe.

Except for some of the coaches' daughters, the wives of sumotori tend to be quite pretty and petite. When asked in a magazine interview why so many rikishi seem to prefer tiny women, one coach replied that after grappling with a heavy opponent during the day, it is nice to deal with something small and light at night.

Sumotori generally wed in their late twenties or early thirties, since the lack of a salary in the apprentice stages serves as major deterrent to early marriages. In addition, although a rikishi ostensibly does not need the permission of his head coach to wed, his relations in the sumo world could be seriously impaired if he did so without consulting with the coach, who, in turn, would be unlikely to approve of any of his charges getting married before reaching a relatively high rank.

Nevertheless, some do get married secretly as low-ranking sekitori or even occasionally in the apprentice stage. They usually either wait until after a significant victory or promotion to break the news to the coach or else confess first to the stable's okamisan who acts as a buffer in relaying the information to her husband. This trend has been growing particularly pronounced in the 1980s.

Four sumo wedding ceremonies held in one year in the mid-1980s, for example, involved couples who had already legally registered their marriages and had even had children together. Yet only one of those weddings had been delayed, understandably, due to the death of the previous head coach. (The Japanese customarily do not hold felicitous ceremonies for a year after a death in the family.)

Divorce is still relatively rare in the sumo world. Although many sumo wives initially have trouble adjusting to having husbands who spend nearly half of the year on the road, once they do get used to the situation, the periods of separation may actually serve to perpetuate the freshness of the relationship. After all, absence is said to make "the heart grow fonder."

13

Referees, Announcers, and Hairdressers

Referees

Just like the sumotori whose matches they officiate, the gyoji, or referees, tend to come into sumo on their own accord or through recruitment, although the former is undoubtedly the most common way. The reason should not be so hard to imagine. Some young men who simply love sumo will take another position associated with the sport if they are not physically suited for the actual fighting.

In fact, a majority of the *urakata* (people behind the scenes)—the referees, match announcers, and hairdressers—is composed of such men. A number of match announcers and hairdressers even worked as active sumotori for a few years before assuming their present positions.

However, very few gyoji have started out as anything but a referee. Aside from being, along with the announcers, the most visible "behind the scenes" post, the referee position is also the most prestigious. The referees are the only urakata whose names appear on the ranking sheets along with all active sumotori and coaches.

As of May 1992, there were forty-one gyoji, all with the assumed professional name of either Kimura or Shikimori. The gyoji's role is believed to date back to the late eighth century, but apparently did not take on its present form until the late sixteenth century when Oda Nobunaga reigned as the most powerful military lord in Japan. The houses of Kimura and Shikimori came into being in 1726 and 1768.

For nearly two centuries there were clear distinctions between the two lines of gyoji. Even now some fine differences exist in the way they hold the gunbai, or war paddles, when calling out the contestants' names. A Kimura keeps his palm down; a Shikimori has it up. Yet nowadays a referee can start out as Kimura, switch over to Shikimori, and go back again to Kimura as he moves up the referee ranks.

Similar to the way several apprentice sumotori perform under their real names, some of the young referees also use their own given name as part of their professional name (such as Kimura Hideki) in the early part of their career. A more old-fashioned sounding name, like Zennosuke or Kandayu, will be assumed by the time they have climbed high enough to officiate matches at the juryo level.

The highest ranking referee is always named Kimura Shonosuke, and the second highest is always known as Shikimori Inosuke. Given the moving between the gyoji families nowadays, this means that the man assuming the name of Kimura Shonosuke was previously known as Shikimori Inosuke, and that he undoubtedly performed under at least one or two different names before that.

The referees must work their way up through the ranks just like the sumotori. The youngest gyoji, like the youngest rikishi, is likely to be fresh out of junior high school. He must be affiliated with one of the sumo stables and, just like the sumotori, is likely to live there until he gets married.

A separate stable once existed for the referees but it was closed in 1973. (However, they still have their own large dressing room inside the Kokugikan.) Now almost all the sumo stables, except for some of the newest or smallest, have one or more gyoji attached to them.

Again similar to the sumotori, the gyoji's promotion through the ranks is based primarily on ability, though seniority can play a small part in the referee's case. Nevertheless, just as an exceptional sumotori like Kitanoumi and Taiho can become yokozuna at age twenty-one, the previous Kimura Shonosuke XXVII—the "grand champion" among referees—was promoted to the position at the extraordinarily early age of fifty-two. For some years, Shonosuke XXVII had a second-hand man, Shikimori Inosuke XXIV, who was about six years his senior. Inosuke XXIV reached the mandatory retirement age of sixty-five at the end of 1983; Inosuke XXV was a bit younger and became Shonosuke XXVIII in 1991.

There are some differences between the ways the sumotori and the referees climb through the ranks. Whereas all sumotori, except yokozuna and ozeki, are constantly moving within the ranks in reflection of their scores in the most recent tournament, promotions of gyoji are made only once a year, if at all. Furthermore, there are no demotions, per se, of referees. If a gyoji is deemed to have performed badly—to have made an unforgivable number of misjudgments (*sashichigai*), he will simply be passed by for the next advancement. This happened to Shikimori Isaburo, who unfortunately tended to make more mistakes than other referees, and was at the time of his death in 1987 older than both Shonosuke XXVII and Inosuke XXIV.

In addition, while there can be four or even five ozeki or yokozuna, the number of ranks at the top of the referee hierarchy is strictly limited to never more than one Kimura Shonosuke and one Shikimori Inosuke each. In fact, sometimes after one Shonosuke reaches the mandatory retirement age, the Sumo Association may even wait a year before designating his replacement.

Advancement for referees is painfully slow. Most do not reach the level to officiate over juryo matches—the gyoji equivalent of sekitori status—until they are about forty years old. Thus, with limited places at the top, some referees may never climb all that far, despite their ability.

On the other hand, the referees are not past their prime and ready for retirement in their early thirties like most sumotori. Due to the limited places at the top and the slow rate of attrition among high-ranking referees, some gyoji even end up holding the rank of "makunouchi level" or "juryo level" while actually handling juryo or makushita bouts.

The referees dress and receive salaries in accordance with their official rank. Just as only the sekitori are allowed to wear silk mawashi and the more elaborate style of topknot, only the gyoji ranked in the juryo and makunouchi levels are allowed to don silk costumes and wear tabi on their feet. Young referees officiating matches from the jonokuchi to makushita divisions wear cotton kimono and enter the ring barefoot. However, the last several bouts in the makushita division tend to be overseen by juryo-level referees decked out in silk and wearing tabi.

The gyoji costumes called *hitatare* date back around six hundred years to what was favored by the nobility of the Ashikaga period. In the mid-1980s, it cost around ¥15 million to outfit a gyoji newly promoted to the juryo level with one hitatare, a new paddle, tabi, and a pointed hat called *eboshi*.

While it is easy to distinguish, by costume alone, the sekitori-level referees from those in the lower ranks, a person must look more closely to tell a juryo-level gyoji from one officiating upper-division bouts. Those seeing black-and-white pictures of sumo

Makunouchi and juryo referees dressed in silk costumes and wearing tabi.

may have a hard time telling the difference at all, as the most visible distinction lies in the color of the rosettes on various parts of their costumes and the tassels hanging from their paddles. The rosettes and tassels of juryo-level referees are green and white; those of makunouchi-level gyoji are red and white. The rosettes and tassels used by lower-level referees are solid green. Black is also permitted for the lower-ranking referees, but seems to have fallen out of favor in recent times.

Further distinctions exist within the makunouchi ranks of gyoji. Those designated san'yaku level have solid red rosettes and tassels. They are allowed to wear straw sandals in addition to their tabi in the ring. But depending on the number of sumotori ranked in san'yaku in a particular tournament, these referees may or may not actually officiate any komusubi or sekiwake bouts.

Moreover, similar to the way only ozeki and yokozuna are permitted to have purple fringe on their decorative aprons, only the two highest ranking referees are allowed to use that color in their rosettes and tassels. Inosuke uses a combination of purple and white, while the supreme Shonosuke alone is permitted solid purple. These gradations date back to the Heian period, when purple held the highest position within a strict color-ranking system established by the imperial court.

Shonosuke and Inosuke ranks are called the tate-gyoji, meaning they are allowed to officiate yokozuna matches. (When there are four or more grand champions, one or two of such matches will inevitably by handled by the third-ranking referee.)

The two tate-gyoji are required to keep a dagger tucked into their obi as a constant reminder of the seriousness of their job. If a tate-gyoji is deemed to have made a misjudgment, he is expected to hand in his resignation immediately—a form of symbolic suicide. The letter of resignation is a mere formality and is usually not accepted. But there have been a few cases in the past in which the resignation was accepted because the Sumo Association was anxious to get rid of that particular referee. The most recent example occurred in January 1972, when Shonosuke XXV joined the judges' deliberations uninvited and even argued with them over their reversal of his decision. (A gyoji is not supposed to join the deliberations unless his opinion is expressly requested.)

Otherwise, once in the ring, the referee is virtually the master of it. Referees in the lower divisions get anywhere from five to twelve matches to officiate, depending on the number of both sumotori and fellow gyoji at the time. All juryo- and makunouchi-level referees handle two bouts each, with the exception of Kimura Shonosuke who oversees only the last match every day.

The referee begins the proceedings by pointing his paddle to the east and then to the west (or vice versa on even-numbered tourney days) to announce the names of the contenders. He directs the two fighters during the warm-up period and ultimately gives the signal for them to make their initial charge. If the tachiai is faulty in any way, he can stop the fight and order them to start over.

While the match is in progress, the referee repeatedly cries in a high-pitched voice, "Nokotta, Nokotta, Nokotta" to indicate that the two opponents are still in the ring. If the proceedings come to a standstill, with the two sumotori locked in a hold and neither able to get the upper or lower hand, the gyoji will yell out, "Hakkeyoi"—literally, "Put some spirit into it!" If the stalemate lasts for a couple of minutes, the referee may even halt the match temporarily to give the two rikishi a break for some water. Such water breaks are seldom seen nowadays. More likely to be viewed during the course of tournament is a gyoji stopping two rikishi at grips with each other to tighten their belts.

The referee must constantly keep his eyes on the action, and particularly the feet of the fighters, for he must turn his paddle to the winning side within a split second after one of them touches the ground or steps out of the ring. Occasionally a sharp-eyed gyoji will notice a sumotori's toe, for example, stepping out of the ring so briefly that neither he nor his opponent has even noticed it in the midst of their heated fight.

Sometimes the referee will accidentally turn his gunbai to the wrong side, or else change his mind, and quickly swing it around in the opposite direction. This procedure is called *mawashi-uchiwa*, literally "turning fan"—a term originating from the fact that gunbai were once used as samurai commanders' fans; they have assumed a stylized paddlelike shape in sumo.

The referee must turn the paddle to one of the sides in every match he officiates, even the ones in which the two opponents seem to have fallen or stepped out of the ring simultaneously, leaving no clear-cut winner. In such cases, the judges sitting around the ring usually climb into it to deliberate whether the referee was right, the match was too close to decide and should be done over, or the gyoji was wrong and the other man is the winner. It is only the "wrong decisions" that can adversely affect a referee's career.

Nevertheless, one unfortunate referee was pressured into taking a temporary "leave of absence," which became permanent, after he failed to make any decision at all in a bout in the late 1970s. Fudenosuke, a gyoji barely 150 centimeters tall, was knocked out of the ring in a match between Tamanofuji (now Kataonami Oyakata) and Arase (now a television personality) before he could see its conclusion, so the judges had to climb into the ring to tell him which way to turn his paddle.

Fudenosuke turned out to be suffering from a bad case of diabetes and had been unable to move swiftly enough to stay out of the behemoths' way. Although his name was kept on the ranking sheets, he never returned to the ring and died in 1983. This unfortunate incident made sumo officials all the more aware that physical as well as mental alertness is necessary in a referee. Thereafter, a physical fitness program was established for them.

Another job of some of the gyoji is to conduct the entrance into the ring ceremonies. In addition, every day during the break coming between the yokozuna dohyo-iri and the beginning of the upper-division matches, Kimura Shonosuke or Shikimori Inosuke reads the list of the following day's bouts.

Less visible is a young gyoji, dressed in everyday clothing, who announces over a microphone the name—and rank, if in san'yaku—of each rikishi mounting the ring for the dohyo-iri.

Another referee, wearing ordinary clothing, announces the names of the winners of matches over the stadium's public address system. Two announcer-gyoji work together to determine which technique was used to win the bout.

The referees, furthermore, keep records of wins and losses in a room called *wariba*. They are also required to write the ranking sheets and the Sumo Association calendar in the highly stylized characters. Most of the referees indeed have exquisite calligraphy and often handle official and unofficial letter-writing duties for the Sumo Association and coaches in their stables.

Match Announcers

As the literal meaning of the term yobidashi ("beckoners") indicates, the main duty of these men is to call the fighters into the ring. A yobidashi, dressed in a *tattsuke-bakama*, a traditional workman's outfit with kimono sleeves and tight leggings, does this by pointing his fan to the east side of the ring, while calling out higashi (east) and the name of the next fighter who will enter the ring on that side in a distinctively drawn-out, singsong voice. Then he points his fan to the west, and sings out nishi (west) followed by the opponent's name. (On the even-numbered days of the tournament he starts with the west side.)

Yet a yobidashi is more than a mere match announcer: he serves as a super handyman or jack-(as well as master)-of-all-trades around the ring. In fact, the ring in the stadium, as well as those in the sumo stables, is first of all built by a group of yobidashi before each tournament. During the tourney, the yobidashi, in addition to summoning the rikishi, sweep the ring and sprinkle it with water between matches, carry banners listing the names of the sponsors who have put money on a bout, and offer towels to the fighters.

Some of the yobidashi also clap wooden boards together before the entrance into the ring ceremonies and the last matches in the juryo and makunouchi divisions. The clappers are usually made of cherrywood, but each yobidashi chooses his preferred type of cherry tree as well as the section of it to make his own individual set. Zenzaburo, for instance, prefers a piece taken from the very inner core of a cherry tree with the reddest wood, which in his opinion produces the best sound.

On the Saturday prior to the opening of a tournament, the yobidashi are divided into small groups and sent around to various

Announcements of the following day's matches.

parts of town as well as to the stables to beat *fure-daiko* drums and announce the first day's line-up in the upper division. In addition, around 6 P.M. every day during a tourney one of these men beats a *yagura-taiko* (a drum on a tower right outside the stadium) to signify that the matches for the day have ended. Another yobidashi is stationed as liaison in the press club room inside the sumo stadium.

Some yobidashi also perform drumming demonstrations at sumo exhibitions and retirement ceremonies. Others both write and perform colorful songs about sumo life, famous sumotori, and the various spots visited on tour. When actually on the road, the yobidashi take charge of such duties as transporting equipment, setting up and taking down tents, and so forth. They also may take care of various random chores around the stable.

In other words, the yobidashi virtually never have a free moment. Their work is so variegated that probably none of them could actually describe it in full.

The yobidashi role, like that of the referee, is believed to have originated in the Heian period. At that time, the position was

Match announcers visit Takasago-Beya before the start of the tournament. Left, next to the drum, to right are Takamiyama, Fujizakura, and Ozeki Asashio.

called *fusho,* and its main duty was to announce the names of the fighters to the emperor. The job, in fact, was not always distinct from that of the gyoji in those times. The duties of the two became clearly separated only in the seventeenth century. The first record of the name yobidashi dates back to the early eighteenth century, and the term became fixed in the late nineteenth century.

Although the yobidashi have origins in common with the gyoji, they are not ranked on the banzuke-hyo like the referees. Actually, for a while in the nineteenth century, and again from May 1949 to January 1963, their names did appear on the ranking sheets—in the latter case mostly due to the efforts of Yobidashi Taro, a famous character who tried hard to raise the prestige of the position.

There is a hierarchy among the yobidashi, just like almost everything else in sumo. They are ranked into five classes similar to the gyoji; the ones in the lower grades serve as announcer for far more matches than those calling sekitori into the ring. Yet, although fresh-faced teenage yobidashi do announce the lowest level matches, seniority alone will not necessarily guarantee a man a position at the top. In other words, inevitably some particularly talented yobidashi reach the equivalent of "sekitori" level at an earlier age than others. Kankichi, for example, who is the yobidashi equivalent of the tate-gyoji handling the

Left, an announcer painting the starting lines of the ring. Right, an announcer on his tiptoes—ready to spring into action whenever the occasion demands.

yokozuna bouts, is three years younger than the eldest of his subordinates.

The mandatory retirement age for yobidashi is sixty-five—the same as that for referees. The Sumo Association has fixed the number of such positions at "not to exceed thirty-eight." As of May 1992, there were thirty-four yobidashi—less than the number of sumo stables. Given the increasing tendency toward establishing new stables in the 1980s and 1990s, which in effect means more dohyo to be built, it seems likely that the Association will eventually have to reconsider its quota on the superhandymen known as yobidashi.

Hairdressers

The chonmage, or topknot, has become the aesthetic symbol of professional sumotori—not to mention a source of considerable sexual appeal to women. Though some star players in other sports may not be so easily recognizable out of uniform, in sumo even a low-ranking apprentice can never disguise his profession as long as he has a topknot.

The men who arrange this precious symbol of sumo life are called *tokoyama*, a word which originally designated the specialized

*A hairdresser adjusting Chiyonofuji's chonmage
just before his tournament match.*

hairdressers for Kabuki. The chonmage was the normal male hairstyle in Japan during the Edo period. However, the Meiji Restoration
government issued an order in 1871 for Japanese men to cut off
their topknots and to adopt the more modern Western hairstyles.

An exception to this ruling was made for sumotori, who need
the extra hair to buffer their heads when absorbing the shock of a
hard fall. Yet, with the passing of time, the number of ordinary

barbers who could fix topknots decreased markedly. At first the sumo stables arranged for Kabuki hairdressers to help out occasionally, but eventually they came to have their own tokoyama.

Like everything else in sumo, there is a hierarchy to the tokoyama, who are ranked into six grades. The apprenticeship can be long (over ten years), and only tokoyama in the top two grades are allowed to dress a sekitori's hair into the more elaborate oicho-mage style of topknot. A hairdresser in the third rank may handle the oicho part of the way through.

Seven small instruments are used to put the elaborate oicho together and fan it out to resemble a gingko leaf. A skilled tokoyama can do the job within about fifteen minutes.

The quota of tokoyama positions was thirty-five until the mid-1980s; the number was expanded to forty-five in the wake of the increased number of sumo stables. As of May 1992, there were forty-four hairdressers. All are on the Sumo Association's payroll, but each, just like the referees and yobidashi, is affiliated with one of the stables. The mandatory retirement age for hairdressers is the same as that for yobidashi and gyoji: sixty-five.

Unfortunately, the distribution of the tokoyama can be far from even among the forty-four sumo-beya. Takasago-Beya, for example, had four hairdressers in 1989, while its affiliate Kokonoe-Beya had only two young, low-ranked tokoyama; and some stables have none at all. This does not matter so much in everyday life in the stables, for all sumotori, except the newest recruits who still have shortish hair, wear their locks in a simple topknot for practice. In stables without a hairdresser the apprentices straighten chonmage for each other and the sekitori (if there are any).

However, since an apprentice sumotori is even less qualified than low-ranked tokoyama to fix an oicho for sumo tournaments and exhibitions, stables with sekitori but without hairdressers usually borrow one from a heya in the same camp. An extreme example is Tokokatsu. After years of being on loan to Futagoyama-Beya from Hanaregoma-Beya (and originally from the now defunct Hanakago-Beya), he was finally officially transferred to Futagoyama-Beya in 1987. On the other hand, Kokonoe-Beya privately hired a veteran tokoyama out of retirement to fix the hair of its luminaries such as Chiyonofuji and Hokutoumi.

All tokoyama adopt names prefixed with Toko. Often the second half of the name is taken from part of their own real given or family name. For example, a man whose real name is Watanabe Kunio is known in the sumo world as Tokokuni, and Tanigawa Katsumi has become Tokotani. Sometimes the suffix may refer to the stable

*Ozeki Wakashimazu having his hair dressed
with the fragrant hair oil called bintsuke.*

in some way, such as Tokosado who is affiliated with Sadogatake-
Beya, or Tokotaka from Fujishima-Beya (which is headed by the
former Takanohana). Nevertheless, some of the naming seems to
be rather arbitrary—such as Tokomine, who hails from Miyagino-
Beya and whose real name is Kato Akira, or Futagoyama-Beya's
Tokokatsu, whose real name is Sumiya Koji.

Several of the tokoyama originally approached the sumo
world with the ambition of becoming a rikishi, but, unable to pass
the requirements for minimum weight, height, or both, took the
job as an alternative. Tokokatsu is one such example; however, his
dream of becoming a sumotori was passed on to his son, who
joined Futagoyama-Beya as a rikishi in 1988. A few other tokoyama,
such as Tokosado, were originally accepted for sumo but switched
to hairdressing after an injury or coming to the realization that
they lacked great fighting potential. Tokotani is unique—perhaps
surprisingly—in that he trained as a regular barber before joining
the sumo world.

14

Organization of the Sumo Association and Heya

The Nihon Sumo Kyokai, Japan Sumo Association, is a juridical foundation that oversees all matters pertaining to professional sumo. The organization is comprised of approximately twelve hundred people, including all the coaches or elders, sumotori, referees, wakaimono-gashira, sewanin, yobidashi, hairdressers, and about thirty-two general clerical workers. However, the decisive core consists of the coaches, the top two referees, and four sumotori representatives (usually yokozuna and ozeki) elected by the Rikishi-kai, an organization of sekitori.

At the very top of the hierarchy are up to ten *riji*, or directors of the board; three *kanji*, or supervisors; and two or three other executives, the *yakunin taigu*. The work of the Sumo Association is organized into seven divisions (Training, Personal Guidance, Operations, Judging, Out-of-Tokyo Tournaments, Performance Tours, and Security) and five committees or sections (Press Relations, the Training School for New Recruits [Sumo Kyoshujo], Physical Examination for New Recruits, Judging Public Injuries [Kosho Nintei], and Management of the Sumo Museum). All coaches have positions in at least one of these divisions or groups.

The post of *rijicho* (chairman or managing director) is usually filled by a former yokozuna. In February 1992, former Grand Champion Sadanoyama (Dewanoumi Oyakata) succeeded to the post after Wakanohana I (Futagoyama Oyakata) voluntarily stepped down. Four years earlier, Futagoyama had become rijicho when his rival from his days as an active sumotori, Tochinishiki (Kasugano Oyakata), voluntarily resigned, too. Kasugano, a former yokozuna, served as chairman of the Sumo Association from 1974 to 1988—the longest reign since the organization officially took the name Nihon Sumo Kyokai. His predecessor at the association's helm was the late Musashigawa, a former maegashira known for his business education—something rare in the sumo world. Like Musashigawa and Kasugano before him, Futagoyama Oyakata became director of the Sumo Museum upon stepping down as chairman of the Sumo Association, which he also serves as special adviser.

The Sumo Association's chairman and other executives are all ostensibly chosen in elections held after the January tournament every other year. However, since there is actually a fixed number of chairs alloted per *ichimon* (group of affiliate stables), the real selection process occurs within the groups, so that the candidates they put up automatically get elected. The only real balloting goes on for the supervisor positions.

The breakdown of riji by ichimon since 1986 has normally been two each for the Dewanoumi, Nishonoseki/Futagoyama, Takasago, Tokitsukaze, and Tatsunami/Isegahama camps. Prior to 1986, the Tatsunami/Isegahama ichimon had three riji and Takasago had only one. The allotment was adjusted in recognition of the growing importance of the Takasago ichimon and the decline of the Tatsunami group.

Sumo Stables

As of July 1992, there were forty-four sumo stables. Their number is expected to increase, as more ex-sumotori these days have been showing interest in opening their own heya.

There are reasons both for and against opening up one's own stable or succeeding to the leadership of an established one. First of all, the advantages are that the stablemaster, not the oyakata working under him, generally gets the credit and glory for raising strong sumotori. One coach, who opened his own stable in 1986, explained that it is "the only way to earn real respect." Needless to say, if a stable proves successful, the head coach will reap various financial benefits as well. It was estimated that Kokonoe Oyakata, for example, received about ¥40 million from the Sumo Association alone in 1989. Glory or money aside, some coaches truly enjoy training young sumotori.

On the other hand, it costs a lot of money to construct a new stable or to buy an already established one in Tokyo, where the land prices are undoubtedly the most expensive in the world. Most coaches simply cannot branch off without strong and continued financial support from their patrons. Even after the land and construction costs are paid off, until a sekitori is produced the outlay involved in running a stable and taking care of several hungry young behemoths can be higher than the income and stipends received from the Sumo Association.

The previous okamisan of Mihogaseki-Beya, who is also the mother of the present head coach, mentioned in an interview how in the stable's poorer days she used to carry salable items to a pawnshop in a baby buggy to prevent her neighbors from taking notice. The situation underwent a change for the better after Mihogaseki-Beya produced a sekitori in Dairyugawa. Later, with the advent of Yokozuna Kitanoumi, the stable was even able to reconstruct and modernize its quarters.

But not all stables are so fortunate, and running one can prove more than just a financial burden on the coach's family. Ozeki Kotogahama (Oguruma Oyakata) reportedly declined an offer to take over Sadogatake-Beya because it would have meant lack of privacy for his family and, moreover, too much extra work for his wife. He remained a coach with the stable until his death in 1981.

Running a stable can be a physical burden on the coach as well. Stables have been known to fold due to the poor finances or poor health of the stablemaster.

There also can be problems with the widow or heirs, or both, of the previous coach when succeeding to the leadership of an established stable. The Sumo Association has set regulations concerning who can become oyakata; but the heirs of a coach, whether a stablemaster or an assistant, have the right to choose among qualified bidders for the stock. Moreover, even though the Sumo Association may occasionally join in the negotiations a bit to see that the highest ranking bidder gets the stock, the heirs of a stablemaster still have the right to do as they please with the stable property. Several successors to stables in the past two decades have rebuilt the heya elsewhere because the widow of the previous coach either asked an unreasonable sum for the property or declined to sell it in the first place.

The Ichimon and Heya

Unlike baseball players, who are regularly traded among teams and are also allowed to become free agents to negotiate for contracts, a sumotori is expected to stay in the stable he chose to join. (Sumo does not have a drafting system like baseball.) The only exception is when a rikishi is allowed to follow the coach who scouted him into a new independent heya. Even then, the coach normally does not take along everyone he has brought into the parent stable. Usually the most amicable way to arrange a parting is for the coach who is branching off to take only comparatively new recruits with him and let the master of the parent stable keep all the sekitori—even the ones discovered by the former. Sometimes, when the parting is not so amicable, the Sumo Association ends up intervening to decide which rikishi must stay with the old stable and which can transfer to the new one.

In the past, rikishi from the same ichimon were not pitted against each other in a tournament. The regulations were changed in 1965 so that only sumotori from the same stable do not fight each other. Therefore, after a coach breaks off to set up a new heya, sometimes men who had formerly been stablemates in the parent stable will suddenly find themselves facing each other in tournament bouts.

Even though the bonds within the ichimon are, thus, not as strong as they used to be, they still carry weight in matters beyond just the distribution of the Sumo Association's board members. For example, when a sumotori has a wedding ceremony or a party to celebrate promotion to ozeki or yokozuna, he is expected to invite all the sekitori and coaches in his camp of stables. Likewise, all oyakata and sekitori from the ichimon are expected to attend or at least send their formal regrets. They must also attend the funeral of someone in their group or send wreaths if on the road. Members of the ichimon also help make a yokozuna cord for a grand champion. A makunouchi member of the same group may even flank a yokozuna during his dohyo-iri, when the latter's heya is short of qualified rikishi. Furthermore, when a serious problem such as a succession dispute arises, the elders from the same ichimon usually try to settle it before the highest authorities in the Sumo Association intervene.

The five ichimon and the heya in them are outlined in the following section.

Dewanoumi Ichimon

Dewanoumi-Beya was founded by Dewanoumi, a makunouchi rikishi of the late eighteenth century. The great Yokozuna

Hitachiyama made it into an important stable after his retirement from the ring in 1914. As the fifth Dewanoumi Oyakata, former Hitachiyama trained three grand champions (Onishiki Uichiro, Tochigiyama, and Tsunenohana) and had two hundred sumotori under his tutelage at the stable's peak. Dewanoumi-Beya has remained a leading stable, producing five ensuing grand champions, and has been a powerful presence in the Sumo Association ever since.

More than any other ichimon, Dewanoumi has tended not to permit branching off. After the death of the seventh Dewanoumi Oyakata (former Tsunenohana) in 1960, ex-Yokozuna Chiyonoyama expected to take over the stable. Since it was decided that he, at age thirty-three, was too young for the responsibility, Musashigawa Oyakata (ex-Maegashira Dewanohana) became what was supposed to be the interim head of the stable. After Yokozuna Sadanoyama married Musashigawa's daughter, Chiyonoyama saw his hopes of becoming the Dewanoumi-Beya oyakata dashed and asked to form his own independent Kokonoe-Beya. The permission was granted only on the condition that he would leave the Dewanoumi camp. He left in February 1967, taking Ozeki (later yokozuna) Kitanofuji and nine others with him. Kokonoe-Beya since then has been part of the Takasago Ichimon. The sekitori in Dewanoumi-Beya in July 1992 were Ryogoku, Kushimaumi, Oginohana, Mainoumi, Oginishiki, and Tsunenoyama.

Kasugano-Beya is believed to have been originally founded by a mid-eighteenth-century sumotori named Kasugano Gunpachi. It was inactive for a number of decades, as there were no successors to it. In the Meiji period, a referee, Kimura Soshiro, became the stablemaster—a practice no longer allowed. Kimura adopted as his son Yokozuna Tochigiyama, who was permitted to leave Dewanoumi-Beya and become the eighth Kasugano Oyakata. Tochigiyama, in turn, adopted Yokozuna Tochinishiki who, upon the death of the former in 1959, became the ninth Kasugano Oyakata while still an active grand champion. (*Nimai-kansatsu,* or serving in two capacities, is another practice which is no longer permitted.)

Nakadachi Oyakata (former Tochinoumi) of Kasugano-Beya was the only former yokozuna from the past two decades who did not succeed promptly to the leadership of a stable, whether an old established or a newly independent one. However, after more than twenty years as an assistant coach, he took over when former Tochinishiki died in January 1990. The sekitori in July 1992 were Tochinowaka, Tochinofuji, and Tochitenko.

Mihogaseki-Beya was established in Osaka in the 1760s. After relocating in Tokyo in 1927, it became a rather tiny stable for a long while. Former Ozeki Masuiyama I became the eighth Mihogaseki Oyakata in 1950. After nearly two decades of struggle, he managed to develop some sekitori including the great Yokozuna Kitanoumi and his own son, Ozeki Masuiyama II, who became the ninth Mihogaseki in 1986. Higonoumi, a former collegiate champion, was its only sekitori in July 1992.

Musashigawa-Beya was formed in 1981 by the former Yokozuna Mienoumi, who was permitted to branch off from Dewanoumi. Sekitori in July 1992 were Musashimaru and Wakanoyama.

Kitanoumi-Beya was established in 1985 by the former Yokozuna Kitanoumi, who branched off from Mihogaseki-Beya.

Tamanoi-Beya was founded in 1990, by former Sekiwake Tochiazuma, who branched off from Kasugano-Beya.

Nishonoseki/Futagoyama Ichimon

This ichimon is perhaps the most complicated to explain, as it has been the most receptive to the creation of branch stables.

Nishonoseki-Beya was established in the late eighteenth century around the same time as Dewanoumi-Beya, but it was inactive for a while. It was reestablished in 1918 and enjoyed a golden age in the 1930s under the leadership of Tamanishiki, who was still an active grand champion. After Tamanishiki's untimely death in 1938, Sekiwake Tamanoumi I (later a sumo commentator) took over the stable for a while; he trained Komusubi Kotonishiki and Sekiwake Tamanoumi II, both of whom established their own independent stables, and Sekiwake Rikidozan, who later became a pro wrestler.

Tamanoumi I was succeeded by Saganohana who, as the eighth Nishonoseki Oyakata, produced Yokozuna Taiho, Ozeki Daikirin, and other sekitori. After Saganohana's death in 1975, an interim stablemaster was appointed. However, later that year Saganohana's widow arranged the engagement of her second daughter to one-time Sekiwake Kongo, who retired in 1976, at age twenty-seven, to take over the stable. The daughter ran out on Kongo before he could register the marriage officially, so the widow adopted Kongo as her foster son. Thus, the woman who was supposed to be Kongo's wife has ended up as his stepsister. The stable's only sekitori in July 1992 was Daizen.

Yokozuna Taiho left Nishonoseki-Beya in 1971 to open his own Taiho-Beya near the garden-park of Kiyosumi Teien in Koto-ku, a short taxi or bus ride from Ryogoku. The retirement of Ozutsu left it with no sekitori in July 1992. Kitanoumi-Beya is now located just down the street—perhaps an interesting coincidence that two of the greatest grand champions since the end of World War II have set up new stables so close to each other.

Oshiogawa-Beya was established in October 1975 by former Ozeki Daikirin, who left Nishonoseki-Beya in a fairly hostile succession dispute. The former ozeki expected to take over the stable after Saganohana's death, but he and the latter's widow could not agree on the financial arrangements for the property. After Kongo's engagement to Saganohana's daughter was announced, Oshiogawa Oyakata realized there was no hope of becoming the head of Nishonoseki, so he broke off. He was followed by some sympathetic sekitori, like Aobajo and Tenryu, but Nishonoseki-Beya protested this loss. The Sumo Association finally intervened to settle the dispute. It agreed to recognize the independence of Oshiogawa-Beya, as long as Tenryu and a few others were returned to Nishonoseki. Aobajo was allowed to stay with Oshiogawa. Tenryu, unhappy about being forced back to Nishonoseki, quit sumo a year later and went into pro wrestling. Oshiogawa-Beya sekitori in July 1992 were Enazakura, Saganobori, and Hitachiryu.

Sadogatake-Beya was opened in 1955 by former Komusubi Kotonishiki, who took Sekiwake Kotogahama (later promoted to ozeki) with him when he branched off from Nishonoseki-Beya. Yokozuna Kotozakura had been preparing to break off from Sadogatake to set up a new stable in 1974, when the head coach suddenly died. Kotozakura became the master of Sadogatake shortly after his own retirement from the ring and has since made it into one of the largest stables. Its sekitori in July 1992 were Kotogaume, Kotoinazuma, Kotofuji, Kotonishiki, Kototsubaki, Kotonowaka, and Kotobeppu.

Former Ozeki Kotokaze broke off amicably from Sadogatake-Beya to open his own Oguruma-Beya in 1987.

Kataonami-Beya was established by former Sekiwake Tamanoumi II, who went independent from Nishonoseki in 1962 and took seventeen rikishi, including Tamanoshima (later Yokozuna Tamanoumi). As Tamanoumi II was approaching the mandatory retirement age, he had already made arrangements for former Sekiwake Tamanofuji to succeed him. So when Tamanoumi II suddenly died on the last day of the September tournament in 1987, Tamanofuji's succession to the stable's helm went smoothly. This stable seems to have a tradition of career women for the okamisan. Tamanoumi's second wife was a professional singer and teacher of traditional Japanese music; Tamanofuji's wife is the president of a trading company specializing in marine products. Kataonami-Beya's only sekitori in July 1992 was Tamakairiki.

Futagoyama-Beya was set up in 1962 by Yokozuna Wakanohana I, who had branched off from the now defunct Hanakago-Beya. Hanakago Oyakata (formerly Onoumi) originally took then Maegashira Wakanohana with him when he branched off from Nishonoseki in 1953 to establish the first stable in Tokyo's residential Suginami Ward. Two years after Wakanohana converted his home near the Minami Asagaya subway station into Futagoyama-Beya, the stable produced its first sekitori, and later komusubi, Futagodake. The stable proceeded to bring up Ozeki Takanohana (the coach's own youngest brother), grand champions Wakanohana II and Takanosato, and Ozeki Wakashimazu. The retirement of Wakashimazu in July 1987 left Futagoyama-Beya without anyone in san'yaku for the first time in over fifteen years. But Daijuyama returned to the sekiwake rank in 1988, and Misugisato became komusubi in January 1989. Futagoyama sekitori, as of July 1992, were Takamisugi, Misugisato, Wakashoyo, and Naminohana.

Fujishima-Beya was opened in 1982 by former Ozeki Takanohana, the youngest brother of Futagoyama Oyakata. It produced two sekitori in 1987, Akinoshima and Takanohama (now Toyonoumi), and later Takatoriki, Takanonami, as well as Takahanada and Wakahanada (Takanohana's two sons who joined the stable in 1988). Since Futagoyama-Beya now lacks a strong successor, it may possibly merge with Fujishima-Beya upon Futagoyama Oyakata's retirement in 1993.

Magaki-Beya was established in 1984 by former Yokozuna Wakanohana II, who for about a year and a half was Futagoyama Oyakata's son-in-law. Just before he retired from the ring in 1983, Wakanohana II divorced the coach's daughter and later that year married his longtime club hostess girlfriend. Unlike the previous Hanakago-Futagoyama offshoots before it, Magaki-Beya is located in sumo's traditional Ryogoku heartland. Wakatosho became its first sekitori in July 1992.

Former Yokozuna Takanosato broke off amicably from Futagoyama-Beya to open his own Naruto-Beya in February 1989, the first stable to be located in Matsudo, Chiba Prefecture.

Hanaregoma-Beya was set up by ex-Ozeki Kaiketsu, who branched off from Hanakago in 1981, just before Yokozuna Wajima married the coach's daughter and became Hanakago Oyakata. In its heyday Hanakago-Beya produced two yokozuna and ozeki each as well as several other san'yaku rikishi. Once it had as many as six men in the top division, but under Wajima the stable declined to the point where it did not have anyone in makunouchi for a while. Hanaregoma-Beya, in the meantime, produced a fine sekitori in Onokuni (later a grand champion).

Wajima lacked leadership qualities and was also the only head coach to live away from his stable and commute to it. He was temporarily demoted from a sumo judging position after his wife tried to commit suicide in 1982. In 1985, he was pressured by the elders of the Nishonoseki/Futagoyama camp to resign from the Sumo Association altogether after it was revealed that he was heavily in debt and had put up his Hanakago stock as collateral on a loan. (It is against the Sumo Association regulations to pass on toshiyori-kabu to anyone outside the sumo world.) Since an appropriate successor to Hanakago could not be found, it was totally absorbed by Hanaregoma-Beya. Wajima was, thereafter, divorced by his wife and became a pro wrestler to pay off his debts. The only Hanaregoma-Beya sekitori in July 1992 was Hananokuni. Hanakago-Beya is being rebuilt by Daijuyama of Futagoyama-Beya and will open in late 1992.

In December 1988, former Maegashira Misugiiso amicably departed from Hanaregoma-Beya to set up Minezaki-Beya in the Nerima ward of Tokyo. In January 1989, Misugiiso's younger brother joined the stable.

Early in 1990, former Ozeki Wakashimazu broke off amicably from Futagoyama-Beya to open his own Matsugane-Beya.

Takasago/Kokonoe Ichimon

Takasago-Beya was established in 1878 by Takasago Uragoro, who had led a movement to reform the payment system for sumotori after they lost their daimyo patrons. He was temporarily dismissed from the Tokyo Sumo Association. After being allowed back, he produced grand champions Nishinoumi I and Konishiki as well as three ozeki and came to wield great power in the organization. The fifth Takasago Oyakata (former Yokozuna Asashio) died of a stroke in October 1988, not long after a dispute with Samoan-born sekitori Nankairyu prompted the latter to leave the sumo world. Former Komusubi Fujinishiki thereupon succeeded to the helm of the stable. In May 1986, Takasago-Beya absorbed the small Oyama-Beya, which did not have any sekitori, upon the death of its stablemaster (former Ozeki Matsunobori). Takasago-Beya's sekitori in July 1992 were Konishiki, Mitoizumi, and Kumao.

Takadagawa-Beya was set up in 1974 by former Ozeki Maenoyama, who branched off from Takasago. Its sekitori in July 1992 were Kiraiho and Kenko.

In early 1986, the Hawaiian-born former Sekiwake Takamiyama was granted permission to go independent from Takasago and set up his own Azumazeki-Beya. In March 1990, Akebono (Chad Rowan) became a sekitori.

Later in 1986, Fujizakura, another former sekiwake from Takasago, left to establish Nakamura-Beya. It had not produced any sekitori by July 1992.

Wakamatsu-Beya dates back to around 1815, but it did not produce a makunouchi rikishi until some fifty years later. It enjoyed a golden age in the Taisho period. However, after a succession dispute, it was taken over in 1926 by Irimigawa, formerly of Takasago-Beya, who later adopted Maegashira Shachinosato as his son. Shachinosato, in turn, married his daughter off to Sekiwake Fusanishiki, who served as the eleventh Wakamatsu Oyakata. The former Fusanishiki resigned from the Sumo Association because of poor health in 1990 and passed the stable over to ex-Ozeki Asashio of Takasago-Beya. It had no sekitori in July 1992.

The Takasago ichimon has benefited considerably by letting Kokonoe-Beya into its camp when Chiyonoyama was forced to leave the Dewanoumi group in 1967. After Chiyonoyama died in 1977, leaving no strong successor in Kokonoe-Beya, his former prize pupil, ex-Yokozuna Kitanofuji, was asked to take over. Kitanofuji gladly assumed the Kokonoe name, amalgamated his Izutsu-Beya with Kokonoe, and gave up the Izutsu title. In 1987, Kokonoe-Beya became the first stable since Takasago-Beya in 1948 to have two yokozuna simultaneously: Chiyonofuji and Hokutoumi. Chiyonofuji became Kokonoe Oyakata in April 1992. The stable's only sekitori in July 1992 was Tomoefuji.

Tokitsukaze Ichimon

Tokitsukaze is originally the name of a stable founded in Osaka in 1769. It enjoyed a golden era during the Taisho period. However, after the sumo associations in Osaka and Tokyo were amalgamated, Tokitsukaze declined into a small heya with a bad reputation. The great Futabayama moved out of Tatsunami-Beya to assume the leadership of Tokitsukaze in 1941 when he was still an active yokozuna. After Futabayama's death in 1968, former Yokozuna Kagamisato assumed leadership of the stable for a while. But in 1969, he was asked by Futabayama's widow to relinquish the Tokitsukaze name to ex-Ozeki Yutakayama, the first former college champion to reach professional sumo's second-highest rank. Tokitsukaze-Beya's sekitori in July 1992 were Tokitsunada, Daigaku, Aogiyama, and Yutakafuji.

Tatsutagawa-Beya dates back to the mid-eighteenth century and was an important stable in Tanikaze's times. It later became inactive but was reestablished in 1971 by former Kagamisato after he left Tokitsukaze-Beya. Upon reaching the mandatory retirement age in April 1988, Kagamisato transferred the stable's leadership to ex-Sekiwake Aonosato. One of Aonosato's sons joined the stable in 1988. Tatsutagawa-Beya had no sekitori in July 1992.

Minato-Beya was established in 1982 by Komusubi Yutakayama, a former member of Tokitsukaze-Beya. He, like that stablemaster, is a graduate of Tokyo Agricultural University. Because of the academic inclinations of Minato Oyakata, this stable was the first one to set up a reading room on its premises. It had one sekitori in July 1992: Minatofuji.

Isenoumi-Beya dates back to the mid-eighteenth century. It produced Yokozuna Tanikaze in the late 1700s and a number of other sumo greats. This heya developed a tradition of passing on the leadership to a sekitori named Kashiwado. However, as the previous stablemaster (ex-Maegashira Kashiwado) was still somewhat young and in good health when Yokozuna Kashiwado retired, the latter branched off to found a different stable in 1970. The present stablemaster, former Sekiwake Fujinokawa, took over Isenoumi-Beya in 1982. The name Fujinokawa was passed on to Hattori, who had joined professional sumo after capturing a record, at that time, of seventeen titles in amateur and collegiate sumo. But he turned out to be very injury prone and never went beyond the maegashira rank. Although Hattori, still in his mid-twenties, was qualified to become an oyakata, he decided to quit the sumo world altogether and seek a new profession in 1987. The only Isenoumi-Beya sekitori in July 1992 was Kitakachidoki.

Kagamiyama-Beya was opened by ex-Yokozuna Kashiwado in 1970. In September 1984, Tagaryu, a maegashira and later sekiwake in the stable, captured the championship in the last tourney held in the Kuramae Kokugikan. The only other Kagamiyama sekitori in July 1992 was Kirinishiki.

Izutsu-Beya dates back to the mid-eighteenth century, but it did not really come into the spotlight until Nishinoumi I became its sixth master. He produced Nishinoumi II and several other san'yaku. Nishinoumi II, as the seventh Izutsu Oyakata, in turn produced Nishinoumi III, Ozeki Toyokuni, and other sekitori. After the death of the ninth Izutsu Oyakata (ex-Maegashira Tsurugamine), former Maegashira Hoshikabuto briefly assumed leadership of the stable; however, after some difficulties with the previous coach's widow, he left to found another stable.

Former Sekiwake Tsurugamine also coveted the Izutsu stock, but he too was unable to reach an agreement with the widow; for a while, he set up his own Kimigahama-Beya. The Izutsu stock was then sold to Kitanofuji of the Takasago Ichimon. But, after taking over Kokonoe-Beya, Kitanofuji traded the Izutsu stock for the Kimigahama stock held by Tsurugamine. Thereupon, Kimigahama-Beya was renamed Izutsu-Beya. (Kimigahama is now the name of a coach in Kokonoe-Beya.) Izutsu Oyakata's three sons, Sakahoko, Terao, and Tsurunofuji, have been members of this stable; the former two are in the top division. The other sekitori in July 1992 were Kirishima and Sasshunada who hail from Kyushu, the coach's native prefecture of Kagoshima.

Michinoku-Beya was established by Hoshikabuto in 1974 after he returned the Izutsu stock to his former stablemaster's widow. Upon reaching the mandatory retirement age in 1991, the former Hoshikabuto passed the stable on to ex-Maegashira Hoshiiwato. In September 1992, Hoshitango of Argentina was promoted to juryo, and Hoshiandesu was approaching that rank.

In spring 1989, former Maegashira Daiyu and his own sumotori son left Michinoku-Beya to set up Kabutoyama-Beya.

Shikihide-Beya was founded in May 1992 by former Komusubi Oshio, who branched off from Tokitsukaze-Beya.

Tatsunami/Isegahama Ichimon

Tatsunami-Beya was founded in 1876 by a makunouchi sumotori named Onigazaki. The fourth Tatsunami Oyakata (former Komusubi Midorijima) led it to its first days of glory when it had Yokozuna Futabayama and Haguroyama as well as Ozeki Nayoriiwa under its wing. Haguroyama married the coach's daughter and succeeded to the leadership of the stable. He brought Tatsunami-Beya to another golden age by producing Ozeki Wakahaguro as well as Sekiwake Kitanonada, Tokitsuyama, and Annen'yama.

Annen'yama married the coach's daughter and was later granted the name Haguroyama. Upon his father-in-law's death in

1969, he inherited the stable as well as Asahikuni and Kuro-himeyama, who became ozeki and sekiwake, respectively, in the 1970s. Yet for a couple of years in the 1980s the once glorious Tatsunami-Beya was without any men in the top division and without any sekitori at all for a while. Kitao (later Yokozuna Futah-aguro) finally arose to fill that gap in 1984, but he was forced to resign from the sumo world at the end of 1987. Tatsunami-Beya later produced Sekitori Daishoyama in 1990, and Daishoho and Tatsuhikari in 1991.

Oshima-Beya was set up early in 1980 by former Ozeki Asahikuni, who had a rather hostile parting from Tatsunami-Beya. Although Asahikuni did not take any high-ranking sumotori with him, Tatsunami Oyakata still was very opposed to his going independent. The two coaches apparently did not even speak to each other until Oshima-Beya's Asahifuji was promoted to ozeki in September 1987. The stable's sekitori in July 1992 were Kyokudozan, Kyokugozan, and Asahizato.

Isegahama-Beya was founded in 1859 by former Komusubi Arakuma. The sixth Isegahama Oyakata was former Yokozuna Terukuni, who married the daughter of the fifth stablemaster (ex-Sekiwake Kiyosegawa). Since Terukuni, prior to his death in 1977, had already designated former Ozeki Kiyokuni as his succes-sor, the leadership transition went smoothly. However, Terukuni's widow did not want to sell her property, so a new heya was built in another part of Tokyo. Isegahama's wife and children were killed in the Japan Airlines' airplane crash of August 1985 (the biggest single plane accident at that time). He later remarried and relocated his stable. Isegahama-Beya's only sekitori in July 1992 was Wakasegawa.

Tomozuna-Beya was set up in 1892 by former Maegashira Kaizan of Osaka-zumo. It is one of the most inbred stables. Its current head coach is former Sekiwake Kaiki. The previous stable-master was ex-Juryo Ichinishiki, and the one before that was former Komusubi Tomoegata. (They both married daughters of the eighth head of the stable.) Thus, the ninth and tenth men to lead Tomozuna-Beya were brothers-in-law. Kaiki, in turn, married Ichinishiki's daughter. The stable's only sekitori in July 1992 were Tachihikari and Kaio.

Miyagino-Beya was founded by Miyagino Kinnosuke at around the beginning of the nineteenth century. This stable is said to have a tradition of picking fair-skinned, good-looking men as its leaders; this is perhaps best exemplified by former Yoshibayama, the eighth Miyagino Oyakata. During his heyday, Yoshibayama produced several sekitori. They include Sekiwake Myobudani and Mutsuarashi as well as Komusubi Hirokawa who, with his delicate fair skin and round face, was said to look like a sumo doll. Hirokawa became stablemaster after Yoshibayama's death in 1977. After Hirokawa's death in June 1989, this stable was taken over by former Maegashira Chikubayama. It had no sekitori as of July 1992.

Former Sekiwake Mutsuarashi married Yoshibayama's daughter, and for a while seemed the heir apparent to Miyagino-Beya. However, the couple got divorced just after Mutsuarashi's topknot-cutting ceremony in early 1977. Mutsuarashi thereupon moved to Tomozuna-Beya for about two years and then opened his own Ajigawa-Beya in 1979. Ironically, he later remarried his former wife, but by that time it was too late to take over Miyagino-Beya. Ajigawa has yet to produce a sekitori on its own, but it inherited Kasugafuji from Kasugayama-Beya when the latter folded upon the stablemaster's retirement at age sixty-five.

Kise-Beya's official name is actually Kimura Sehei-Beya. Originally led by top gyoji Kimura Shonosuke, it has a complicated history with the leadership passing back and forth between referees and retired sumotori. Its ninth master, former Maegashira Katsuragawa, resigned from the Sumo Association in good health in 1967 to devote more time to kendo; at that time, he passed the stable leadership to his son-in-law, ex-Maegashira Kiyonomori. Both Kiyonomori and his father-in-law hold the dubious record of chalking up fifteen straight losses in one of their tourneys in the top division. The stable remains unique in that it is open not only for sumo practice to amateurs as well as professionals but for kendo and other martial arts training as well. It had no sekitori in July 1992.

Asahiyama-Beya was founded around 1770 and originally flourished in Osaka. Since the sixteenth master of this stable (ex-Sekiwake Futasegawa) died fairly young, his successor (former Maegashira Futaseyama) tried to make it a little livelier by bringing some Tongans into the stable as sumotori. But he himself died in his fifties in 1975; and the Tongans got entangled in a succession dispute between his widow and his successor (former Komusubi Wakafutase), which they probably did not fully comprehend.

It seems that Wakafutase could not afford to buy the Asahiyama stock outright but had already made an agreement with Futaseyama's widow to rent it and the stable for five years for a hefty sum of money. The widow tried to renege on the agreement when a better offer was made by Ryuo, a one-time maegashira from the stable who had fallen into the makushita division. The Sumo Association intervened to see that the promise to Wakafutase was kept. However, the stable property, of course, was the widow's. Five of the six Tongans, who had regarded her as their sort of surrogate mother in Japan, refused to leave her to follow the new coach. (The sixth Tongan was in the hospital recovering from a broken bone at the time.) The Sumo Association ultimately dismissed them all, though the one in the hospital was never really questioned about his intentions. Ryuo, unable to acquire any stock of his own, left the sumo world altogether in 1976 and set up a couple of restaurants specializing in chanko-nabe and Okinawan food. Asahiyama-Beya had no sekitori in July 1992.

Onaruto-Beya was founded by former Sekiwake Kotetsuyama, who branched off from Asahiyama-Beya in 1975. The coach's wife is a ballet instructor and is not around the stable as much as other okamisan. The stable had no sekitori in July 1992.

Kumagatani-Beya originally dates back to the mid-eighteenth century, but it went out of existence for a while. It was established in its current form by former Maegashira Yoshinomine, who branched off from Tomozuna-Beya in 1978 because his son had entered sumo and he wanted to take full responsibility for training him. When Takashima-Beya folded in 1982, due to the poor health of the head coach (former Ozeki Mitsuneyama), Kumagatani-Beya inherited a handful of sumotori, including one-time Sekiwake Koboyama. Yoshinobori, trained only by Kumagatani himself, was its only sekitori in July 1992.

15

Present Sumotori

One of the inevitable perils of writing a book on sumo is that some of the information will already be outdated by the time of publication. Yet, since sumo is a living sport, this book would lose some of its worth as a guide without an introduction to at least the leading figures in sumo at the time of its writing.

Listed on the ranking sheets for the Natsu Basho held in May 1992 were one yokozuna, two ozeki, two sekiwake, and four komusubi. However, though on the banzuke, Yokozuna Hokutoumi announced his retirement prior to the opening of the tourney, and Akebono was officially promoted to ozeki after it.

Below are brief profiles of active sumotori who were in san'yaku in recent years as well as a few others who can be expected to reach such a rank in the near future—perhaps by the time this book is published. Please forgive me if some of these predictions turn out to be off the mark.

The following data appears after the respective numbers, followed by a brief personal comment. Unless otherwise noted, the personal name part of the sumotori's ring name is the same as his actual given name. Except for the deletion of Hokutoumi and Akebono's listing as ozeki, the ranks appear as they were in the 1992 Natsu Basho:

(1) Real name
(2) Heya
(3) Height, weight
(4) Birthdate
(5) Hometown
(6) Professional debut
(* indicates debut in makushita)

(7) Marital status   (8) Number of yusho
(9) Awards   (10) Favored techniques

Ozeki Konishiki Yasokichi

(1) Salevaa Atisanoe   (2) Takasago
(3) 187 cm., 264 kilos   (4) December 30, 1963
(5) Oahu, Hawaii   (6) July 1982
(7) Married   (8) 3
(9) 4 Shukunsho, 5 Kantosho,   (10) tsukioshi
     1 Ginosho

The first man of completely foreign birth and parentage to become ozeki, Konishiki is also the heaviest sumotori on record. His hobbies are disco dancing, trumpet playing, and listening to music. He rents a garage which he uses as a private gymnasium for working out with weights, barbells, and other athletic equipment. His original ambition was to become a lawyer, and he was also offered a music scholarship to Syracuse University. In his spare time, he studies the piano and Spanish, because "there are a lot of Hispanics in the United States." Konishiki has eight sisters and brothers, one of whom became a pro wrestler. In 1992, he married a former fashion model from Hokkaido and applied for Japanese citizenship.

Ozeki Kirishima Kazuhiro

(1) Yoshinaga Kazumi   (2) Izutsu
(3) 187 cm., 127 kilos   (4) April 3, 1959
(5) Makizono-cho,   (6) March 1975
     Kagoshima Pref.
(7) Married, one child   (8) 1
(9) 3 Shukunsho, 1 Kantosho,   (10) hidariyotsu, uwatenage,
     4 Ginosho   yori

As one the lightest members of the top division for a long time, Kirishima quickly became famous for his handling of heavyweights like Onokuni and Konishiki. In fact, he remained Konishiki's number-one nemesis for years until Akinoshima took over that honor. As if normal sumo practice were not enough to maintain his fine musculature, Kirishima also works out with barbells and weights at a private gymnasium. In the year prior to becoming ozeki, he made special efforts to gain weight by eating several bananas a day and drinking a high-calorie, high-protein drink concocted by his wife, Naoko, before retiring every night. Kirishima is known to be particularly devoted to his wife, and often brings her along to out-of-Tokyo tournaments and on jungyo. One of the best-looking rikishi, he was introduced as the "Alain Delon of sumo" during the performance in Paris in 1986.

Ozeki Akebono Taro

(1) Chadwick Rowan	(2) Azumazeki
(3) 204 cm., 200 kilos	(4) May 8, 1969
(5) Oahu, Hawaii	(6) March 1988
(7) Single	(8) 1
(9) 4 Shukunsho, 2 Kantosho	(10) tsukioshi, migiyotsu, yori

Akebono, the second non-Asian ozeki, made the rank in a record twenty-four tournaments from jonokuchi. Indeed, his progress through the ranks has been so fast that it is almost hard to believe that his stablemaster initially did not want to accept him because of his long legs, which are generally viewed as a disadvantage in sumo. Having never seen snow before coming to Japan, Chad adjusted to Tokyo winters by reminding himself that hundreds of other young sumotori were getting up early in the morning in the cold just like himself. While he did not like the sumo diet so much at first, he now prefers chanko-nabe to steak. Although Chad never studied Japanese formally, he has became quite conversant by picking up what he could learn from living in the heya and from watching samurai dramas on television. For relaxation, Akebono listens to all kinds of music—even classical.

Sekiwake Tochinowaka

(1) Kaseda Kiyotaka	(2) Kasugano
(3) 190 kilos, 146 kilos	(4) May 22, 1962
(5) Shimozu-cho, Wakayama Pref.	(6) March 1985*
(7) Single	(8) 0
(9) 2 Shukunsho, 3 Kantosho, 1 Ginosho	(10) hidariyotsu, oshi, yori

Tochinowaka is the first graduate of Meiji University to succeed in professional sumo. He was once runner-up in the national collegiate yokozuna competition, yet he is proving to be more successful than the person who took that title (Hattori, who quit professional sumo in 1987). In July 1987, Tochinowaka and Ryogoku became the first rivals from college days to be promoted simultaneously to a san'yaku position. His ambition in junior high school was to become a professional baseball player, but by high school he was getting a bit too heavy for baseball and so he switched to sumo. His grandmother was a sumo fan and named him Kiyotaka after the great Yokozuna Tochinishiki Kiyotaka, Tochinowaka's previous stablemaster in Kasugano-Beya. Injuries prevented Tochinowaka from making his expected drive toward ozeki promotion in 1988 and again in 1992.

Komusubi Akinoshima Katsumi

(1) Yamanaka Katsumi   (2) Fujishima
(3) 176 cm., 140 kilos   (4) March 16, 1967
(5) Akitsu-machi,   (6) March 1982
    Hiroshima Pref.
(7) Single   (8) 0
(9) 5 Shukunsho, 5 Kantosho, (10) migiyotsu, yori
    1 Ginosho

Akinoshima has been known for his diligence about training since he was in the lowest divisions, so nobody was surprised when he became Fujishima-Beya's first sekitori. Though a bit on the short side, he has fine legs and hips for sumo and a fairly well-rounded technique. Moreover, Akinoshima, at his father's behest, started practicing both sumo and judo as a young boy. Since he hails from the same hometown as the champion women's golfer Okamoto Ayako, he says he is determined to catch up with her in fame. Akinoshima defeated three ozeki and one yokozuna in his first tournament (September 1988) facing all the san'yaku. He currently holds the all-time kinboshi record and remains Konishiki's number-one nemesis. His hobbies are listening to popular music, going to horse races, and watching videotapes. He does not drink liquor.

Komusubi Mitoizumi

(1) Koizumi Masahito   (2) Takasago
(3) 195 cm., 183 kilos   (4) September 2, 1962
(5) Mito, Ibaragi Pref.   (6) March 1978
(7) Single   (8) 1
(9) 1 Shukunsho, 6 Kantosho (10) migiyotsu, yorikiri,
                                  oshidashi, kotenage

Although Mitoizumi's technique is far from polished, his fighting spirit is one of the greatest among the sekitori. Unfortunately, he has been plagued with a series of injuries since he was in the lower ranks. As his father died while he was a schoolboy, Mitoizumi joined sumo in part to ease the financial strains on his mother. He was discovered in a department store by Jesse Takamiyama. His younger brother, Umenosato, later entered Takasago-Beya as well. Mitoizumi is a real crowd pleaser for the huge handfuls of salt he throws during the shikiri. He also has a reputation as one of the greatest eaters in sumo today.

Komusubi Kotonishiki Katsuhiro
(1) Matsuzawa Hideyuki   (2) Sadogatake
(3) 177 cm., 140 kilos   (4) June 8, 1968
(5) Misato-machi, Gunma Pref. (6) March 1984
(7) Married, one child   (8) 0
(9) 4 Shukunsho, 2 Kantosho, (10) tsukioshi, morozashi,
     2 Ginosho   yorikiri

Kotonishiki was in the news in the first half of 1991 for the scandal he created by proposing to one woman while already secretly wed to another. He finally settled down with his legal wife, who went on to bear him a baby daughter. In the latter half of the year, Kotonishiki was again in the news for capturing his first yusho. Like Akinoshima, Kotonishiki was forced by his father to take up both sumo and judo at an early age. Although he did not emerge victorious in the National Junior High School Sumo Championships at age fourteen, he encountered Sadotagake Oyakata there, and that meeting led to his career in sumo. Off the dohyo, Kotonishiki is good friends with fellow "shorties" Akinoshima and Kasugafuji.

Komusubi Musashimaru Koyo
(1) Fiamalu Penitani   (2) Musashigawa
(3) 190 cm., 177 kilos   (4) May 2, 1971
(5) Oahu, Hawaii   (6) September 1989
(7) Single   (8) 0
(9) 1 Kantosho, 1 Ginosho   (10) tsukioshi, yorikiri,
                                      shitatenage

A former football player and Greco-Roman-style wrestler in high school, Musashimaru now does weight training in addition to his regular sumo practice. Though born in Samoa, he was raised from age ten in Hawaii. While Fiamalu likes chanko-nabe, he had some trouble with raw fish upon coming to Japan and still prefers American-style steak and thick sandwiches. Musashimaru dislikes most Japanese television and karaoke, but he enjoys reggae music and will belt out Elvis Presley's "Love Me Tender" when asked to sing at parties. His Samoan nickname is Fia, and he is called Maru in his heya. He has also been dubbed "Saigo-san" because of his facial resemblance to the nineteenth-century hero Saigo Takamori.

The following men all held maegashira positions in July 1992. They are listed in alphabetical order rather than by rank.

Daishoho
(1) Murata Masami
(2) Tatsunami
(3) 188 cm., 144 kilos
(4) May 7, 1967
(5) Sapporo, Hokkaido
(6) January 1990*
(7) Single
(8) 0
(9) 0
(10) tsuppari, migiyotsu, uwatenage

The future Daishoho was put up in Tatsunami-Beya when he came to Tokyo to participate in the National Junior High School Sumo Championships as a third-year student, an experience that led to his decision to enter the stable after graduation from Nihon University. Up until high school, he mainly played basketball; and being from an area with famous ski slopes, he took up skiing as a young boy. However, his father did amateur sumo and encouraged him to try it, too. At Nihon University, Murata majored in economics. Even though he did not hold many collegiate titles, he never considered any job after graduation other than professional sumo. Daishoho is terribly near-sighted and always wears glasses outside the vicinity of the ring.

Daishoyama
(1) Yamazaki Naoki
(2) Tatsunami
(3) 182 cm., 179 kilos
(4) July 7, 1966
(5) Anamizu-machi, Ishikawa Pref.
(6) January 1989*
(7) Engaged
(8) 0
(9) 0
(10) migiyotsu, yorikiri, shitatenage

Daishoyama, the holder of eleven sumo titles, including collegiate yokozuna and amateur yokozuna while a student at Nihon University, also served as captain of the school team. Like Daishoho, he was put up in Tatsunami-Beya as a junior high school boy, but he also has a connection with the stable dating back to the time he was held as a baby by former Komusubi Wakanami (Tamagaki Oyakata). This led him to become the first Nihon University graduate to join Tatsunami-Beya. However, he has been plagued by hip injuries since makushita and is the only one of the quartet (including Akebono, Takatoriki, and Wakahanada) making their makunouchi debut in September 1990 who has yet to reach a san'yaku rank.

Kotofuji

(1) Kobayashi Takaya	(2) Sadogatake
(3) 192 cm., 145 kilos	(4) October 28, 1964
(5) Chiba, Chiba Pref.	(6) March 1980
(7) Married, one child	(8) 1
(9) 2 Kantosho	(10) hidariyotsu, yorikiri, uwatenage

In July 1991, Kotofuji became the first maegashira to capture the yusho in nearly seven years, defeating Asahifuji, Kirishima, and Konishiki in doing so. His scores since then have been far from spectacular, and he failed to achieve kachikoshi in his two attempts at sekiwake. A sociable personality, he often serves as the master of ceremonies at various heya-related parties. During the time Canadian-born Kototenzan was in Sadogatake-Beya, Kotofuji made the greatest effort of anyone in the stable to talk to him in broken English. Kotofuji also enjoys golfing, watching horse races, and singing—particularly at hanazumo functions.

Kotonowaka

(1) Konno Mitsuya	(2) Sadogatake
(3) 192 cm., 163 kilos	(4) May 15, 1968
(5) Obanazawa, Yamagata Pref.	(6) May 1984
(7) Single	(8) 0
(9) 0	(10) tsuppari, hidariyotsu, yorikiri

Already 187 centimeters at age fourteen, Kotonowaka was scouted into sumo by a supporter of Sadogatake-Beya. He intended to join in March 1984, along with Kotonishiki, but at first failed the physical because of high blood pressure. In junior high school, he practiced judo and shotput, and once participated as the representative for Yamagata Prefecture in the All Tohoku Shotput Championships. Blessed with well-defined facial features, Kotonowaka has developed a following among female sumo fans. He is also good-natured and kind to children, but sometimes seems to lack fighting spirit in the ring. While Kotonowaka will drink apple juice, the sound of munching on the fruit bothers him more than just about anything else.

Kushimaumi

(1) Kushima Keita
(2) Dewanoumi
(3) 188 cm., 190 kilos
(4) August 6, 1965
(5) Shingu, Wakayama Pref.
(6) January 1988*
(7) Engaged
(8) 0
(9) 1 Kantosho
(10) migiyotsu, yorikiri, kimedashi

Before joining Dewanoumi-Beya, Kushimaumi served as captain of the Nihon University sumo club and captured a record number of twenty-eight amateur and collegiate sumo titles. In fact, he was the first person ever to become amateur yokozuna while still in high school. Nevertheless, he has yet to reach san'yaku. In fact, it took him seven tournaments just to progress from makushita to juryo. In his off hours, Kushimaumi enjoys singing—particularly Japanese *enka* music.

Kyokudozan

(1) Hata Kazuyasu
(2) Oshima
(3) 183 cm., 104 kilos
(4) October 14, 1964
(5) Tokunoshima-cho, Kagoshima Pref.
(6) May 1980
(7) Single
(8) 0
(9) 1 Kantosho, 1 Shukunsho
(10) hidariyotsu, shitatenage

Kyokudozan made a very exciting debut in the makunouchi division in January 1989, for which he was awarded the Kantosho. Because of his comparatively slim, muscular body and handsome face, he was naturally compared to the young Chiyonofuji or Takanohana. Kyukodozan was actually born in Tokyo but moved to his mother's hometown as a small child. Since he grew up on an island, it seems only natural that he is a good swimmer. Kyokudozan also excelled at running and volleyball; in fact, he was offered a volleyball scholarship to high school, which he declined in order to enter the sumo world. Kyokudozan's younger brother is Kimura Hisayuki, a referee affiliated with Oshima-Beya.

Mainoumi

(1) Nagao Shuhei
(2) Dewanoumi
(3) 171 cm., 97 kilos
(4) February 17, 1968
(5) Tsugaru-gun, Aomori Pref.
(6) May 1990*
(7) Single
(8) 0
(9) 2 Ginosho
(10) hidariyotsu, shitatenage, uchimuso

Since Mainoumi lacked the necessary height for professional sumo, he had arranged to become a high school teacher in Yamagata Prefecture after graduation from Nihon University, where he was an economics major. The sudden death of a friend from the university's sumo club in their senior year inspired him to try to fulfill his friend's dream of succeeding in professional sumo. Nagao originally failed the physical examination for new recruits because of his size. But one basho later, the Sumo Association decided to make special exceptions for sumo hopefuls lacking the height or weight but with ample amateur or college experience in the sport. Mainoumi is the only person to have received the Ginosho during his maku-nouchi debut, and he has become a true crowd pleaser for his unusual tachiai and wide array of techniques.

Misugisato

(1) Okamoto Koji
(2) Futagoyama
(3) 185 cm., 153 kilos
(4) July 1, 1962
(5) Shigaraki-cho, Shiga Pref.
(6) January 1979
(7) Married, one child
(8) 0
(9) 1 Kantosho
(10) migiyotsu, uwatenage

Misugisato dropped out of high school to enter Futagoyama-Beya. He was scouted into sumo in Tokyo while on his way to participate in a Greco-Roman wrestling competition in Ibaragi Prefecture. In January 1989, he became one of the rare sumotori to be promoted to san'yaku without having faced any san'yaku himself. Although Misugisato's komusubi debut was not successful, his power is widely regarded as being of san'yaku class. Having been brought up in an area famous for pottery, Misugisato is naturally interested in ceramics. His other hobbies are light reading and listening to a vast range of records.

Oginohana

(1) Koiwai Akikazu	(2) Dewanoumi
(3) 189 cm., 146 cm.	(4) November 18, 1967
(5) Ichikawa, Chiba Pref.	(6) July 1983
(7) Single	(8) 0
(9) 0	(10) migiyotsu, uwatenage

Oginohana is the elder son of former Sekiwake Oginohana (Takasaki Oyakata), and physically he bears a great resemblance to ex-Yokozuna Wakanohana II (Magaki Oyakata). Like Wakanohana II, he has quite a following among female sumo fans. He had originally planned to go into sumo after graduation from high school, but ultimately dropped out to enter Dewanoumi-Beya. His younger brother, Oginishiki, later joined the stable, too. Oginohana is blessed with a well-proportioned and highly supple physique, but he seems to have lost a lot of fighting spirit ever since the sudden death in 1990 of his good friend and rival in the heya, Ryukozan.

Ryogoku

(1) Kobayashi Hideaki	(2) Dewanoumi
(3) 185 cm., 178 kilos	(4) July 30, 1962
(5) Nagasaki, Nagasaki Pref.	(6) March 1985*
(7) Single	(8) 0
(9) 1 Shukunsho, 1 Kantosho	(10) migiyotsu, yori, shitatenage

A graduate of Nihon University, Ryogoku captured six major collegiate titles but not the most prestigious, collegiate yokozuna, before going into professional sumo. Despite his present gigantic size, Ryogoku was a premature baby—smaller than usual, but not quite tiny enough to require special care in the maternity ward. He started growing larger than his peers in the third grade. Ryogoku showed interest in sumo as a young boy, but since his junior high school did not offer training in it, he took up soccer until high school. His highest rank has been komusubi.

Takahanada

(1) Hanada Koji
(2) Fujishima
(3) 186 cm., 130 kilos
(4) August 12, 1972
(5) Tokyo
(6) March 1988
(7) Single
(8) 1
(9) 3 Shukunsho, 2 Kantosho, 3 Ginosho
(10) migiyotsu, yorikiri, uwatenage

The younger son of former Ozeki Takanohana (Fujishima Oyakata) and his former starlet-cum-beauty-queen (ex-Miss Oita Prefecture) wife, Noriko, Takahanada has rewritten the records for youngest in various accomplishments in sumo, including new juryo, shinnyumaku, shinsan'yaku, sansho winner, and makunouchi yusho. Aged eighteen when he faced Chiyonofuji in May 1991, he also became the youngest sumotori ever to beat a yokozuna in a tournament. Takahanada began practicing sumo in elementary school and later became a junior high school yokozuna. In contrast to the fine physique he has now, Takahanada was a veritable butterball as a youngster. In his off-hours, he listens to Japanese pop music and dons Armani T-shirts.

Takamisugi

(1) Kaneo Takashi
(2) Futagoyama
(3) 179 cm., 147 kilos
(4) March 1, 1961
(5) Kawasaki, Kanagawa Pref.
(6) March, 1976
(7) Married
(8) 0
(9) 0
(10) tsuppari, oshidashi

Because Takamisugi practiced judo in elementary and junior high school and also due to his large size, he was frequently invited to join group sumo competitions as a schoolboy. His team invariably placed within the top three, so perhaps it was only natural that he would decide to give professional sumo a try. Takamisugi is blessed with one of the finest singing voices in sumo, which he never hesitates to display at various hanazumo functions. He is also known as one of the heartiest eaters in sumo at present. In school, Takamisugi was good at painting and artwork, too. He is nicknamed "Doraemon" because of his resemblance to the popular plump cat robot cartoon character. His wife, Rumiko, is a former radio disk jockey.

Takanonami

(1) Namioka Sadahiro	(2) Fujishima
(3) 196 cm. 152 kilos	(4) October 27, 1971
(5) Misawa, Aomori Pref.	(6) March 1987
(7) Single	(8) 0
(9) 0	(10) hidariyotsu, yorikiri, uwatenage

Takanonami stunned the sumo world for a while during his makunouchi debut in November 1991 by becoming the first new maegashira to take the lead in the first week of the tourney and by beating Kotonishiki, the winner of the previous tournament. However, he started losing during the second week and finished with a score of 8–7. He was originally introduced by the mayor of Misawa to Fujishima Oyakata, who had inquired about boys with strong physiques while in the city to give a speech. Although Takanonami first took up sumo in elementary school, he had not been thinking of it as a profession and was hoping to work eventually in a local government office like his father. An easy-going personality, Takanonami likes reading books about famous swordsmen of the past.

Takatoriki

(1) Kamakiri Tadashige	(2) Fujishima
(3) 181 cm., 144 kilos	(4) September 28, 1967
(5) Kobe, Hyogo Pref.	(6) March 1983
(7) Single	(8) 0
(9) 1 Shukunsho, 3 Kantosho	(10) tsukioshi, nichonage

Takatoriki was such a big fan of former Ozeki Takahanada that after finishing elementary school he ventured to Tokyo and lived with the Hanada family for a while. He officially joined Fujishima-Beya only after completing junior high school, where he originally practiced judo. Takatoriki was awarded the Kantosho in his makunouchi debut, and his highest rank has been sekiwake. He was the only makunouchi rikishi in 1991 to achieve winning scores throughout the year and the last person to fight (and beat) Chiyonofuji. Out of the ring, he enjoys mimicking well-known Japanese television personalties, going to horse races, and other forms of gambling. While in London in October 1991, Takatoriki is said to have visited a casino near his hotel every night.

Terao Tsunefumi

(1) Fukuzono Yoshifumi
(2) Izutsu
(3) 185 cm., 114 kilos
(4) February 2, 1963
(5) Tokyo (birth registered in Kagoshima)
(6) July 1979
(7) Single
(8) 0
(9) 1 Kantosho, 1 Shukunsho, 1 Ginosho
(10) hidariyotsu, tsukioshi, yori

The third son of Izutsu Oyakata, Terao quit high school to go into sumo just after his mother (the daughter and granddaughter of former sumotori) tragically died of cancer at age forty-three. His long-time shikona, Terao Setsuo, was based on her maiden name, Terao Setsuko; but in November 1987, on the advice of a fortuneteller, he changed it to Terao Tsunefumi. His highest rank has been sekiwake. Out of the ring, Terao is good friends with former Sekiwake Masurao and Kotogaume. He enjoys listening to Japanese "new music" and can be a heavy drinker despite a heart condition.

Tomoefuji

(1) Kurosawa Toshihide
(2) Kokonoe
(3) 192 cm., 142 kilos
(4) January 27, 1971
(5) Shikazuno, Akita Pref.
(6) May 1986
(7) Single
(8) 0
(9) 1 Kantosho
(10) hidariyotsu, uwatenage, yorikiri

Tomoefuji was scouted by former Yokozuna Chiyonofuji after he won numerous children's sumo tournaments as a youngster in Akita Prefecture. One of his rivals in junior high sumo was the present Wakahanada. In January 1991, Tomoefuji effectively broke the jinx that performers of the yumitori-shiki do not succeed in sumo when he captured the Kantosho as a new maegashira. After the Natsu Basho in May 1992, he became the only sekitori in Kokonoe-Beya, which had two yokozuna just a year earlier.

Wakahanada

(1) Hanada Masaru
(2) Fujishima
(3) 180 cm., 126 kilos
(4) January 20, 1971
(5) Tokyo
(6) March 1992

(7) Single   (8) 0
(9) 1 Shukunsho, 3 Ginosho   (10) hidariyotsu, yorikiri,
                                         uwatenage

Wakahanada had originally planned to go into professional
sumo after completing high school. However, upon hearing that
his sibling, Koji (Takahanada), was joining their father's heya,
he dropped out of the Meiji University High School so as not to
lag behind his younger brother in sumo. Compared to Takahanada, Wakahanada is fairly talkative. In fact, he sometimes
answers questions from the media for his brother. He was never
interested in the idea of a regular office job and claims that if he
had not gone into sumo, he would have become a comedian.
Wakahanada is particularly interested in automobiles and
enjoyed seeing a collection of antique cars at a private manor in
England in 1991. His dream is to own a Ferrari.

*The following men also held maegashira positions in the Natsu Basho of
May 1992.*

Kasugafuji	**Kiraiho**	**Kirinishiki**
Kitakachidoki	**Kototsubaki**	**Sakahoko**
Tamakairiki	**Tatsuhikari**	**Tokitsunada**
Toyonoumi	**Tsunenoyama**	**Wakanoyama**
Wakasegawa	**Wakashoyo**	

The Record Book

Dates are listed in months, years, and decades according to the Western calendar whenever possible. Era names refer to the reigns of the respective emperors: Meiji (1868–1912), Taisho (1912–26), and Showa (1926–89).

Most Consecutive Wins

NUMBER	NAME	DATES
69	Futabayama Sadaji	7th day/1/1936–3rd day/1/1939
63	Tanikaze Kajinosuke	1st day/3/1778–6th day/2/1782
58	Umegatani Totaro I	1st day/4/1876–8th day/1/1881
56	Tachiyama Mineemon	9th day/1/1912–7th day/5/1916
53	Chiyonofuji Mitsugu	7th day/5/1988–15th day/11/1988

Most Consecutive Kachikoshi Tournaments

NUMBER	NAME	DATES
50	Kitanoumi Toshimitsu	7/1973–9/1981
28	Wakanohana Kanji II	7/1976–1/1981
27	Tamanoumi Masahiro	5/1967–9/1971

Most Tournament Championships (six tourneys a year system)

NUMBER	NAME	DATES
32	Taiho Koki	1960–71
31	Chiyonofuji Mitsugu	1981–90
24	Kitanoumi Toshimitsu	1972–84
14	Wajima Hiroshi	1971–81

Most Tournament Championships (before & during World War II)

NUMBER	NAME	DATES
12	Futabayama Sadaji	1936–43
10	Tsunenohana Kan'ichi	1921–30
9	Tamanishiki San'emon	1921–36

Most Wins in Makunouchi Division

NUMBER	NAME	DATES
807	Chiyonofuji Mitsugu	1975–5/91
804	Kitanoumi Toshimitsu	1972–84
746	Taiho Koki	1960–71
683	Takamiyama Daigoro	1968–84
620	Wajima Hiroshi	1971–81

Most Kinboshi

NUMBER	NAME	DATES
14	Akinoshima Katsumi	1988–92
12	Takamiyama Daigoro	1968–78
10	Ozutsu Takeshi	1979–89
10	Annenyama Sojo	mid 50s–mid 60s
10	Dewanishiki Tadao	late 40s–early 60s
10	Kitanonada Noboru	1950s
10	Tsurugamine Akio	mid-50s–mid 60s

Most Tournaments in Makunouchi

NUMBER	NAME	DATES
97	Takamiyama Daigoro	1968–84
84	Kirinji Kazuharu	1974–88
81	Chiyonofuji Mitsugu	1975–91

Most Tournaments as Yokozuna

63	Kitanoumi Toshimitsu	1974–85

Most Years as Yokozuna

12	Haguroyama Masaji	5/1941–9/53

Most Tournaments as Ozeki

50	Takanohana Toshiaki (Mitsuru)	11/1972–1/81

Most Appearances in Makunouchi

NUMBER	NAME	DATES
1,398	Takamiyama Daigoro	1968–84
1,221	Kirinji Kazuharu	1974–88
1,128	Tsurugamine Akio	1953–67

Most Consecutive Appearances in Makunouchi

NUMBER	NAME	DATES
1,231	Takamiyama Daigoro	1/1968–9/1981
1,170	Ozutsu Takeshi	3/1979–1/1992
1,065	Kurohimeyama Hideo	1/1969–7/1981

Most Consecutive Appearances from Jonokuchi

NUMBER	NAME	DATES
1,630	Aobajo Yukio	5/1965–7/1986
1,543	Fujizakura Yoshimori	5/1964–1/1984
1,425	Takamiyama Daigoro	5/1964–9/1981

Most Wins Annually (six tourneys a year)

NUMBER	NAME	YEAR
82	Kitanoumi Toshimitsu	1978
81	Taiho Koki	1963
80	Chiyonofuji Mitsugu	1985

Youngest Yokozuna

NAME	AGE AT PROMOTION	DATE
Kitanoumi Toshimitsu	21 yr., 2 mo.	July 1974
Taiho Koki	21 yr., 3 mo.	Sept. 1961
Kashiwado Tsuyoshi	22 yr., 11 mo.	Sept. 1961

Oldest Yokozuna (18th–19th century)

NAME	AGE AT PROMOTION	DATE
Kinmenzan Tanigoro	43	1869
Tanikaze Kajinosuke	39	1789
Shiranui Dakuemon	39	1840
Umegatani Totaro I	39	1884

Oldest Yokozuna (20th century)

NAME	AGE AT PROMOTION	DATE
Nishinoumi Kajiro I	36	1916

Youngest Ozeki

NAME	AGE AT PROMOTION	DATE
Taiho Koki	20 yr., 6 mo.	Jan. 1961
Kitanoumi Toshimitsu	20 yr., 10 mo.	Mar. 1974
Kashiwado Tsuyoshi	21 yr., 11 mo.	Sept. 1960

Youngest New Makunouchi

NAME	AGE AT PROMOTION	DATE
Takahanada Koji	17 yr., 9 mo.	May 1990
Kitanoumi Toshimitsu	18 yr., 8 mo.	Jan. 1972
Takanohana Mitsuru	18 yr., 9 mo.	Sept. 1968

Youngest New Juryo

NAME	AGE AT PROMOTION	DATE
Takahanada Koji	17 yr., 3 mo.	Nov. 1989
Kitanoumi Toshimitsu	18	May 1971
Takanohana Mitsuru	18 yr., 1 mo.	Mar. 1968

Fastest Progress to Makunouchi (prewar)

NAME	TOURNAMENTS
Haguroyama Masaji	6

Fastest Progress to Makunouchi from Jonokuchi (postwar)

NAME	TOURNAMENTS
Itai Keisuke	12
Konishiki Yasokichi	12

Fastest Progress from Jonokuchi to Makunouchi Yusho
(six tournaments a year system, excluding makushita tsukedashi)

NAME	TOURNAMENTS	DATE
Takahanada Koji	23	Jan. 1992
Akebono Taro	25	May 1992
Kitanoumi Toshimitsu	42	Jan. 1974
Hoshi (Hokutoumi) Nobuyoshi	42	Mar. 1986
Asahifuji Seiya	42	Jan. 1988

Slowest Progress to Makunouchi

NAME	TOURNAMENTS	DATES
Hoshiiwato Yuji	115	5/1970–7/89

Slowest Progress to Ozeki

NAME	TOURNAMENTS	DATES
Kirishima Kazuhiro	91	3/1975–5/90

Slowest Progress to Yokozuna

NAME	TOURNAMENTS	DATES
Mienoumi Tsuyoshi	97	7/1963–7/79

Most Sansho

NUMBER	NAME	TECHNIQUE (GINOSHO)	PERFORMANCE (SHUKUNSHO)	SPIRIT (KANTOSHO)
14	Tsurugamine Akio	10	2	2
14	Asashio Taro	1	10	3
11	Takamiyama Daigoro	-	6	5
11	Daiju Hisateru	6	4	1
11	Kirinji Kazuharu	3	4	4
11	Hoshi Nobuyoshi	5	2	4
11	Akinoshima Katsumi	1	5	5
10	Dewanohana Soichi	4	5	1
10	Tochinishiki Kiyotaka	9	1	-
10	Kitanonada Noboru	5	4	1
10	Tochiazuma Tomoyori	6	4	-
10	Kaiketsu Masateru	1	2	7

Tallest Rikishi

NAME	HEIGHT (CM.)	YEAR
Ikezuki Geitazaemon	229	1830s
Ozora Shikizaemon	228	1820s
Ryumon Kogoro	226	1820s

Tallest Ozeki

NAME	HEIGHT (CM.)	YEAR
Shakagatake Kumoemon	223	1760s

Tallest Yokozuna

NAME	HEIGHT (CM.)	YEARS
Futahaguro Koji	199	1986–87

Heaviest Rikishi

NAME	WEIGHT (KG.)	YEAR
Konishiki Yasokichi	264	1992
Hidenoumi Wataru	229	1992
Onokuni Yasushi	211	1989

Shortest Sekitori

NAME	HEIGHT (CM.)	ERA	RANK
Tamatsubaki Kentaro	158	Meiji	sekiwake
Kohitachi Yutaro	158	Meiji	sekiwake
Ryogoku Kajinosuke	159	Meiji	sekiwake

Shortest Ozeki

NAME	HEIGHT (CM.)	ERA
Onosato Mansuke	160	Taisho

Lightest Rikishi

NAME	WEIGHT (KG.)	ERA OR YEAR	RANK
Koyogawa Koichi	71	Taisho	komusubi
Fujimidake Toranosuke	71	Meiji	maegashira
Tamatsubaki Kentaro	73	Meiji	sekiwake
Kiryugawa Mitsuo	73	1947–61	maegashira
Kiryuzan Raihachi	73	Meiji	maegashira

Elevator Record of Going Between Makunouchi and Juryo

NAME	NUMBER	DATES
Oshio Kenji	13	1971–83

Sumo Name	Real Name	Native Prefecture	Birth/ Death	Height/ Weight (cm./kg.)
1. Akashi Shiganosuke	?	Tochigi	?	250/160?
2. Ayagawa Goroji	?	Tochigi	?	188/105?
3. Maruyama Gontazaemon	Haga Gindayu	Miyagi	1713–50	200/150?
4. Tanikaze Kajinosuke	Kaneko Yoshiro	Miyagi	1750–95	189/169
5. Onogawa Kisaburo	Kawamura Kisaburo	Shiga	1758–1806	176/116
6. Onomatsu Midorinosuke	Sasaki Jokichi	Ishikawa	1791–1851	173/135
7. Inazuma Raigoro	Nemoto Saisuke	Ibaraki	1795–1877	188/142
8. Shiranui Dakuemon	Kinkyu Shinji	Kumamoto	1801–54	176/135
9. Hidenoyama Raigoro	Kikuda Tatsugoro	Miyagi	1808–62	164/135
10. Unryu Hisakichi	Sato Hisakichi	Fukuoka	1823–91	179/135
11. Shiranui Koemon	Harano Minematsu	Kumamoto	1825–79	176/124
12. Jinmaku Kyugoro*	Ishigura Shintaro	Shimane	1829–1903	174/139
13. Kimenzan Tanigoro	Tanaka Shin'ichi	Gifu	1826–71	186/146
14. Sakaigawa Namiemon	Udagawa Daijiro	Chiba	1843–87	176/128
15. Umegatani Totaro I	Koe Totaro	Fukuoka	1845–1928	176/128
16. Nishinoumi Kajiro I	Kosono Kajiro	Kagoshima	1855–1908	176/128
17. Konishiki Yasokichi	Iwao Yasokichi	Chiba	1867–1914	168/143
18. Ozutsu Man'emon	Kakuhari Manji	Miyagi	1869–1918	197/131
19. Hitachiyama Taniemon	Ichige Tani	Ibaraki	1874–1922	174/147
20. Umegatani Totaro II	Oshida Otomatsu	Toyama	1878–1927	168/158
21. Wakashima Gonshiro	Takahashi Gonshiro	Chiba	1876–1943	178/116
22. Tachiyama Mineemon	Oimoto Yataro	Toyama	1877–1927	188/150
23. Okido Morieemon	Uchida Mitsuzo	Hyogo	1877–1930	177/120
24. Otori Tanigoro	Takida Akira	Chiba	1887–1936	174/112
25. Nishinoumi Kajiro II	Makise Kyuhachi	Kagoshima	1880–1931	185/135
26. Onishiki Uichiro	Hosokawa Uichiro	Osaka	1891–1941	175/143
27. Tochigiyama Moriyama	Nakata Moriya	Tochigi	1892–1959	171/103
28. Onishiki Daigoro	Yamada Kisaburo	Aichi	1883–1943	176/113
29. Miyagiyama Fukumatsu	Sato Fukumatsu	Miyagi	1895–1943	173/113
30. Nishinoumi Kajiro III	Matsuyama Isesuke	Kagoshima	1890–1933	185/124
31. Tsunenohana Kan'ichi	Yamanobe Kan'ichi	Okayama	1896–1960	177/117
32. Tamanishiki San'emon	Nishiuchi Yasuki	Kochi	1903–38	173/135
33. Musashiyama Takeshi	Yokoyama Takeshi	Kanagawa	1909–69	186/120
34. Minanogawa Tozo	Sakata Tomojiro	Ibaraki	1903–71	193/154

YOKOZUNA

Stable	Debut	Promoted to Yokozuna	Tourney Titles	Makuuchi W–L–Draws	Mo./Yr. Retired	Elder Name
?	?	?	?	?	?	?
?	?	?	?	?	?	?
Nanatsumori		1749	?	?	(died as yokozuna)	
Isenoumi	4/1769	11/1789	21	258–14–36	(died as yokozuna)	
Onogawa	10/1779	12/1789	8	144–13–17	1798	Onogawa
Takekuma	10/1816	2/1828	5	140–31–33	1835	Onomatsu
Sadogatake	10/1821	9/1830	10	130–13–18	1840	(quit sumo)
Urakaze	11/1830	11/1840	1	48–15–6	1844	Minato**
Hidenoyama	11/1827	9/1845	4	112–21–35	1850	Hidenoyama
Oitekaze	11/1847	9/1861	6	127–32–20	1865	Oitekaze
Sakaigawa	11/1850	10/1863	3	119–35–24	1869	Minato**
Hidenoyama	2/1851	1/1867	5	87–5–20	1867	
Takekuma	2/1852	2/1869	7	143–24–24	11/1870	
Sakaigawa	11/1857	12/1876	5	118–23–76	1/1881	Sakaigawa
Tamagaki	3/1870	3/1884	9	116–6–20	2/1885	Ikazuchi
Takasago	1/1882	3/1890	2	127–37–29	1/1896	Izutsu
Takasago	5/1883	3/1896	7	119–24–16	1/1901	Hatachiyama
Oguruma	1/1885	4/1901	2	98–29–55	1/1908	Matsuchiyama
Dewanoumi	5/1891	6/1903	7	150–15–24	5/1914	Dewanoumi
Ikazuchi	12/1891	6/1903	4	168–27–49	5/1915	Ikazuchi
Nakamura	5/1890	4/1905	5	87–33–13	1/1907	Wakashima*
Tomozuna	5/1900	2/1911	11	195–27–15	1/1918	Azumazeki*
Minato	9/1869	2/1912	10	143–20–10	5/1914	Minato**
Miyagino	1/1903	2/1915	2	108–49–15	5/1920	Miyagino**
Izutsu	1/1900	2/1916	1	136–38–36	5/1918	Izutsu
Dewanoumi	1/1910	3/1917	5	119–16–3	1/1923	(Quit sumo)
Dewanoumi	1/1911	2/1918	9	166–23–11	5/1925	Kasugano
Asahiyama	1/1903	4/1918	4	158–48–22	1/1922	(Quit sumo)
Takadagawa	5/1910	2/1922	4	192–94–10	3/1931	Shibatayama
Izutsu	1/1910	4/1923	1	134–60–4	4/1928	Asakayama
Dewanoumi	1/1910	2/1924	10	221–58–14	3/1929	Dewanoumi
Nishonoseki	1/1920	10/1932	9	308–92–3	(died as yokozuna)	
Dewanoumi	1/1926	5/1935	1	174–69–2	4/1939	Dekiyama*
Takasago	1/1924	2/1936	2	247–136–1	1/1942	Minanogawa*

35. Futabayama Sadaji	Akiyoshi Sadaji	Oita	1912–68	178/128
36. Haguroyama Masaji	Kobayashi Masaji	Niigata	1914–69	178/139
37. Akinoumi Setsuo	Nagata Setsuo	Hiroshima	1914–79	177/130
38. Terukuni Manzo	Suga Manzo	Akita	1919–77	173/161
39. Maedayama Eigoro	Hagimori Kanematsu	Ehime	1914–71	181/120
40. Azumafuji Kin'ichi	Inoue Kin'ichi	Tokyo	1921–73	180/179
41. Chiyonoyama Masanobu	Sugimura Masaji	Hokkaido	1926–77	191/131
42. Kagamisato Kiyoji	Okuyama Kiyoji	Aomori	1923–	176/165
43. Yoshibayama Junnosuke	Ikeda Junnosuke	Hokkaido	1920–77	179/161
44. Tochinishiki Kiyotaka	Otsuka Kiyotaka	Tokyo	1925–90	178/126
45. Wakanohana Kanji I	Hanada Katsuji	Aomori	1928–	179/105
46. Asashio Taro	Yonekawa Fumitoshi	Kagoshima	1929–88	189/145
47. Kashiwado Tsuyoshi	Togashi Tsuyoshi	Yamagata	1938–	188/132
48. Taiho Koki	Naya Koki	Hokkaido	1940–	187/146
49. Tochinoumi Teruyoshi	Hanada Shigehiro	Aomori	1938–	177/107
50. Sadanoyama Shinmatsu	Sasada Shinmatsu	Nagasaki	1938–	182/122
51. Tamanoumi Masahiro	Takeuchi Masao	Aichi	1944–71	177/130
52. Kitanofuji Katsuaki	Takezawa Katsuaki	Hokkaido	1942–	185/138
53. Kotozakura Masakatsu	Kamaya Norio	Tottori	1940–	182/155
54. Wajima Hiroshi	Wajima Hiroshi	Ishikawa	1948–	184/132
55. Kitanoumi Toshimitsu	Obata Toshimitsu	Hokkaido	1953–	180/164
56. Wakanohana Kanji II	Shimoyama Toshihito	Aomori	1953–	188/135
57. Mienoumi Tsuyoshi	Ishikawa Goro	Mie	1948–	181/135
58. Chiyonofuji Mitsugu	Akimoto Mitsugu	Hokkaido	1955–	183/122
59. Takanosato Toshihide	Takaya Toshihide	Aomori	1952–	181/151
60. Futahaguro Koji	Kitao Koji	Mie	1963–	199/157
61. Hokutoumi Nobuyoshi	Hoshi Nobuyoshi	Hokkaido	1963–	181/144
62. Onokuni Yasushi	Aoki Yasushi	Hokkaido	1962–	189/203
63. Asahifuji Seiya	Suginomori Seiya	Aomori	1960–	189/143

Tatsunami	3/1927	5/1937	12	276–68–1	11/1945	Tokitsukaze
Tatsunami	5/1934	5/1941	7	321–94–1	9/1953	Tatsunami
Dewanoumi	2/1932	6/1942	1	142–59–0	11/1946	Fujishima*
Isegahama	1/1935	6/1942	2	271–91–0	1/1953	Isegahama
Takasago	1/1929	6/1947	1	206–104–0	9/1949	Takasago
Takasago	1/1936	10/1948	6	261–104–2	9/1954	Nishikido*
Dewanoumi	1/1942	5/1951	6	366–149–2	1/1959	Kokonoe
Tokitsukaze	1/1941	1/1953	4	360–163–0	1/1958	Tatsutagawa
Takashima	5/1938	1/1954	1	304–151–1	1/1958	Miyagino
Kasugano	1/1939	10/1954	10	513–203–1	5/1960	Kasugano
Hanakago	11/1946	1/1958	10	546–235–4	5/1962	Futagoyama
Takasago	10/1948	3/1959	5	431–248–0	1/1962	Takasago
Isenoumi	9/1954	9/1961	5	599–240–0	7/1969	Kagamiyama
Nishonoseki	9/1956	9/1961	32	746–146–0	5/1971	Taiho
Kasugano	9/1955	1/1964	3	315–178–0	11/1966	Kasugano
Dewanoumi	1/1956	1/1965	6	435–164–0	3/1968	Dewanoumi
Kataonami	3/1959	1/1970	6	496–211–0	(died as yokozuna)	
Kokonoe	1/1957	1/1970	10	592–294–0	7/1974	Jinmaku
Sadogatake	1/1955	1/1973	5	345–253–0	7/1974	Sadogatake
Hanakago	1/1970	5/1973	14	620–213–0	3/1981	Hanakago*
Mihogaseki	1/1967	7/1974	24	804–248–0	1/1985	Kitanoumi
Futagoyama	7/1968	5/1978	4	512–234–0	1/1983	Magaki
Dewanoumi	7/1963	7/1979	3	532–413–1	1/1980	Musashigawa
Kokonoe	9/1970	7/1981	31	807–253–0	5/1991	Kokonoe
Futagoyama	7/1968	7/1983	4	464–332–0	1/1986	Naruto
Tatsunami	3/1979	7/1986	0	197–87–0	12/1987***	
Kokonoe	3/1979	5/1987	8	465–206–0	5/1992	Hokutoumi
Hanaregoma	3/1978	9/1987	2	426–288–0	7/1991	Onokuni
Oshima	3/19/81	7/1990	4	487–277–0	1/1992	Asahifuji

Note: In case of changes in name or stable affiliation, only the final one is listed.
* Left the sumo world.
** Active in Osaka sumo.
*** Forced to resign while yokozuna.

Addresses and Telephone Numbers of Sumo Stables and Stadiums

Nihon Sumo Kyokai (Japan Sumo Association) and Kokugikan
    13-28 Yokoami, Sumida-ku, Tokyo 130
    Tel. 3623-5111

All the following addresses are in Tokyo (telephone area code 03) unless specified otherwise. Some telephone numbers or addresses may be changed in the future because of a stable's relocation or amalgamation.

Ajigawa   1-7-4 Mori, Koto-ku, 135
                    3634-5514

Asahiyama   4-14-21 Kita Kasai, Edogawa-ku 132
                    3686-4950

Azumazeki   4-6-4 Higashi Komagata, Sumida-ku 130
                    3625-0033

Dewanoumi   2-3-15 Ryogoku, Sumida-ku 130
                    3632-4920

Fujishima   3-10-6 Honcho, Nakano-ku 164
                    (not available for publication)

Futagoyama   3-25-10 Narita Higashi, Suginami-ku 166
                    3316-5939

Hanaregoma   3-12-7 Asagaya Minami, Suginami-ku 166
                    3391-9748

Isegahama	227 Matsugazaki, Kashiwa-shi, Chiba Prefecture 277 (not available for publication)
Isenoumi	3-8-80 Harue, Edogawa-ku 132 3677-6860
Izutsu	2-2-7 Ryogoku, Sumida-ku 130 3634-9827
Kabutoyama	5-19-7 Hongo, Bunkyo-ku 113 3811-9080
Kagamiyama	8-16-1 Kita Koiwa, Edogawa-ku 133 3673-3474
Kasugano	1-11-11 Ryogoku, Sumida-ku 130 3634-9828
Kataonami	1-33-9 Ishihara, Sumida-ku 130 3622-8001
Kise	2-35-21 Hongo, Bunkyo-ku 113 3811-6365
Kitanoumi	2-10-11 Kiyosumi, Koto-ku 135 3630-9900
Kokonoe	1-16-1 Kamezawa, Sumida-ku 130 3621-0404
Kumagatani	1-6-28 Minami Koiwa, Edogawa-ku 133 3671-9511
Magaki	3-8-1 Kamezawa, Sumida-ku 130 3623-7449
Matsugane	16 Gaikuno 1, Kosaku-cho, Funabashi-shi, Chiba Prefecture 273 0473-38-3081
Michinoku	4-23-18 Horie, Urayasu-shi, Chiba Prefecture 272-01 0473-81-4725
Mihogaseki	3-2-12 Chitose, Sumida-ku 130 3632-4767
Minato	2-20-10 Shiba Nakata, Kawaguchi-shi, Saitama Prefecture 333 0482-66-0015
Minezaki	2-20-3 Tagara, Nerima-ku 177 5997-3601

Miyagino	4-16-3 Midoricho, Sumida-ku 130 3634-6291
Musashigawa	4-27-1 Higashi Nippori, Arakawa-ku 116 3802-6333
Nakamura	4-1-10 Chuo, Edogawa-ku 132 3655-1808
Naruto	183 Hachigasaki, Matsudo-shi, Chiba Prefecture 270 0473-46-1500
Nishonoseki	4-17-1 Ryogoku, Sumida-ku 130 3631-0179
Oguruma	4-27-30 Inari, Soka-shi, Saitama Prefecture 340 0489-36-2889
Onaruto	2-22-14 Kitakata, Ichikawa-shi, Chiba Prefecture 272 0473-34-9677
Oshima	3-5-3 Ryogoku, Sumida-ku 130 3631-9708
Oshiogawa	2-7-17 Kiba, Koto-ku 135 3642-4362
Sadogatake	4-18-13 Taihei, Sumida-ku 130 3625-6951
Shikihide	Sanuki-cho Mokuda 168-1, Ryugasaki-shi, Ibaragi Prefecture 301 (not available for publication)
Taiho	2-8-3 Kiyosumi, Koto-ku 135 3630-4243
Takadagawa	2-1-15 Ichinoe, Edogawa-ku 132 3656-5604
Takasago	1-16-5 Hashiba, Taito-ku 111 3876-7770
Tamanoi	4-12-14 Umeda, Adachi-ku 123 3852-4333
Tatsutagawa	3-2-10 Iidabashi, Chiyoda-ku 102 3222-0128
Tatsunami	3-26-2 Ryogoku, Sumida-ku 130 3631-2424
Tokitsukaze	3-15-3 Ryogoku, Sumida-ku 130 3634-8549

Tomozuna	1-20-7 Mori, Koto-ku 135
	3631-6390
Wakamatsu	3-5-4 Honjo, Sumida-ku 130
	5608-3223

Haru Basho: Osaka Furitsu Taiikukan (Osaka Prefectural Gymnasium)
3-4-36 Nanbanaka, Naniwa-ku, Osaka 556
Tel. 06-631-0120, 641-0770

Nagoya Basho: Aichi Kenritsu Taiikukan (Aichi Prefectural Gymnasium)
1-1 Ninomaru, Naka-ku, Nagoya 460
Tel. 052-971-0015

Kyushu Basho: Fukuoka Kokusai Sentaa (Fukuoka International Center)
2-2 Chikko Honmachi, Hakata-ku, Fukuoka 812
Tel. 092-291-9311, 291-9312

Glossary

agari-zashiki: The elevated tatami area overlooking the practice ring.
akeni: Bamboo luggage trunks, painted red and green, which hold the personal effects of sekitori. Only the sekitori are allowed to have them, but they are usually transported by their attendants. Grand champions alone are permitted to have three trunks.
anko (-gata): A blubbery sumotori.

banzuke (-hyo): Ranking sheets.
basho: Sumo tournament.
bintsuke: The fragrant pomade used in dressing a sumotori's topknot.

chanko (-nabe): A sort of stew or rich chowder which is the main course of a sumo meal. There is almost an infinite number of varieties. Chanko, without the suffix nabe, can also be used loosely to refer to any meal in a sumo stable.
chiho basho: Any or all of the regular tourneys held outside of Tokyo—specifically, the Haru (Osaka) Basho, Nagoya Basho, and Kyushu (Fukuoka) Basho.
chikara-gami: "Power paper" for purification given after chikara-mizu during the warm-up period before a match.
chikara-mizu: "Power water," given from a pail affixed to an edge of the ring, for good luck and purification purposes to the two sumotori who are about to fight.
chonmage: Topknot.

danpatsu-shiki: Topknot-cutting/retirement ceremony. Also see *intai-zumo*.

dohyo: The sumo ring.

dohyo-iri: Entrance into the ring ceremony performed by juryo, makunouchi, or yokozuna.

dotai: Written with the characters for "same body," this word is used to describe a bout in which the two sumotori seem to have fallen or stepped out of the ring simultaneously. Such bouts almost always result in a rematch.

ebisuko (ga tsuyoi): Sumo slang for a particularly hearty eater.

fusen: Written with the characters for "no fight," this refers to a default. A loss by default is fusenhai; a win earned through the opponent's default is fusensho.

Ginosho: Technique Prize.

gottsuan (desu): "Thank you" in sumotori slang.

gunbai: The war paddle held by the referee. Also called *uchiwa*.

gyoji: Referee.

haigyo: Quitting, leaving the sumo world altogether.

hanamichi: Literally "flower paths," this term refers to the aisles in the sumo stadium. In the Heian period (794-1185) the sumotori made their entrance to the ring from aisles decorated with flowers. But now this term can mean any sumo stadium aisle, including those used by spectators.

hanazumo: Any sumo performance other than a regular tourney.

hansoku: A violation of the rules. This usually results in an automatic loss for the sumotori who committed it in the ring.

haridashi: Position projected out on the sides of the ranking sheets. Ostensibly, there are supposed to be only two holders of each rank on the banzuke-hyo, so any extra names are projected outside of the regular line-up. The haridashi rikishi usually had the lowest score in the previous tournament, or else were able to retain the rank while absent for one tournament under the Public Injury System. Also see *Kosho Seido*.

heya (-beya): Sumo training house with communal living facilities.

heya-gashira: The highest ranking sumotori in a heya.

higashi (-gawa): The east side or eastern side of the ring, stadium, or a division on the ranking sheets. On the ranking sheets, this is the more prestigious side; those ranked on higashi most likely had a higher score in the previous tourney.

hikae-rikishi: Any or all of the four sumotori sitting below the ring waiting for their bouts.

hikiwake: A draw.

hon-basho: Any or all of the six, fifteen-day regular tournaments held each year.

hon-wari: A regular match—not a playoff or an exhibition bout.

hyosho-shiki: Awards ceremony.

ichimon: A group or camp of related stables. There are five ichimon: Dewanoumi, Nishonoseki/Futagoyama, Takasago, Tokitsukaze, and Tatsunami/Isegahama.

intai: To retire from the ring and take a coaching position within the Sumo Association.

intai-zumo: Retirement ceremony. Also see *danpatsu-shiki*.

isamiashi: Literally "overbrave feet," this is when the seeming winner of a match loses by inadvertently putting a foot over the edge of the ring before he manages to get his opponent out. In ordinary Japanese, this term means "to step out of the bounds of propriety" and is especially used to describe events in the political world.

jonidan: The second lowest division.

jonokuchi: The lowest, or "beginning," division.

jungyo: Exhibition tour.

juryo: The second highest division or any man in it. Members of this division and those in the makunouchi division are known as sekitori.

kabu: See *toshiyori-kabu*.

kachikoshi: A winning record, a score with more wins than losses.

kadoban: An ozeki who, following a losing tournament, will face demotion unless he achieves a winning record.

Kantosho: The Fighting Spirit Prize.

keiko: Sumo practice.

keikoba: The practice area.

kensho-kin: The money placed by outside sponsors on top division bouts. The winner takes all in white envelopes before he leaves the ring.

kesho-mawashi: Decorative aprons worn by juryo and makunouchi rikishi during the dohyo-iri.

kettei-sen: Play-off.

kimarite: Any technique used to win a bout. There are seventy officially recognized kimarite.

kinboshi: "Gold star," accompanied by a monetary bonus, given to a maegashira who has upset a yokozuna. In sumo slang, it also means a beautiful woman—something equally desirable as a kinboshi earned in the ring.

koenkai: Group of patrons. Also see *tanimachi*.

Kosho Seido: The Public Injury System allowing for a rikishi who has been injured in the ring during a regular tournament to sit out the next tourney without any effect to his rank.

komusubi: Sumo's fourth highest rank, sometimes translated as "junior champion, second class."

kuroboshi: Literally, "black star." A loss.

kyujo: Absence from a tourney.

kyukin: A sekitori's tournament stipend, calculated from his total number of wins, winning tourneys, kinboshi, championships, and so on. Also called *mochi-kyukin* and *hoshokin*.

kyukin-zumo: A match on which achieving a winning record in the tourney depends. Winning the bout will raise the rikishi's stipend—a process also called *kyukin-naoshi* (literally, "stipend revising").

maegashira: The majority of the members of the makunouchi division not ranked in san'yaku, and numbered from one to twelve, thirteen, or fourteen since the mid-1960s. (The numbers went to about twenty before then.)

maezumo: Pre-sumo, not listed on the ranking sheets. Also called *banzuke-gai* and *shin-jo*.

makekoshi: A record with more losses than wins.

makunouchi: The top of six divisions in professional sumo, having no more than forty members. Also called *makuuchi* and *naka-iri*.

makushita: The third highest division, having no more than 120 official members.

makushita tsukedashi: A special privilege for sumotori who are college graduates allowing them to make their debut at the bottom of makushita, though their names will not appear on the ranking sheets until the next tourney.

man'in onrei: "Full house, thank you." Banners saying this are lowered before the start of the makunouchi matches on days during a regular tournament when the tickets have sold out.

masu-zeki: Matted box seats in the stadium. Also called *sajiki-seki*.

matawari: Sumo-style splits.

matta: "Wait." Called by a rikishi who does not feel ready to join his opponent in the initial charge. Since the fall of 1991, members of makunouchi or juryo guilty of matta have been fined. A gyoji matta is when a referee halts a bout, usually to tighten a lose belt on one of the rikishi.

mawashi: Also called shimekomi, this is the belt worn by sumotori for doing sumo. Rikishi in the four lower divisions wear the same black canvas mawashi both in practice and tournaments. Sekitori wear white canvas mawashi (also called *keiko-mawashi*) for practice, and colored silk belts for tournament and exhibition matches.

mizu-iri: When the referee temporarily halts a particularly long stalemated bout to give the two rikishi a breather and a chance to drink some water. Also called *mizu ga hairu*.

mono-ii: Conference called by the judges, or rarely by a hikae-rikishi, to dispute or discuss a referee's decision after a close match or a clear mistake on the referee's part.

muko-jomen: Opposite the main side of the stadium.

musubi no ichiban: The last match of the day during a tournament.

nage: Any of the throws in sumo.

nakabi: The middle day of a tournament.

niramiai: The glaring "contest" which precedes a sumo match. Also called *niramekko*.

nishi (-gawa): West or western side of the sumo ring, stadium, or of a division on the ranking sheets.

oicho (-mage): An elaborate topknot fanned out to resemble a ginkgo leaf—a hairstyle reserved almost exclusively for sekitori.

oiri-bukuro: Little red and white envelope containing a coin (ten yen in the 1980s) passed out to reporters and special patrons of sumo on days during a regular tournament when the stadium draws a full house. Also see *man'in onrei*.

okamisan: The coach's wife.

ongaeshi (on o kaesu): To repay one's debt to another. In the sumo world, this usually means to repay a senior who has helped train oneself by beating him in the ring—in other words, to show him just how good his training has been.

oyakata: Sumo coach.

ozeki: Sumo's second highest rank, sometimes translated as "champion."

rensho: Consecutive wins. Official records are kept only of consecutive wins in a tournament.
rikishi: "Strong man." Sumotori.

sandanme: The third lowest division.
san'yaku: Komusubi, sekiwake, ozeki, and yokozuna, or any one of these positions. These men are also called *yaku-rikishi*.
sansho: The three prizes (Technique, Fighting Spirit, Outstanding Performance) awarded on the last day of a tournament. Recipients must have a winning record and be ranked below ozeki.
sashichigai: An incorrect decision made by a referee. Also see *mono-ii*.
sei: Proper holder of a position, as opposed to the ones projected out, on the ranking sheets. Also see *haridashi*.
sekitori: Full-fledged, salaried sumotori in juryo and makunouchi.
sekiwake: Sumo's third highest rank, sometimes translated as "junior champion."
senshuraku: The last day of a sumo tournament.
sewanin: Caretaker and performer of various odd jobs. A position within the Sumo Association offered to up to eight former sumotori who were unable to become regular coaches.
shikiri: The warm-up process before a bout.
shikiri-sen: Starting line.
shiko: Sumo-style stomping.
shikona: Ring name adopted by a sumotori.
shinnyumaku: Newly promoted member of the makunouchi division.
shiroboshi: Literally, "white star." A win.
shisho: The head coach, who can also be called oyakata. Shisho is used when it is necessary to distinguish the head of a stable from other coaches. He can also be referred to as *heya-mochi* oyakata, but shisho is more respectful.
shitaku-beya: One of the dressing rooms at the stadium.
shobu shinpan (-in): Any or all of the judges sitting around the ring. Formerly called *kensa-yaku*.
shokkiri: Comic sumo, performed at hanazumo exhibitions.
shomen: The main side of the stadium.
shonichi: The first day of a tournament.
Shukunsho: ("Prize for Meritorious Deeds" or "Outstanding Performance Prize") This is generally awarded to the man ranked sekiwake or below who has beaten the most yokozuna, ozeki, or strong candidates for the tourney championship.
soppu (-gata): A comparatively lean sumotori.
sumo ga sukisugiru: Literally "to like sumo too much," this is used in reference to sumotori who tend to be slow in the ring

and have long, drawn-out matches. In other words, they love sumo so much that they want to be in the ring as long as possible.

sumo ni katte, shobu ni makeru: "To win at sumo, but lose the match." This expression is used to describe a rikishi who had the winning force in a bout but ultimately lost, either inadvertently by isamiashi or by being struck or flung down in a last-second move of desperation by his opponent.

suna-kaburi: ("Sand-covered"). These are the first five rows around the ring in the stadium. Also called *tamari-seki*.

tachiai: The initial charge in a match.

tachi-mochi: Sword-bearer during the yokozuna dohyo-iri.

tanimachi: A patron of sumo.

tate-gyoji: The top two referees or either one of them.

tawara: Rice-straw bales forming and demarcating the ring.

tegatana (o kiru): The sign of thanks made to the three gods of creation by the winner of a tournament bout.

Tenno-hai: The Emperor's Cup, the first of several trophies given to the winner of a tourney in the top division.

tenran-zumo: Sumo in the presence of the emperor or crown prince.

tokoyama: Sumo hairdresser.

torikumi: Sumo bout.

torikumi-hyo: List of bouts for the day.

torinaoshi: A match which is to be taken over because there was no clear winner to the previous one. Also see *mono-ii*.

toshiyori-kabu: "Elder stock" necessary for remaining in the Sumo Association as a coach.

tsukebito: Apprentice serving as a sort of attendant to sekitori. A tsukebito serves meals, runs errands, does various other things to help a sekitori (putting on his mawashi, carrying luggage, and doing whatever is requested).

tsukioshi (-zumo): Pushing and shoving moves.

tsunauchi-shiki: The ceremony to make the white hawser worn by the yokozuna.

tsuppari: Series of slapping.

tsuyu-harai: Literally the "dew-sweeper," the herald during the yokozuna dohyo-iri.

wakaimono-gashira: Trainer of apprentice sumotori and performer of various odd jobs for the Sumo Association. A position held by no more than eight former sumotori who were unable to become regular coaches. Also called *kashira*.

wakaishu: Apprentice nonsalaried sumotori in any of the four lowest divisions (jonokuchi, jonidan, sandanme, makushita). Also called wakaimono, toriteki, or fundoshi-katsugi.

yaocho: A fixed match. This term can be used to describe fixed matches in all kinds of sports. *Chusha* (literally, "injection"), an alternate term, is unique to the sumo world.

yatchin ga takai: Literally, "the rent is too high." This refers to a rikishi who is ranked too high for his skills or strength and is having trouble holding his own in the position.

yobidashi: "Beckoner." A sumo announcer, who performs various other chores, such as building the dohyo, carrying banners for kenshokin, and so on.

yokozuna: Sumo's highest rank, often translated as "grand champion." Also the name of the white hawser donned by holders of this rank.

yorikiri: "Drive out." The technique most commonly used to win tournament matches.

yotsu-zumo: The style of sumo in which two opponents grip each other's belt.

yumitori-shiki: The bow ceremony performed at the end of the day.

zensho: All wins.

zensho yusho: A tournament championship with a perfect score.

The "weathermark" identifies this book as a production of Weatherhill, Inc., publishers of fine books on Asia and the Pacific. Editorial supervision: Meg Taylor. Book design and typography: Miriam F. Yamaguchi. Text composition: H. Roberts, New York City. Printing and binding: Arcata/Kingsport, Tennessee.